1956

1956

THE YEAR THAT CHANGED BRITAIN

FRANCIS BECKETT
AND TONY RUSSELL

Biteback Publishing

First published in Great Britain in 2015 by
Biteback Publishing Ltd
Westminster Tower
3 Albert Embankment
London SE1 7SP

ISBN 978-1-84954-912-7

10 9 8 7 6 5 4 3 2 1

A CIP catalogue record for this book is available from the British Library.

Set in Quadraat

Printed and bound in Great Britain by
CPI Group (UK) Ltd, Croydon CR0 4YY

CONTENTS

CHAPTER 1

AIN'T IT ALL A BLEEDING SHAME?

If it were possible to buy package holidays to the early '50s, there might not be many takers. After a few hours of looking around, vacationers would probably be clamouring to come home – even those of us, like the present authors, who have visited before. (We were very young at the time.)

Tourists from the twenty-first century would have to be careful about their behaviour, and guides would warn them of quaint and primitive local customs. It would have to be explained to them that if two men had any physical contact in public beyond a handshake, this could cause a scandal, unless they were fighting, in which case it was probably OK.

Women would have to be careful about their clothing and their behaviour, as if they were visiting a strict Muslim country, and would be expected to regard sex as a commodity to be traded for a wedding ring. To prepare visitors for the culture shock, a thoughtful tour company might equip them with a copy of David Lodge's 1980 novel *How Far Can You Go?*, where they would discover that, 'in the fifties, everyone was waiting to get married'.

In Lodge's book, Roman Catholics Dennis and Angela wait for many years for their wedding, while they get their degrees, he does his National Service, they get jobs and save money. In 1952, he puts a hand on her breast outside her blouse. In 1953, he strokes her leg to stocking-top height. In 1954, he puts a hand inside her blouse and on to her bra. Angela tires of 'acting as moral referee over their endearments, blowing the whistle at every petty infringement'.

The early '50s may have been a time – there is no way this can be proved – when more people married as virgins than at almost any time before or since, for its prudery was new. Compared with the early '50s, the decades between the two world wars had been years of joyful sexual liberation. Prudery came with austerity and rationing and bad cooking.

The place would seem to us dirty and uncared-for. London and other cities would still have great tracts of bare ground, where wartime bombs had destroyed the buildings and nothing had yet replaced them.

In December 1952, a thick and polluted fog fell on London, killing many people, bringing road, air and rail transport to a virtual standstill, and even – so it was said – choking cows to death in fields near the city. Around the Isle of Dogs, the 'smog', as it was called, was so thick that people could not see their feet. It was just the worst of a series of smogs to hit the dreadfully dirty and polluted capital in the first half of the '50s.

You would have to be careful what reading you took with you to the early '50s. You could get into trouble for possessing books proscribed by the Obscene Publications Act, such as Vladimir Nabokov's *Lolita*, which was banned in the UK until 1959, or D. H. Lawrence's *Lady Chatterley's Lover*, finally legalised after a famous court case in 1960. In the '50s, if you wanted to read those books, you had to purchase them in France and try to smuggle them into the UK in your holiday luggage.

It was illegal to get an abortion, have a homosexual relationship or put on a play without first obtaining permission from the Lord Chamberlain, who would vet the script carefully for banned words.

It was the world of Dennis Potter's 'great greyness' – the 'feeling of the flatness and bleakness of everyday England'. It was a world of convention. 'Short back and sides,' a man would say as he walked into the barber; it would have been unmanly to say anything else. The man, if he was middle class and it was a working day, would have worn a grey suit, white shirt and tie, and his turn-ups would have been baggy with the dust of the week's work.

'The early 1950s were grim, dull years,' wrote Royston Ellis in *The Big Beat Scene*:

> There were no coffee bars, no commercial television stations, no juke boxes, and no teenage singing stars. The young people of those years were the same as they had been for generations previous. They were quiet, ordinary embryo-adults plodding without interference towards maturity.
>
> Their spare time was spent on sport, ballroom dancing, or on visits to the cinema. Slumped in the stalls of the local 'fleapit' they came face to face with celluloid glamour transporting them to the fantasies of filmdom. Their idols were film, not record, stars.[1]

For the tourist from the future, perhaps the worst thing would be the food. The residue of wartime shortages and rationing, on top

1 Royston Ellis, *The Big Beat Scene* (London: Four Square Books, 1961), p. 15.

of Britain's traditional culinary conservatism, made for dreadfully plain fare. Conversation at mealtimes often turned wistfully to the good things you could get before the war, such as real cream, thick and glutinous.

Visitors who wanted to find out how people lived might ask to be taken to the schools where their children were educated, and these would come as a shock.

For those at the poshest schools – the expensive private fee-charging schools, confusingly called public schools to this day – and the grammar schools, where brainy middle-class children went, there were long hours of stifling boredom, parsing sentences, chanting Latin declensions and memorising capital cities.

For those who failed the eleven plus and went to secondary modern schools, education was relentlessly skill-based. There was thought to be little need to bother with literature and history for those who were to spend their whole working lives doing menial jobs.

The school system enshrined the class system. In Church of England schools, they still sang the verse from 'All Things Bright and Beautiful' that is now banned:

The rich man in his castle
The poor man at his gate
God made them, high and lowly,
And ordered their estate.

Boys (and often girls) in '50s schools expected to be beaten regularly, like carpets. In a few schools, they were caned only occasionally and on special occasions, but in many, especially private fee-charging schools, it was a commonplace, if not daily, feature of life.

In many of these schools, beatings were formally administered not just by teachers but by older children too. Seventeen-year-olds were empowered to beat fifteen-year-olds; in many preparatory schools, twelve-year-olds were empowered to beat nine-year-olds. It was an unusually docile boy, or one who attended an unusually liberal school, who had not received a formal beating by the time he was eight, and there would be many more to come.

At many schools, the regime was merciless. The Catholic order of the Christian Brothers ran schools that were notorious for sustained brutality. Masters, as male teachers were routinely called in schools of the period, regularly beat their pupils to a pulp with their fists and any weapon that came to hand. Everyone knew it, and no one seemed to think anything should be done about it.

A lot of schools had on their staff a resident sadist. The children all knew who he was (it was generally, though not always, a man) and learned to avoid him, and the rest of the staff looked the other way. A very large number of schools – we are only just beginning to realise how many – also had on their staff at least one sexual predator who liked them young. Again, the children knew who he was, and who his victims were; and if his colleagues knew, they liked to pretend to themselves that they did not.

For, intolerant as the '50s were about most things, the tourist would find the mood of the times very tolerant towards sadistic teachers, as well as to violence in the home against both women and children.

They were tolerant about drink-driving too. Your attentive host would routinely offer you 'one for the road', and the tourist would be well advised not to venture on to the roads after the pubs closed, for a large proportion of the cars must have been driven by people who were too drunk to stand up.

They were tolerant towards racism. Many people now in their sixties can remember, as children, hearing grown-ups refer routinely to 'nips', 'wogs', 'dagos', 'yids' and 'niggers'. But they would have been horrified if anyone had said 'fuck'.

The class system would take some getting used to. Social classes had the rigidity of castes. Middle-class men and women talked quite openly of 'servants', and even the phrase 'below stairs' still meant something. The middle class, by and large, did not *keep* servants as they might have done between the wars, but they still talked as though one day, when the war had been forgotten and the welfare state had withered away, they might have them once again.

Those at the top of the caste system had some leeway with the rules, which was not granted to their social inferiors. Members of the upper classes could procure a safe abortion or a rapid divorce, carry on affairs, and get hold of banned books. Pretty well anything was available, pretty well anything was permissible, if you were rich or aristocratic, or a top journalist or politician. And people knew it, but they did not seem to mind. Class was just a fact of life.

Wine? It was unknown in most households, but it was well known that Winston Churchill began his morning in bed with champagne, and floated through each day on a sea of the very best wines, whiskies and brandies.

Sex? The political class knew, but kept discreetly silent, about the many affairs among their own kind, both heterosexual and homosexual.

Everyone was aware that there were different rules for the rich. They didn't like it, but they thought it was just how the world was, and there was nothing to be done about it. After a few pints of beer in a grubby old pub they might lurch home singing the old music-hall song:

It's the same the whole world over,
It's the poor what gets the blame,
It's the rich what gets the pleasure,
Ain't it all a bleeding shame?

There's a dreadfully misplaced nostalgia for the '50s, mostly to be found among expensively educated children of Thatcherism. They see the '50s as a glorious Indian summer, before free love and protest and egalitarianism, and 1956 and then 1968, came along to ruin it. Sometimes Thatcher's children sound as though they want to take us back to it – but they have never been there. If they had, they'd know better.

Ironically, Thatcher's children would recoil from the things the tourist might find attractive. The early '50s were the high-water mark of British public services. The public sector was respected and respectable, and offered much-sought-after careers in robustly unionised workplaces.

That's why, if you should have the misfortune to fall ill during your stay in the early '50s, you would find yourself instantly whisked off to a hospital that had all the latest equipment, and doctors and nurses who were proud of their work and their calling. The National Health Service was in the best shape in its history.

The visitor would not see many beggars. Unemployment, low throughout the early '50s, reached a record low of 1.2 per cent in 1955. The visitor would be amazed at how constantly human contact was made. You talked to human beings all the time: when buying railway tickets (you bought one for every journey, and a human being sold it to you and said good morning); when you were unsure which road to take; when you made a purchase of any sort; when you boarded a bus and spoke to the conductor (who sold tickets and left the driver free to drive). If you told the locals that, where you came from, you frequently had to be satisfied with an automated voice saying, 'Your call is important to us,' they would have thought your homeland must be a terribly primitive place. You would feel safe in the streets, because every so often you would come across a policeman, ambling along, looking around and ready to direct you if you were unsure of the way. All this human contact meant work for most of the population.

And if the visitor from the twenty-first century was unfortunate enough to get caught short in the streets of the early '50s, and require a lavatory faster than it would take to get back to the hotel, it would not be necessary to pay through the nose for a coffee the tourist did not want in order to gain access to the vendor's facilities, for you could find a public toilet more or less everywhere. Gentlemen's urinals were generally free; ladies needed, in the words of the contemporary euphemism, to spend a penny.

But, despite this, the early '50s were, taken all in all, the worst of times: dreary, conformist, class-ridden, complacent and directionless in a way that neither the '30s nor the '40s had been. The relative liberalism of the '30s had been closed down in the grey postwar years. Britain in the '50s was a much more repressed and conformist society than it had been before.

There was a sense of daring impropriety about the '30s, and one of idealism and common endeavour about the '40s, but both of these had run out of steam by 1950. The country had the scars of war all over it, but it lacked the spirit that drove the war itself.

That wartime spirit had gained a new lease of life at the 1945 general election. The Second World War had enabled the classes to mix, and war films harped on the theme of the naïve gentleman officer gaining new respect for the working class by associating with his cleverer and more worldly NCOs.

The idea that the 1945 general election might be a landmark that would change the face of Britain seems never to have occurred to most contemporary pundits. 'This is not the election that is going to shake Tory England,' said the *Manchester Guardian*, while the *News Chronicle*, faced with a Gallup poll giving Labour a six-point lead, found it so hard to credit that they ran the story as a low-key single-column item, full of caveats. The majority of Conservatives thought Churchill would pull them through.

Most elections are decided by fear; the 1945 election may have been the only one in the twentieth century to be decided by hope. Men who had fought for Britain for six years were saying that they were not going to go back to the old, unfair society of the '30s. They believed in better, which is why they got something better.

Most elections are won with a bit of razzmatazz; the 1945 election was won partly by the absence of razzmatazz. Churchill travelled the country in a cavalcade, arriving at each meeting in style amid great clamour, to address huge audiences. Labour leader Clement Attlee travelled in the passenger seat of the family Hillman, with his wife Vi at the wheel, an atlas on his knees if they were unsure of the route, the *Times* crossword when they knew the way.

Most elections are followed by disillusion as election promises dissolve like the morning mist. The Attlee government, inheriting a war-ravaged economy, set out to implement their very expensive promises to a deadline of 5 July 1948. It was the work Attlee had dreamed of being able to do ever since he published *The Social Worker* in the early '20s, quoting Blake in the introduction:

> *I will not cease from mental fight,*
> *Nor shall the sword sleep in my hand:*
> *Till we have built Jerusalem,*
> *In England's green and pleasant land.*

So, on 5 July 1948, Attlee broadcast to the nation, and he sounded deeply contented:

> Tomorrow there will come into operation the most comprehensive system of social security ever introduced into any country ... When I first went to work in east London, apart from what was done by voluntary organisations and by private charities ... the only provision

> for the citizen unable to work through sickness, unemployment or old age was that given by the Poor Law ... The Poor Law was designed to be, and indeed it was, the last refuge of the destitute.

Four acts, he said, were to come into force: the National Insurance Act, the Industrial Injuries Act, the National Assistance Act and the National Health Service Act. They were all based on a new principle:

> We must combine together to meet contingencies with which we cannot cope as individual citizens ... [They are] part of a general plan and they fit in with each other ... They are comprehensive and available to every citizen. They give security to all members of the family ... [The NHS] gives a complete cover for health by pooling the nation's resources, and paying the bill collectively.[2]

The Attlee government also took the first crucial step towards dismantling the British Empire by granting independence to India and Burma. Yet, at the start of the '50s, Britain still seemed not to understand the epoch-making significance of this. If the tourist were to ask most of the people he met in the streets about the country they lived in, they would say that Britain was a great imperial power. Schoolchildren were still proudly shown maps of the world on which vast tracts of territory were coloured red; they were taught about the empire upon which the sun never sets, and many of them learned by heart Rudyard Kipling's 'The White Man's Burden':

> *Take up the White Man's burden –*
> *Send forth the best ye breed –*
> *Go bind your sons to exile*

---

2 Francis Beckett, *Clem Attlee* (London: Haus Publishing, 2015).

To serve your captives' need;
To wait in heavy harness
On fluttered folk and wild –
Your new-caught, sullen peoples,
Half-devil and half-child.

Churchill had provided the inspiration to fight the war; the unlikely figure of little Clement Attlee, who looked and sounded like a suburban bank manager, provided the inspiration for the people to take control of their own nation.

A friend who was ill in a military hospital in India has told us how, when the news of the election result came through, men confined to bed got up and danced in the wards.

Iris Murdoch wrote to a friend: 'Oh, wonderful people of Britain! After all the ballyhoo and eyewash, they've had the guts to vote against Winston. I can't help feeling that to be young is very heaven.'

Soon after the election, a blazer-wearing, straw-boatered, fourteen-year-old public schoolboy, John Rae, stood on Bishop's Stortford station platform with his trunk, and called out, 'My man!'

'No,' said the station porter quietly, 'that sort of thing is over now.'[3]

The Labour victory and the Attlee government sustained the spirit that had fought the war. They sustained it through hardship, austerity and economic crisis, through the coldest and bleakest winter in living memory in 1946–47, and through the unexpected and unwelcome continuation of wartime rationing and National Service.

But a national spirit of optimism is a frail and sensitive plant, and it was wilting badly by 1951, when Labour was narrowly defeated. (Actually, the party got more votes than the Conservatives, but it piled up votes in Labour seats, and the Conservatives won a parliamentary majority.)

3 David Kynaston, *Austerity Britain* (London: Bloomsbury, 2008), pp. 77, 80.

The spirit that drove the Attlee settlement was not dead, but it was less obvious, and you had to look beyond politics to see it at work. A few good things that had been the preserve of the rich and powerful were opened up to those below them. The stuffy old West End theatres, whose prices alone excluded the vast majority of the population, opened their doors just a crack to the *hoi polloi* when, in 1950, the Whitehall farces, presented by Brian Rix, replaced the prewar Aldwych farces – the first was *Reluctant Heroes*. They made their money on a new kind of audience, the coach trade, with local clubs or pubs putting together a sufficiently large party to earn a discount at the box office. The same trade sustained Agatha Christie's *The Mousetrap*, which opened in 1952 and is still running in 2015.

Yet the start of the '50s remains one of the bleakest moments in Britain's social history. The spirit of optimism, of working to make a better world – the spirit of the war, of the Attlee settlement and of the New Jerusalem – had largely gone; but the hardship, social conservatism, conformism and austerity had not. Hardship without hope is not a good combination.

This is why so much was invested in the coronation of Queen Elizabeth II in 1953: it had to do duty for optimism and vision. Rather hopefully, a lot of people talked about a 'new Elizabethan age' to rival the era of the first Elizabeth.

Neil Kinnock was a schoolboy at the time:

> I remember our teacher really focusing on this business of the New Elizabethan Age. Because of jet travel, climbing Everest, because of all kinds of developments associated with full employment, the health service, there was this idea that there was a parallel [with] the days of John Hawkins and Walter Raleigh.

There were, it's true, certain resonances with the age of the first Elizabeth. Eight years earlier, Britain had emerged from war a victor against long odds. The novelist and short-story writer H. E. Bates, in his introduction to Paul Brickhill's collection of wartime escape stories *Escape – Or Die*, wrote: 'It has been said, and I think with a great deal of truth, that the RAF were the new Elizabethans, fighting and adventuring in the air, as the great navigators had fought and adventured in the seas.'

Despite wartime and postwar restrictions, despite the defeat of the Attlee government and despite recurrent economic crises, there was still an air of adventure in 1953. Intellectual adventure was manifested in the discovery of the DNA double helix, and physical adventure in the conquest of Everest, reported by the British press on the day of the coronation. 'Be proud of Britain on this day,' trumpeted the *Daily Express*, though the two members of the British-led expedition who reached the summit, Edmund Hillary and Tenzing Norgay, were actually from New Zealand and Nepal.

No matter. Lord Beaverbrook's *Daily Express* was keen to foster a feeling that, from this point on, the '50s would be an age of discovery, entrepreneurism, self-reliance and right-little-tight-little-islandism. How much better that was, Beaverbrook thought, than the statist, look-after-the-weakest sentimentality of the Attlee settlement.

But, as the comparison with the time of Elizabeth I might suggest, there would be only a very cautious rocking of the social boat. It was not to be expected that this new epoch should offer a platform for any young hobbledehoy with a point of view. The sort of men who gathered behind the young Queen to fanfare her new age were the 54-year-old historian Arthur Bryant, author of *English Saga* and many other works of patrician history, and one of the founders of the Right Book Club ('We are as much the countrymen of Nelson, Wesley and Shakespeare as of our own contemporaries'); the 76-year-old former war correspondent and right-wing social commentator Philip Gibbs, who published *The New Elizabethans* in that year; and the 49-year-old literary scholar A. L. Rowse, whose *An Elizabethan Garland* also appeared in 1953, and who attempted to allay his unease at the postwar democratisation of culture with a vision of a new literary and artistic elite.

This version of New Elizabethanism would be an antidote to what Churchill and other Tories considered the 'shoddy socialism' fostered by the Attlee government and its welfare state. (Though Attlee, too, had gone on record expressing hope that Britain was 'witnessing the beginning of a new Elizabethan age no less renowned than the first'.)

'I never fell for that,' said the writer and broadcaster Ludovic Kennedy, recalling New Elizabethanism. 'In fact I felt it was bogus at the time and I remember thinking: "Oh, this is just a political ploy and there's no truth in it."'

Still, there was this feeling in the air. Consider that perceptive witness of the period, Nigel Molesworth, the curse of St Custard's and hero of an ongoing school saga in the books *Down with Skool!* (1953) and *How to Be Topp* (1954) by Geoffrey Willans, illustrated by Ronald Searle. The third book in the sequence, *Whizz for Atomms* (1956) (parts of which had actually appeared in a magazine called *New Elizabethan*), opened with a chapter titled 'How to be a young Elizabethan': 'No one kno wot to do about anything at the moment so they sa the future is in the hands of YOUTH ... it is up to us boys becos the grownups hav made such a MESS of it all.'[4]

If you were just a little older than Molesworth, however, New Elizabethanism took a very bad fourth or fifth place behind the sex you were not getting. 'Did you know you were a New Elizabethan, Michael?' asks one of David Lodge's young female students in *How Far Can You Go?*, but Michael neither knows nor cares; he is 'gazing lustfully at an unclothed and headless mannequin in a shop window'.

Nor could New Elizabethan optimism shield Britain for long from

---

4 Geoffrey Willans and Ronald Searle, *The Compleet Molesworth* (London: Max Parrish, 1958), p. 212.

the hurricanes of international change. In the words of the historian and politician Tristram Hunt:

> It was a telling prelude to a reign which would see the eclipse of Britishness as a default form of national identity. The natural, instinctive, 1950s sense of British nationhood – forged through two world wars, a Protestant faith and an imperial project which suffocated the tensions of internal UK differentiation – would not see out the second Elizabeth's reign.[5]

Rationing finally ended in 1954. The next year provided a new Prime Minister, Anthony Eden, and a new Leader of the Opposition, Hugh Gaitskell, as well as the chance for a clean break with the past. No one had any idea how cataclysmic and final the break would prove to be.

The old Prime Minister and opposition leader, Churchill and Attlee, were politicians of the interwar years. So was Eden, but Hugh Gaitskell was of the new postwar generation; he had entered Parliament in 1945.

At the start of 1955, Nikita Khrushchev emerged the winner from Moscow's power struggle, and, by the start of 1956, we knew a lot that had been hidden from us throughout the Stalin years. We knew that Hitler and Eva Braun really had died in the *Führerbunker* in 1945, and the Allies had not allowed them to escape, as Stalin had suggested. Khrushchev released Hitler's pilot Hans Bauer after ten years in prison, and Bauer knew the truth.

We knew that the Yugoslav leader Tito was not a traitor to communism after all, because Khrushchev went to see Tito in Belgrade and announced that there were, in fact, 'different roads to socialism'. And if Tito was not a traitor, then everything Britain's

---

5 Tristram Hunt, 'Dreams of a new Elizabethan age faded into the end of empire', *The Guardian*, 31 May 2013.

communists had been saying for ten years about him was garbage. And if that was garbage, then the execution of Hungarian former interior minister László Rajk, and that of many other eastern Europeans, applauded by British communists, was judicial murder.

It was not immediately clear that communism, which had established itself as the home for idealistic and impatient youth, was unravelling; but it was to become so quite soon.

Yet perhaps the most important step on the road to 1956 was taken by the British and American governments in 1953.

Two years earlier, Iran had acquired its first (and, as it turned out, its last) democratically elected Prime Minister – Mohammad Mossadegh. He quickly introduced popular reforms: unemployment pay; sickness benefits for ill and injured workers; an end to forced labour; and rural housing. But then he made the fateful decision to nationalise his nation's oil and take control of the oil companies' assets.

On 21 June 1951, he told his nation:

> With the oil revenues we could meet our entire budget and combat poverty, disease and backwardness among our people. Another important consideration is that by the elimination of the power of the British company, we would also eliminate corruption and intrigue, by means of which the internal affairs of our country have been influenced. Once this tutelage has ceased, Iran will have achieved its economic and political independence. The Iranian state prefers to take over the production of petroleum itself. The company should do nothing else but return its property to the rightful owners.

This brought him into immediate confrontation with Churchill's government in London, which did everything possible to make it impossible for Iran to sell its oil, and managed to bring the Iranian oil industry to a virtual standstill. Britain's oil companies doubled their production in Saudi Arabia, Kuwait and Iraq to make up for lost production in Iran, so that no hardship was felt in Britain.

Nonetheless, nationalising the nation's oil made Mossaddegh a hero to his people. He brought in measures to strengthen the democratic political institutions that he knew would sustain his government: limiting the powers of the monarchy; cutting the Shah's personal budget; transferring royal lands back to the state; and weakening the political power of the landed aristocracy.

Churchill's government decided Mossaddegh had to go. At first, the Americans declined to help, but, in late 1952, the Republican Dwight Eisenhower replaced Democrat Harry Truman as President, and Churchill told Eisenhower that Mossaddegh could become dependent on a pro-Soviet party in Iran.

British and American security services started to work together to achieve Mossaddegh's overthrow, joining forces with his conservative and pro-Shah domestic enemies and using agents inside the Iranian government. The plot succeeded, Mossaddegh was overthrown, the CIA's choice for Prime Minister was installed in his place by the Shah, and Mossaddegh was sentenced to three years' solitary confinement in a military prison, and then kept under house arrest until his death in 1967.

The British Foreign Secretary at the time was Anthony Eden, and, when he became Prime Minister in 1955, he quickly found himself confronting yet another ruler in the Middle East who thought his people, rather than a British company, should own its nation's assets. As he contemplated how he might deal with this, Eden must have remembered the overthrow of Mossaddegh and thought he could bring down Egypt's Nasser too. 'I want him destroyed, don't you understand?' he told a close colleague.

The removal of Mossaddegh enabled a British company to keep control of Iran's oil, but the damage it did to the development of Iranian democracy can be seen in the country even today. Eden seems never to have understood the Middle East, nor what harm he might do there.

He was not the first, and certainly not the last, British Prime Minister to tinker in the Middle East without understanding what he was doing. To this day, Iranians think of Mossaddegh as a hero. More than half a century later, the recently retired Prime Minister Tony Blair urged Britain once again to attack the country Mossaddegh had briefly ruled. Broadcaster Jon Snow interviewed Blair and said, 'Of course, the problems of Iran go back to Mossaddegh, don't they?'

Blair looked blank. 'I'm sorry,' he said. 'You're going to have to remind me who that is.'

CHAPTER 2

ROCKING THE ESTABLISHMENT

When the record shops opened for business on 2 January in the deep fog that greeted the new year in London, 'Rock Around the Clock', by the American rock 'n' roller Bill Haley and his Comets, had elbowed aside local boy Dickie Valentine's 'Christmas Alphabet' to reoccupy the number-one slot it had claimed briefly in the dying weeks of 1955.

Rock 'n' roll was rough, raucous and dangerous, a strange and alien American sound that made some of the older, stuffier musicians and commentators look very foolish, very fast. 'I don't think the rock 'n' roll craze will come to Britain. It is primarily for the coloured population. I can't see it ever becoming a real craze,' said bandleader Ted Heath early in 1956.

Its arrival on the same day as Prime Minister Sir Anthony Eden's New Year message seems to mock the 58-year-old statesman's studied steady-as-she-goes calm.

Sir Anthony told cinema audiences on Pathé News:

> This is the season when we, each one of us, try to prepare our resolutions for the new year. We're determined to keep full employment – we're all agreed about that. We're also determined to maintain our high standard of living. But if we are to do these things, we have got to sell more abroad ... And then there's the question of peace – always, in all our minds. You can be sure we shall do everything we can to reduce tension between the nations at any time and at every opportunity. And we shall stand stoutly and firmly with our friends.

By the end of the year, the Prime Minister's remark about peace looked even more out of touch than the bandleader's one about rock 'n' roll.

One of the most characteristic attitudes of the '50s was deference, and, at Sandringham on New Year's Day, you got a vivid sense of its grip upon the nation. *The Queen* magazine told its readers:

> A crowd of about 5,000 saw Her Majesty the Queen and other members of the Royal Family leave the parish church after Morning Service. Later, Valerie Simpson, who lives on the Royal Estate at Anmer, went to Sandringham to receive from the Queen the bible that Her Majesty presents each year to the pupil of Dersingham Secondary School considered most proficient in religious knowledge.

Every year, teacher Richard Hackford selected a pupil and passed his or her details to Sandringham House so that the Queen could be briefed. The headmaster accompanied Valerie Simpson and her parents to morning service at Sandringham Church, and later presented Valerie to Her Majesty. He then met the eager press – including, no doubt, the correspondent of *The Queen* – outside a side entrance to Sandringham House to tell them all about his star pupil, before Valerie emerged to be photographed with the signed presentation Bible.

The magazine followed this with many pages of court news – charity balls, hunt balls, the Duke of Edinburgh leading the guns on a pheasant shoot – and a comment piece saying that, while the future was hard to predict, 'we should, by every means in our power, induce trade union leaders to be reasonable in their wage demands'.

But the editor of *The Queen* saw a ray of light in the New Year Honours list: 'A reminder that despite the democratic tendencies of the age, recognition by the sovereign of special services to the community still makes a popular appeal.'

Indeed, the idea that 'democratic tendencies' were necessarily a good thing was very far from being a given in 1956. On 6 January, Britain's Catholic newspapers reported with disgust the French election victory of Pierre Mendès-France's radicals and Guy Mollet's socialists because they intended to abolish state subsidies to Church schools. The pro-Catholic Popular Republican Movement lost sixteen seats. *The Universe*'s headline was: 'The people fail France again.'

It was, after all, only eleven years since Labour's 1945 election victory was greeted by a lady diner at the Savoy Hotel – so the story goes – with the words: 'This is terrible – they've elected a Labour government, and the country will never stand for it.'[6]

The same could well have been said of rock 'n' roll. Young people took to it, but it was not at all clear that the country would stand for it. The success of Bill Haley's disc was initially due to its exposure in the movie *Blackboard Jungle*, where 'youngsters were seen bopping

6 D. R. Thorpe, *Supermac: The Life of Harold Macmillan* (London: Pimlico, 2011), p. 241.

in their schoolroom to the background of a reedy voice and honking saxophone exhorting them to "rock!"'. Indeed, 'for many, this was the first personal experience of rock 'n' roll'.[7] It was a sight that was to horrify parents and teachers for the rest of the '50s.

Haley also occupied the number-five slot in that first chart of 1956 with 'Rock-A-Beatin' Boogie'. It would prove to be a remarkable year for Haley and his Comets. Having only been heard in *Blackboard Jungle*, they starred in the films *Rock Around the Clock* and *Don't Knock the Rock*. According to a survey in the *New Musical Express* (NME) of the first half of the year's 'disc biz', the group could rely on 'a guaranteed sale exceeding 100,000 copies ... for each of their releases'.

There was only one week in those six months when Haley had no record in the NME chart. As London's deep fog moved northwards, closing aerodromes throughout the country, bringing traffic to a halt and preventing shipping from moving on the Humber and the Tees, 'Rock Around The Clock' was replaced by the 'wailing saxophone and terrific beat', as the NME reviewer enthused, of 'See You Later, Alligator'. Haley spent more weeks in the chart (with more hits) than anybody had before, or has since. For a spell of eight weeks in the autumn, he had five discs in the Top 30 every week.

In it, but not on top of it. In mid-January Haley moved aside to accommodate Tennessee Ernie Ford's 'Sixteen Tons', another quintessentially American vignette, but, for most of the rest of the year, the number-one ranking was held by mainstream figures with anodyne songs: Dean Martin with 'Memories Are Made of This', Ronnie Hilton with 'No Other Love', Pat Boone, Doris Day, Anne Shelton...

It wasn't very different in the lower reaches of the chart. At number six in the first week of January, just below Haley's 'Rock-A-Beatin' Boogie', was the perky chanteuse from Whitechapel, Alma Cogan,

---

7 Royston Ellis, *The Big Beat Scene* (London: Four Square Books, 1961), p. 20.

with 'Never Do a Tango with an Eskimo'. A ubiquitous sound of early 1956 was 'The Ballad of Davy Crockett', from the movie *Davy Crockett, King of the Wild Frontier*, recorded in competing versions by Billy Hayes (who got as high as number two in January), Tennessee Ernie Ford and, improbably, the comedian Max Bygraves.

Looking back, we can see that rock 'n' roll had put down its marker: it was a new music for a new generation, and nothing afterwards would be the same. But in the music business of early 1956, rock 'n' roll amounted, at the most, to a hill of beans – certainly not a mountain. It is easy to think of artists like Cogan and Dickie Valentine, or their contemporaries David Whitfield and Lita Roza, as the parade's end of pre-rock popular music, but that wasn't how it seemed to the music papers at the time. For the NME, the big news story of spring 1956 was the UK tour of Stan Kenton's West Coast modern-swing orchestra. (And the big one of late summer would be the visit of American singer Mel Torme, greeted by the NME with the headline: 'Tormultuous receptions for fabulous Mel!')

As the NME saw it, records were still predominantly bought by grown-ups. The year witnessed just two further chart-toppers that might be regarded as younger persons' music. The first was 'Why Do Fools Fall in Love' by The Teenagers, a vocal group from New York that was three-fifths African-American and two-fifths Puerto Rican, headed by the wailing thirteen-year-old Frankie Lymon. The second, at the year's end (and stretching the definition of 'younger persons' music' quite a lot), was Johnnie Ray's 'Just Walking in the Rain'.

The influence of American youth culture – fast cars, drive-in movies, soda fountains, casual clothes and hip language, as glimpsed in movies like *Blackboard Jungle* and *Rock Around the Clock* – was undeniably heady, but not everyone got drunk on it. Some found ways to consume it without being consumed. Take, for instance, the curious Anglo-American hybrid called skiffle.

Entering that first January chart at number seventeen was Lonnie Donegan from Glasgow with 'Rock Island Line' – an obscure railroad song from the repertoire of the black American folk-singer Lead Belly, and a harbinger of the skiffle craze. It was the first record fifteen-year-old John Lennon bought, and he took it home very carefully: it was a fragile, precious 78rpm disc.[8] That summer, he got together with some friends from his school, Quarry Bank High, to form a skiffle group – the Quarrymen.

Skiffle was defiantly homemade-sounding music, characterised by acoustic guitars and banjos, clattering washboards, thumping tea-chest basses, the buzz of the kazoo, and, sometimes, the rattle of the lagerphone – a household broom festooned with hundreds of beer bottle-tops, which the player held upright and banged rhythmically on the floor.

Skiffle offered a perfect starting-point for teenagers who wanted to make music and had neither the skill nor the resources – nor, probably, the inclination – to make it according to the stifling conventions of the pop industry. Which was fortunate, because the mediators of British pop music at the time, producers and arrangers like Norrie Paramor and Wally Stott, had learned their trade in the era of the dance band and the Broadway song, and took those lessons into their studio work. For them, a group of youths interpreting the songs of American convicts or coal miners on improvised instruments scarcely counted as music at all.

In the United States, the word 'skiffle' had been around since the '20s, evidently meaning music performed in a loose or informal way. When a group of leading blues artists, including the guitarist Blind Blake and the banjoist Papa Charlie Jackson, gathered in the studio of

---

8 John Wyse Jackson, *The Life of John Lennon: We All Want to Change the World* (London: Haus Publishing, 2008), p. 31.

Paramount Records in 1929 to create the illusion of a phonographic all-star party, the disc was titled 'Hometown Skiffle'.

Skiffle also implied the use of non-standard instruments – like those washboards and tea chests. In the '30s, there had been a brief vogue for washboard bands like the Washboard Rhythm Kings, whose 'I'm Gonna Play Down by the Ohio', issued in the UK on an HMV 78rpm disc, was remembered fondly by Philip Larkin as the second jazz record he ever bought.

In Britain, though, skiffle had no history until 1953, when it emerged, almost by accident, as a sideline of traditional jazz. It began, George Melly recalled, with the bandleader Ken Colyer:

> In order to provide a contrast to an evening's diet of undiluted New Orleans ensemble, he introduced a short vocal session of Negro folk music with himself and his banjo player Lonnie Donegan on guitars, and Chris Barber on bass ... He called these interludes 'Skiffle Sessions', to differentiate them from the more serious activity of playing blues, rags, stomps and marches, and they achieved great, if localized, popularity among the band's followers.
>
> When Ken's band broke up and Chris [Barber] picked up the pieces, he naturally retained the skiffle-session idea. Lonnie Donegan took over the singing and became very popular round the clubs ... His version of 'Rock Island Line', originally part of a *Chris Barber in Concert* LP, was requested so often on the radio that it was put out as a single.[9]

'Rock Island Line' spent twenty weeks in the chart in 1956, and was a Top 10 hit in the United States. Donegan would also do well with

9 George Melly, *Owning Up* (London: Weidenfeld & Nicolson, 1965), pp. 168–9 in 1970 Penguin edition.

his third release, 'Lost John'/'Stewball', which entered the chart in April, and rose in June to number two. 'Lonnie's skiffle is no piffle!' the NME would boast in that month, despite the fact that, at the beginning of the year, the paper had been puzzled by the success of 'Rock Island Line':

> Exactly why this happened is one of those eternal mysteries of show business. But one thing seems fairly certain. The disc has quite accidentally cashed in on two very strong trends in the pop record business. One is the narrative gimmick ... the other is the 'rock an' roll' craze as exemplified by 'Rock Around the Clock' and 'Sixteen Tons'.

Peter Cooley was a student of mechanical engineering at King's College, London:

> I first heard Lonnie Donegan as he featured on at least two tracks of my Chris Barber Jazz Band LP, which I think I bought in about 1954 and practically wore out. I recall 'Rock Island Line' being 'sung' all around college. Much to many people's relief, as soon as *My Fair Lady* arrived in London in 1958, skiffle seemed to be temporarily eclipsed.

George Melly's slant on the birth of British skiffle was that of a jazz insider. Royston Ellis links it also with the folk scene of the early '50s:

> By the beginning of 1956 ... singing guitarists were becoming a standard attraction at certain pubs and cafés. The 'bohemian' characters, art students, actors, and ordinary intelligent people who liked this rambling fifties style folk singing, would drop in

> during the evenings to hear the singers. Their haunts included the Gyre & Gymbal near Charing Cross, the Breadbasket near Middlesex Hospital, and the Two I's Coffee Bar in Old Compton Street.[10]

A key moment, according to skiffleogical legend, was in July 1956, when The Vipers – a skiffle band led by Wally Whyton – played for the Soho Fair parade; soon afterwards, regular skiffle sessions began at the 2i's (as it was spelled on the shopfront at 59 Old Compton Street). Later in the year, The Vipers had some success with a recording of 'Pick a Bale of Cotton' – another song learned from Lead Belly.

In many ways, skiffle was a '50s version of punk rock: iconoclastic, insiderish, informal. Musical simplicity was part of the point. The famous page in a 1977 punk fanzine showing three basic chords, A, E and G, and the instruction 'now form a band' was simply the manifesto of skiffle, twenty years on. The difference was that skiffle drew its inspiration from America and from tradition – entities punk couldn't care less about.

Such was the popularity of do-it-yourself music in 1956–57 that supply faltered behind demand. 'There is a fantastic shortage of Guitars due to the great rock 'n' roll, calypso and skiffle rage,' claimed a 1957 ad placed by Headquarter & General Supplies Ltd, a popular mail-order company that advertised extensively in the music press, *Exchange & Mart* and elsewhere. 'Just try and buy one of this type. We have been lucky in finding 1,000 only – get yours quickly. Full size popular plectrum style, handsomely polished.' One of those 'Professional Style Rock 'n' Roll Guitars' could be yours for just five shillings down and twenty-two fortnightly payments of 10s 3d.

Skiffle didn't last long – two or three years at most – but, for

---

10 Ellis, op. cit., pp. 46–7.

a while, it had its own radio show on the BBC Light Programme called *Saturday Skiffle Club*. After a year or so, the show's producers acknowledged the waning of skiffle and shortened the name to *Saturday Club*. Until the late '60s and the arrival of Radio 1, this was BBC radio's primary showcase for pop music.

The spirit of the age was being driven by the young – with a self-confidence their parents and older siblings could not dream of – and the country could either stand for it or lump it. For the first time, the young had a small amount of money in their pockets and could make consumer decisions. When they did, they were better informed than their elders, because they understood the new advertising-driven world – a strange and frightening one to their parents. The previous year had seen the start of commercial television, and it had brought advertising, for the first time, into the sanctum of the home.

It was as shocking as strobe lighting in a cathedral: a dreadful thing, a precursor of a world viewers were not sure they wanted to live in. In the first-ever TV ad, they saw a tube of toothpaste embedded in a block of ice and a woman brushing her teeth in the approved manner – 'up and down and round the gums' – and the slogan was: 'It's tingling fresh. It's fresh as ice. It's Gibbs SR toothpaste.'

Within a week, Bernard Levin was attempting to draw conclusions in the *Manchester Guardian*, having been

> goaded into incivility by several days of the most idiotic verse imaginable – and in many cases unimaginable ... The childishness of some of these songs is exceeded only by their irritating ability to stick like burrs in the memory ... Messrs. Cadbury['s] advertisement,

> though inept in the extreme, has for two days had me singing the damnably catchy little tune which accompanied it.[11]

Children and teenagers, too, were singing jingles from the advertisements. From the end of 1955 came: 'Murray Mints, Murray Mints, the too-good-to-hurry mints.' And from 1956: 'You'll wonder where the yellow went, when you brush your teeth with Pepsodent.' And who could forget the plaintive cry of the schoolboy as his mother went off to the shops? 'Don't forget the Fruit Gums, Mum!'

ITV conditioned the childhoods of the baby boomers, making them fundamentally different from any earlier generation. Within what seemed to be an amazingly short space of time, advertisements had become everyday currency. The first known joke to revolve around an advertising slogan probably dates from early 1956, and goes like this:

> A man is walking through the desert with a camel and a native bearer when he hears a quiet, insistent sound: 'One, two, three...'
>
> He tells the bearer: 'If you don't stop that, I'll shoot you.'
>
> So when he hears 'twelve, thirteen, fourteen...', he shoots the bearer. Then he hears 'fifty-seven, fifty-eight, fifty-nine...', so he shoots the camel, and is entirely alone. Yet it continues: 'A hundred and forty-five, a hundred and forty-six, a hundred and forty-seven...'
>
> In despair, he sits on a rock and takes out his matches and his packet of Player's cigarettes. Then he remembers: it's the tobacco that counts.

Another celebrated advertisement dates from 1956: the chimpanzees in humans' clothing enjoying a cup of PG Tips tea. The basic idea was

11 Bernard Levin, 'Rhymes without reason', *Manchester Guardian*, 27 September 1955.

nothing new: the 'chimpanzees' tea party' had been a popular attraction at London Zoo since the mid-'20s. Brooke Bond, makers of PG Tips, merely appropriated it, though as well as jackets and frocks they gave the chimps voices, fabricated by well-known comedy performers of the time like Peter Sellers and Bob Monkhouse. The effect of the ad, first aired on Christmas Day, was dramatic: within two years PG Tips rose from fourth place in the British tea sales chart – the tea table, if you will – to become the nation's favourite.

After objections by animal rights groups in the '70s, the chimps were cancelled and retired to their home in Twycross Zoo, but the public missed them and PG Tips's sales fell. The primates returned to prime-time TV, not to leave it until 2002.

In January 1956, easily the most-watched television programme was ITV's *The Adventures of Robin Hood*, with Richard Greene as a dimpled version of the famous outlaw, and a theme song that everyone in Britain over sixty can still sing:

> *Robin Hood, Robin Hood, riding through the glen,*
> *Robin Hood, Robin Hood, with his band of men.*

In two-channel London households it was number one for January 1956 with a staggering 78 per cent audience share. We rushed home from school to watch it, or went to the home of a friend with a television. Did we understand that taking from the rich and giving to the poor was a fairly potent political message for 1956, another way of saying 'redistribution of wealth'? Or that the producers were using the show to undermine Senator Joe McCarthy's House Un-American Activities Committee by using the writers McCarthy had blacklisted to write its scripts under different names? Sadly not. But it was another nail in the coffin of the old order, all the same.

There was a revolution of sorts going on, driven by the young and, we may be pretty sure, unnoticed by the embattled and secretly unwell Prime Minister, whose surface calm concealed not only pain and physical frailty, but also worries and insecurities that gnawed at him during every waking minute. Since his electoral triumph in May the previous year – a month after taking over the premiership from Winston Churchill – it had all been downhill for Anthony Eden, and he had acquired a reputation for dither, weakness and micro-management. When he replaced Foreign Secretary Harold Macmillan with Selwyn Lloyd, partly because he wanted to control foreign policy himself, he telephoned his new appointee thirty times on his first weekend in the job.

Just after he issued his New Year message, he saw that the polls for the first time gave Labour, under its new and much younger leader Hugh Gaitskell, a lead over the Conservatives. On 13 January, the Conservative-supporting *Spectator* said:

> The widespread criticism of the Prime Minister reached a climax last week, with the attack of that faithful party warhorse, the *Daily Telegraph*, and the extraordinary denial from 10 Downing Street of the rumours that Sir Anthony Eden was about to resign. Just why Sir Anthony should think it necessary to deny a rumour originating in a German newspaper and repeated in a popular English Sunday newspaper is obscure.

From the left, the *Manchester Guardian* added: 'It is extraordinary that it had to be made at all about a Prime Minister, who has been in office only since 6 April.'

The wording of Eden's denial certainly had the feel of panic: 'The report is false and without any foundation whatsoever.'

Just at that moment, Mrs Maud Butt, who lived in one of the farm workers' cottages about 400 yards from the Prime Minister's country residence at Chequers, was affronted to receive a message from Eden's wife Clarissa asking her please not to string her washing along her back garden, where it was clearly visible from the house and to foreign visitors, whom Clarissa took for walks in the grounds.

Only a few years earlier, Mrs Butt's mother or older sister would have humbly ceased to display the offending garments, but Mrs Butt instead went to the *Daily Mirror*. The incident offers a first taste of the new spirit 1956 was to inaugurate. According to Clarissa Eden, the newspaper paid Mrs Butt – and it may well have done, though it seems unlikely that Mrs Eden knew for certain. Either way, it was an embarrassment. Clarissa was full of remorse for having added to her husband's troubles, and her husband was so angry that he consulted Sir Hartley Shawcross, the Attorney General, on whether to take legal action against the *Mirror*.[12] This, of course, would have been foolish and self-defeating, and it was an ominous sign that Eden even considered it.

'I don't believe Anthony can do it,' Winston Churchill had said to his doctor, just before resigning as Prime Minister the previous year.[13] But it's at least arguable that no one could have done it, for what a Conservative Prime Minister had to do in 1956 was reconcile the traditional Tory idea of Britain's place in the world with the reality. There was a chasm between the two.

Here, for example, is what an entirely respectable mainstream political commentator, Henry Fairlie, was writing in *The Spectator* on 20 January:

---

12 Cherie Booth and Cate Haste, *The Goldfish Bowl* (London: Chatto & Windus, 2004).

13 John Colville, *The Fringes of Power: Downing Street Diaries 1939–1955* (London: Phoenix, 2005), p. 662.

> I believe with Milner that 'the survival of Britain through the preservation and development of the empire must be the supreme concern of all Britons.' [Viscount Milner was the British High Commissioner for South Africa at the end of the nineteenth century, and held Britons to be racially superior to Afrikaners.] Neither of the two major parties believes this. During the past ten years, when both of them have enjoyed periods of secure office, neither has proposed a single act of policy that has betrayed even the slightest belief that the development of the Commonwealth and Empire should be given priority ... This could be merely the symptom of a country in decline; a country which is decadent instinctively tries both to contract and to ossify. It could, on the other hand, and this is the more hopeful diagnosis, be the symptom of a governing elite in decline. I believe there are good reasons for thinking this is true.

Squaring this with the reality of Britain's position as 1956 opened might have strained a much healthier man, and a much cooler politician, than Sir Anthony. And Fairlie was at the sane end of the empire lobby. At the loopy end was to be found the League of Empire Loyalists (LEL). Its chairman A. K. Chesterton had once been a lieutenant of Sir Oswald Mosley; but he had left Mosley in 1938 and was not to found the National Front until 1967. In the meantime, he was almost a respectable, mainstream figure as literary adviser and authorised biographer of Lord Beaverbrook, and regular writer for the magazine *Truth*, which, before the war, had been the voice of the appeasers in the Conservative Party. Indeed, the LEL had the discreet sympathy and support of several Conservatives.

Chesterton had fallen out with *Truth*, and his LEL created what it hoped would be a replacement. They called it *Candour*. *Candour* was pretty clear where it stood on the empire and on race. On 6 January, commenting on rapes in South African townships, it ran a piece – almost certainly by Chesterton himself, who had spent some of his early years in South Africa – that began:

> There is being reproduced on the Rand, in gangster form, much of the savagery and violence that had been the almost invariable pattern before the Whiteman [*sic*] arrived. As the Whiteman's laws alone had power to stop the internecine tribal warfare, so today only the Whiteman's law, remorselessly enforced, can bring release from their present nightmare to Africans terrorized by the vile creatures of their own race who thus exploit them.

Four days later, the *Manchester Guardian*, exhibiting a rather more modern attitude to colonial peoples, ran a story headed 'Cannibalism in India'. It reported the police discovering that a missing five-year-old boy in Uttar Pradesh had been eaten by a Hindu sect that believed eating boys would ward off evil spirits. Twenty-one sect members, 'living like beasts amid the bones of their victims', had been arrested, and so had a young man in south India who had dragged his mother to the temple steps and decapitated her, earning the respect of the crowd for his devotion to God.

'What does all this mean?' asked the *Manchester Guardian*'s reporter Taya Zinkin:

> Not that India is going back to the days of *suttee*[14] and human sacrifices, but rather the opposite: that orthodoxy is rearing its ugly head in a last fight for survival ... Today it is rare and scandalous and the police interfere. Only two heads have been cut as an offering to the gods during the past year, so far as I recall, and there has only been a *suttee* or two.

---

14 The practice of a Hindu widow throwing herself on her husband's funeral pyre.

Such laid-back tolerance was not for the LEL. Among their adherents were several members of the Greene family of Berkhamsted, whose best-known members were the author Graham Greene and his brother Hugh Carleton Greene, who was to be BBC director-general in the '60s. In January 1956, one of the family, Miss Leslie Greene, became a heroine of the movement after she managed to get herself to the front of the hall while the Prime Minister was speaking at Bradford.

Anthony Eden was, of course, their historic enemy: not just as the Prime Minister who did not seem to value the empire, but also – though they tended not to talk about this much any more – as the man who had stabbed Neville Chamberlain in the back in 1938, and helped scupper the chance of making peace with Hitler.

'Little did Sir Anthony Eden think,' reported *Candour*, 'as he tranquilly embarked upon his speech, that he would be challenged by the LEL at the very microphone through which he was pouring his sedatives into the minds of the thousands of dutifully loyal Tories assembled for that purpose.'

Miss Greene shouted into the microphone, 'The British Empire is the greatest force for peace the world has ever known and you are giving it away.' As she spoke these heroic words, LEL leaflets showered down from an upper gallery in the hall.

The Prime Minister's minders ushered Miss Greene out, and this is what had to do duty for Sir Anthony's riposte: 'I don't think that was a justified observation. After all, I have had some contacts with the British Commonwealth and empire.'

Someone shouted from the gallery: 'You have given the empire away.'

Sir Anthony replied: 'We have not given it away. What has happened is that the people of the Commonwealth are steadily developing towards freedom and self-government.' The strand of thinking represented by the LEL was not one a Conservative government could afford to take lightly.

Another of the indefatigable Greenes, Herbert, wrote a poem *Candour* printed on 13 January – three days after earth tremors were felt in the Midlands and the north-west, which one suspects might have seemed significant to the Greenes:

It's not among the Union Men
Or Bureaucratic spivs;
It's not among the Parties
That the heart of England lives.
You'll find that heart in wayside pubs
And in quiet home retreats,
For there, amidst the smoke and pipes
The heart of England beats.

Mr Greene was clearly trying to capture the tone of A. K. Chesterton's more famous cousin G. K., but was hampered by a lack of literary talent, at least if this poem is a fair example of his *oeuvre*. It would certainly not have passed muster with W. H. Auden, who, in late January, was a candidate for the post of Professor of Poetry at Oxford University. 'There is keen excitement about the election,' Evelyn Waugh confided to his diary. 'Auden and [Harold] Nicolson, both homosexual socialists, and an unknown scholar named Knight. I wish I had taken my degree so that I might vote for Knight.'[15]

---

15 Michael Davie (ed.), *The Diaries of Evelyn Waugh* (London: Weidenfeld & Nicolson, 1976), p. 753.

Waugh's loathing of homosexuals was common in 1956, as we shall see in Chapter 9, but that did not stop Auden winning the election. Alan Bennett attended his inaugural lecture:

> Had I any ambitions to write at that time, the lecture would have been enough to put me off. Auden listed all the interests and accomplishments that poets and critics should properly have – a dream of Eden, an ideal landscape, favourite books, even, God help us, a passion for Icelandic sagas. If writing means passing this kind of kit inspection, I thought, one might as well forget it.[16]

And while Leslie Greene was braving the Prime Minister in Bradford, just 75 miles due east, in Hull, another poet, Philip Larkin, was settling into his new post of University Librarian and enjoying the critical success of his verse collection *The Less Deceived*, which had been published by a small local press the previous November. Early in the new year, before term began, he and his companion Monica Jones visited Chichester Cathedral, where they admired the monument to the Earl of Arundel and his wife. Back in Hull, he immediately began working on what would become 'An Arundel Tomb'.

Poems did not come easily to Larkin in 1956 – he completed only two in the year – and parts of this one gave him trouble. 'I'm absolutely *sick* of my tomb poem,' he wrote to Monica in mid-February. But he persevered, discussing passages with her in letters and cards, particularly its ending. He finally settled upon: 'What will survive of us is love' – little suspecting that it would become one of his most quoted lines.[17]

---

16 Alan Bennett, *Six Poets: Hardy to Larkin – An Anthology* (London: Faber & Faber/Profile Books, 2014), pp. xi–xii.

17 Andrew Motion, *Philip Larkin: A Writer's Life* (London: Faber & Faber, 1993), pp. 273–4 in 1994 paperback edition; Anthony Thwaite (ed.), *Philip Larkin: Letters to Monica* (London: Faber & Faber in association with The Bodleian Library, 2010), pp. 196–9.

'What will survive of us is love.' Perhaps, but the auguries were not good. On 31 January, A. A. Milne, pacifist author whose work soothed generations of children comfortingly to bed, died; while John Lydon, later known as Johnny Rotten of the Sex Pistols, whose work was to jolt a future generation out of its comfort zone, was born.

CHAPTER 3

THE LEFT'S HOME IS TRASHED

Early in February, Harry Pollitt, the veteran leader of the Communist Party of Great Britain (CPGB), addressed a meeting of 'cultural comrades' in High Holborn Hall.

Communism, at the start of 1956, was still a grcat brave cause, and the CPGB still provided a home for the idealistic young. The show trials of the '30s and the trumped-up charges against nine Jewish doctors in 1953 had damaged it, but not as much as you might imagine: idealistic youth in 1956, as ever, badly wanted something to believe in.

Alison Macleod, then a journalist on the *Daily Worker*, recalled the meeting: 'We were harangued by Harry Pollitt and the art critic John

Berger. We had no opportunity for questions or discussion. It must have been the last time Pollitt got away with that.'[18]

Britain's communists, like its capitalists, relied on deference. The 66-year-old Pollitt expected his members to follow the correct line, and he, in turn, took his lead from the Communist International and, ultimately, the Kremlin. He was not to know, when he talked to that meeting in High Holborn Hall, that the respect he had relied on all his political life was about to be destroyed for ever.

Within days of that meeting, Pollitt was off to Moscow for the 20th Congress of the Soviet Communist Party. He had visited Moscow hundreds of times, and been to all the Soviet Communist Party's congresses, but this one was to shake his world.

On 11 February, three days before the start of the 20th Congress, Britain learned where the spies Guy Burgess and Donald Maclean were.

Burgess and Maclean had been recruited as Soviet spies when they were undergraduates at Cambridge University in the '30s, along with Kim Philby and Anthony Blunt, who were not unmasked until many years after 1956, and, it is thought, a fifth person whose identity is still unknown. They had worked their way up to positions that gave them access to secrets worth knowing.

But they were public-school and Oxbridge men from good families, and were never suspected. The security services were far too busy bugging former boilermaker Harry Pollitt's telephone calls and following him about. Quite what use as a spy they thought the best-known communist in Britain would be, it is hard to say, but that's how they spent their time and money.

In the summer of 1951, believing they were on the verge of being discovered, Burgess and Maclean slipped out of the country. No one knew for certain where they had gone, and the Soviet Union

18 Alison Macleod, *The Death of Uncle Joe* (London: Merlin Press, 1997), pp. 46–7.

ferociously denied that it had them. But of course it did, and the Soviet government said as much nearly five years later.

As Burgess and Maclean's whereabouts were revealed to a rather less than astonished world, Harry Pollitt was on his way to Moscow at the head of a three-strong delegation. The second delegate was the grim theoretician Rajani Palme Dutt, a man of Pollitt's own vintage, whose determination to follow the Moscow line far exceeded Pollitt's own, with some even believing him to be the only British communist Moscow entirely trusted. The third was a younger communist, 39-year-old assistant general secretary George Matthews, who had progressed to leadership by way of the National Union of Students.

The 20th Congress opened on 14 February.

The 19th Congress in 1952 had turned out to be Stalin's last. He died in 1953, and the struggle for the succession had been going on ever since. It fell to Nikita Khrushchev, then First Secretary of the Soviet Communist Party, to make the first speech of the 20th Congress, and it lasted six hours – but that was nothing terribly unusual: speeches in communist gatherings were famously interminable.

Speech followed speech. The only sign of what was to come was when the First Deputy Premier Anastas Mikoyan said: 'The principle of collective leadership is elementary for a party of the Lenin type. Yet for twenty years we did not have collective leadership but the cult of the individual. This had a harmful effect.'

On 18 February, it was the turn of the foreign communist parties to deliver their fraternal addresses. 'The workers welcome and salute the brilliant achievements and plans of the Soviet Union,' said Pollitt on behalf of the British delegation, and then he said it again, in different (and rather more) words.[19]

The fraternal address was one of the great set-pieces of world

---

19 Macleod, op. cit., p. 50.

communism, and, saluting the brilliant achievements of the Soviet Union, a conventional piety, used rather in the same way that a Christian or a Muslim will insert a conventionally pious phrase when mentioning the name of God. As the communist students in Cambridge had sung in the '30s:

Dan, Dan, Dan
The Communist Party man
Working underground all day
In and out of meetings
Bringing fraternal greetings
Never seeing the light of day.

Pollitt was the master of the fraternal address. Around the same time as these events, someone wrote a little ditty about him that also became popular among communists. One verse went:

Old Harry went to Heaven, he reached the gates with ease,
Said, 'May I speak with Comrade God, I'm Harry Pollitt please,
I'm Harry Pollitt please, I'm Harry Pollitt please,
May I speak with Comrade God, I'm Harry Pollitt please.'

Naturally, he gets into Heaven and brings the angels out on strike.

But at the 20th Congress, everyone understood that the fraternal addresses were a sideshow. Something big was going on, but Western journalists struggled to understand what it was, because they were excluded from the only speech that really mattered. So they generally got the story completely wrong. Here is *The Spectator* on 24 February:

> As we go to press, the Congress of the Soviet Communist Party is not yet over ... Interest centres on the attacks on leadership by

> an individual, and on Stalin personally. These were made mainly by those least committed to Khrushchev – Suslov, Malenkov and Mikoyan. It seems reasonable to suppose they were directed against Khrushchev, the main immediate contender for individual leadership, and at the same time the most loyal and orthodox Stalinist.

Reasonable supposition maybe, but not at all what was going on. On 25 February, the day after *The Spectator* ran this report, in the early hours of the morning, at a closed session from which foreign communists were excluded, Khrushchev made a four-hour speech, and nothing was ever the same again. Stalin, the man whom British communists had been taught to admire, was revealed as a murderous monster, little better than Hitler.

But it was that contradiction in terms, a secret speech. The British delegation was not there. Most foreign delegates, and all journalists, were excluded. As Alison Macleod put it, British delegates 'were told that the workers of the Caoutchouc factory were longing to hear them make speeches', and 5,000 of them cheered Pollitt as he obliged.

Caoutchouc was a rubber factory. 'Where was I when Comrade K. made that speech?' Pollitt said later, deflecting criticism in vintage Pollitt style when the world learned what had happened. 'I was being conducted round a French letter factory. At my age, I suppose that was a compliment.'

George Matthews was there with him, but Palme Dutt, the most reliable and on-message Stalinist in Britain, was not. Some people thought that Dutt alone had been admitted to the great secret of the Khrushchev speech.[20] It would make sense. Someone had to know, so as to be ready with the party line if it ever leaked, and Moscow did not quite trust Pollitt. We shall probably never know for certain.

---

20 Francis Beckett, *Enemy Within* (London: John Murray, 1995; Merlin Press, 1998), p. 130.

'Stalin, using his unlimited power, allowed himself many abuses,' said Khrushchev:

> Many Party activists who were branded in 1937–38 as 'enemies' were never actually enemies, spies, wreckers etc., but were always honest communists, and often, no longer able to bear barbaric tortures, they charged themselves with all kinds of grave and unlikely crimes ... Of the 139 members and candidates of the Party's Central Committee who were elected at the Seventeenth Congress, ninety-eight persons, i.e. 70 per cent, were arrested and shot.

He quoted personal testimonies. One was Robert Eikhe, a member of the Communist Party since 1905:

> Not being able to suffer the tortures to which I was submitted by Z. Ushakov and Nikolaev – especially by the former, who utilised the knowledge that my broken ribs have not properly mended and have caused me great pain – I have been forced to accuse myself and others. The majority of my confession has been suggested or dictated by Ushakov.

Eikhe was shot in 1940.

'It has been definitely established now that Eikhe's case was fabricated,' said Khrushchev.

It was all down to Stalin. 'Stalin was a very distrustful man, sickly, suspicious,' Khrushchev continued. 'The sickly suspicion created in him a general distrust even towards eminent Party workers whom he had known for years. Everywhere and in everything he saw "enemies", "two-facers" and "spies".'

Khrushchev even offered a personal reminiscence as an example of how Stalin used to humiliate his circle. 'Once he turned to me and said: "Oi, you, *khokhol*, dance the *gopak*." So I danced.' *Khokhol* is a derogatory term for a Ukrainian, while the *gopak* is an intricate dance – the execution of which would have made the portly Khrushchev look ridiculous.

He also denounced Stalin's role in the war, including the Nazi–Soviet Pact and his failure to re-arm or visit the Front.

And no one outside the hall knew – at first. One British journalist, John Rettie of Reuters, had been given an account of parts of the speech by a contact, and Reuters put out the story that became front-page news all over the world. But still, a lot of the detail was missing. It was not until June that the world would learn the full truth.

But Rettie's story was enough to cause heartache in the *Daily Worker* office in London, and editor John Campbell urgently cabled the British delegation asking for more information. Pollitt and Dutt said they were too busy to deal with it, and the task fell to Matthews, who wrote:

> The admission of this most serious mistake has been followed by the most far-reaching measures to strengthen collective leadership ... the cult of the individual, the lack of collective leadership, the activities of Beria and his group – all these did harm. But the vital thing is that the mistakes have been recognised and the wrong policies put right.

This speech marked the beginning of perhaps the strangest part of Harry Pollitt's strange life. He never quite believed Khrushchev, whom he saw as a small man attacking his hero Stalin, and the bust of Stalin in the living room of his small north London home stayed there, defiantly, until Pollitt died four years later.

Pollitt, writes Kevin Morgan, 'unable to grasp the implications of Khrushchev's revelations, continued to deploy long-practised arguments about the dangers of adverse publicity, as if that could now matter to the Russians in the year of the secret speech'.[21] He had always managed to convince at least himself, and sometimes a lot of other people too, that it was enough to say you couldn't make a great revolution without the occasional injustice:

> The thing that mattered to me [about the Russian revolution] was that lads like me had whacked the bosses and the landlords, had taken their factories, their lands and their banks ... for me these same people could never do, nor ever can do, any wrong against the working class. I wasn't concerned as to whether or not the Russian revolution had caused bloodshed, been violent, and all the rest of it.[22]

Yet, telling no one, five months after Khrushchev's speech, Pollitt sent a letter to the Central Committee of the Communist Party of the Soviet Union – one he might have been secretly composing for twenty years. He hoped against hope that they would now tell him what they had done with the woman he loved:

> Dear Comrades,
>
> The relatives of Comrade Rose Cohen asked me to try to obtain some information about her ... In Moscow, she married Comrade Petrovsky. She had a son called Alyosha, who must now be about twenty years old.
>
> In the 1930s Petrovsky was arrested, as was his wife Rose Cohen subsequently. In 1937 or 1938 I personally requested news of Rose Cohen from Comrade Dimitrov and Comrade Manuilsky,

21 Kevin Morgan, entry in *Dictionary of Labour Biography*.

22 Kevin Morgan, *Harry Pollitt* (Manchester: Manchester University Press, 1993), p. 177.

> but received no information. In 1938, the late Beatrice and Sidney Webb were very interested in Rose Cohen, because in 1919–21 she had worked in their office.
>
> Rose Cohen's family has great influence in Jewish circles in Britain. Following the publication of reports of wrongful arrests, they are again raising that question and are bombarding me with requests.
>
> I should be extremely obliged if you would let me have some information about Rose Cohen in order that an unpleasant fuss in the British press may be avoided.

Pollitt was being economical with the truth. Rose's family was not particularly influential in Jewish circles and had not suddenly renewed their requests for information. By then, anyway, Stalin had thrown away all the support and sympathy he'd once had in Britain's Jewish community by fitting up Jewish doctors and torturing them into confessions of a plot to murder top Kremlin figures.

It looks as though Pollitt still clung to some sort of hope that Rose might one day walk out of one of those terrible labour camps, old, bent and ill, no doubt, but still Rose. It must have been a secret, despairing hope that he could never confess to anyone, and he knew Moscow well enough to know that such human considerations would cut no ice there.

The revelations about Stalin destroyed the peace of mind of people who had followed Pollitt through all the twists and turns of Soviet policy for nearly three decades. British Communist Hetty Bower's brother-in-law, George Fles, had disappeared into a Moscow prison many years earlier, and was presumed – rightly, we now know – to have been killed there.

George Fles and his wife Pearl had been living in Moscow, and Pearl had travelled to England to give birth to their son. Hetty, who clung to her communist faith, insisted that George must be guilty of subversion, for surely the socialist state would not arrest an innocent man; and a rift opened up between the sisters that was never healed. To the distress felt by most British communists at the betrayal of their idealism was added a sense that Hetty had betrayed her sister. Yet she and her husband Reg were not quite sure about George Fles. She told one of the present authors:

> We were completely bewildered and totally unable to judge whether, in fact, George had been guilty of any indiscretion or worse, or whether he had been a completely innocent victim of Stalin's madness. Reg and I only knew that somehow we felt guilty personally; that Pearl's tragic circumstances, bereft of her husband and father of her child, was something we had to atone for.

Hetty Bower was fifty-one in 1956, and spoke for many communists of her generation. For those who were young in 1956, there was none of her bewilderment. They saw that communism as a great, generous, radical idea was irretrievably tainted. By the end of 1956, idealistic youth was homeless, and, in a sense, has been so ever since.

On the second day of the Communist Party conference, in Britain, the first ever double yellow lines were painted on roads to prohibit parking. Appropriately enough, they made their debut in Slough, the butt of John Betjeman's 1937 poem 'Slough':

> *Come, friendly bombs, and fall on Slough!*
> *It isn't fit for humans now.*

Meanwhile, the Prime Minister was still recovering from a long transatlantic flight and a difficult visit to Washington. 'Welcome home,' wrote his new Chancellor Harold Macmillan on 8 February:

> You have done a wonderful job. I only hope you are not too exhausted. You have put Anglo-American relations back where they ought to be. We are not one of many foreign countries. We are allies and more than allies – blood brothers. In my short time I have tried to get [US Secretary of State] Foster Dulles towards this concept. You have crowned the work.

This is an interesting early appearance of what became known as the 'special relationship', but nothing in Macmillan's note was quite what it seemed. If Eden was exhausted, it might be because he was not physically up to the job, which was the whisper around Westminster, and 'in my short time' was a reminder that Macmillan had not forgiven the Prime Minister for evicting him from his dream job of Foreign Secretary and sending him to the Treasury instead. But the real purpose of the note was in the next sentence: 'I am afraid on your return you will find a lot of troubles on the home front. I have prepared a cabinet paper setting out my proposals in detail to deal with the economic crisis.'

Macmillan was determined to force his leader into radical economic policies. 'It is defence expenditure which has broken our backs,' he was to write two months later, and, in February, he was already clear that the government must either cut defence spending or raise taxes sharply – or preferably both. (By the end of the year, Macmillan was to be demanding more defence expenditure.) Eden would not allow either.

On 11 February, while Burgess and Maclean were handing their statement to four British journalists in a hotel room overlooking

Moscow's Red Square, and Harry Pollitt was on his way there for the 20th Congress, Macmillan tightened the screws on the Prime Minister. A note marked 'private and confidential' read:

> I feel I ought to let you know how serious I consider the inflationary position and the general weakness of the economy ... We must act swiftly and decisively ... So I really must ask for your support at this critical moment. I am in something of a dilemma. I don't want to appear to threaten the cabinet; I have never tried such tactics in all my service. But I would not like you to be under any misapprehension and afterwards perhaps blame me for not letting you know the depth of my feeling. I must tell you frankly that, if I cannot have your confidence and that of my colleagues in handling this problem in the way that seems to me essential, I should not feel justified in proposing measures that seem insufficient for their purpose. Neither would I be any good to you and the cabinet in such circumstances. One can compromise about minor points of policy that come up all the time in cabinet, but I would not be any good if I were trying to defend policies in which I had no belief.

Seldom can a Cabinet minister's threat to resign and destroy the government have been couched in so silky a manner. A meeting between the two was swiftly arranged, at which Eden suggested dealing with the crisis with a capital gains tax. Macmillan wrote afterwards, on 18 February: 'Dear Anthony, I have thought a great deal about what you said to me this morning ... Naturally I want to help you in any way I can. But I am afraid your proposed package will not do.'[23]

Macmillan wanted to abolish bread and milk subsidies; Eden didn't. The row dragged on for a while, but Macmillan won.

---

23 The National Archives, CAB 103 661.

They were not just watching the economy collapse; they were watching the British Empire collapse, too. Everyone wanted to leave – except Malta, which apparently wanted to draw closer. The new Maltese premier Dom Mintoff was campaigning for a 'yes' vote in a referendum to amalgamate with Britain. On 12 February, the proposal was approved by 77 per cent of those who voted.

The Catholic Church believed that the Maltese people had let the country down yet again. 'Voters ignore the bishop's warning' was the main headline in the Catholic paper *The Universe*: 'Nearly half of the predominantly Catholic electorate has voted in favour of integration with Great Britain, ignoring the Church's wish to have beforehand written guarantees that her rights will continue to be respected and that Catholic morals will not be violated by future legislation.'[24]

It seemed odd to *The Spectator*: 'What does the archbishop want? He wants to limit the power of the Maltese Parliament itself to legislate in matters touching the Church.'[25] But Archbishop Gonzi was livid, denouncing 'those who do not listen to the word of God, those who criticise the behaviour and teaching of the Church, those who continually in the press, in lectures and speeches in Parliament, belittle the authority of the Church'.[26]

Thursday 2 February saw the London première of the American film *Cinerama Holiday*. Cinerama is one of the great might-have-beens of movie history – a technical innovation that promised much but could not sustain itself. What it offered was the point of view not

24 *The Universe*, 17 February 1956.

25 *The Spectator*, 17 February 1956.

26 *The Universe*, 9 March 1956.

of one camera but of three, synchronised so that a scene appeared to viewers not only straight ahead but also on each side, filling their peripheral vision so that they felt as if they were inside the action.

Any cinema planning to show Cinerama films needed a special wide screen and an adapted projection suite. London's Palace Theatre on Cambridge Circus was converted to Cinerama use in 1954 when the first such production, *This Is Cinerama*, was released in the UK. It was called into service again for *Cinerama Holiday*, a glorified travelogue with some spectacular passages, like the bobsleigh ride filmed from the sleigh itself.

The problem with Cinerama was that it was really only suitable for this-wonderful-world subjects. Pointless to go to that sort of expense for a *noir* thriller or screwball romantic comedy. After some more exotica like *Search for Paradise* and *The Wonderful World of the Brothers Grimm*, the novelty evaporated, and Cinerama was supplanted in the '60s by the slightly less breathtaking and more affordable Panavision processes. Today, its original widescreen wonders are displayed at the Pictureville Theatre in the National Media Museum at Bradford – the only remaining cinema in Europe equipped for regular Cinerama projection.

Cinerama turned out to be ephemeral, part of the razzmatazz of 1956, but Free Cinema was part of the revolution. On 5 February, three short films were shown at the National Film Theatre (NFT) in London, and the Free Cinema movement was born. Two were documentaries: *O Dreamland*, directed by Lindsay Anderson and made three years before (but previously unshown), was about an amusement park in Margate, Kent; Karel Reisz and Tony Richardson's *Momma Don't Allow* watched Chris Barber's band and their audience at a jazz club in Wood Green, north London. Alongside those was Lorenza Mazzetti's *Together*, which was a fictional portrayal, though shot in a documentary manner, of two deaf-mutes (played by the artists Eduardo Paolozzi and Michael Andrews) wandering amid the bombsites of London's East End.

Free Cinema's initial members were Anderson, Reisz and Richardson – Mazzetti, Anderson would say later, was 'adopted' – together with Walter Lassally, who shot *Momma Don't Allow*, and John Fletcher, who shot *O Dreamland* and was editor and sound recordist on *Momma Don't Allow*.

A Free Cinema manifesto was presented along with the films, and was mostly written by Anderson, allegedly in the Charing Cross café where Mazzetti worked. It stated:

> These films were not made together; nor with the idea of showing them together. But when they came together, we felt they had an attitude in common. Implicit in this attitude is a belief in freedom, in the importance of people and the significance of the everyday.
>
> As filmmakers we believe that:
> No film can be too personal.
> The image speaks.
> Sound amplifies and comments.
> Size is irrelevant.
> Perfection is not an aim.
> An attitude means a style. A style means an attitude.

The importance of 'the image speaks' was that it elevated image over sound, while the slogan 'an attitude means a style', as Reisz explained, signified: 'A style is not a matter of camera angles or fancy footwork; it's an expression, an accurate expression of your particular opinion.'

The NFT programme was followed by another in September, when the American Lionel Rogosin showed *On the Bowery*, an account of life in New York's skid row district that won a Best Documentary award at the Venice Film Festival and a similar award from the British Film Academy. There were four further Free Cinema programmes over the next three years, showing films like Alain Tanner and Claude Goretta's *Nice Time* and Reisz's *We Are the Lambeth Boys*. The latter, shot by Lassally and edited by Fletcher, depicted a group of south London teenagers, and was praised by Richard Hoggart because 'it sets out to show, not the whole truth, but some aspects of the truth, wholly'. A couple of the programmes were devoted to foreign films, with examples of work by young directors from the French New Wave (Truffaut, Resnais, Varda) and Poland.

Of all the Free Cinema films, *Nice Time* focuses most sharply on 1956. First shown in March 1957, it had been filmed during the previous autumn and winter. For a long series of Saturday evenings, the three-man crew of Tanner, Goretta and cameraman/sound recordist Fletcher hung round Piccadilly Circus filming Londoners at play, or at work providing the play. Cinema queues for *War and Peace* and *X the Unknown*; Teds and tarts; spivs and street entertainers; balloon sellers and hot-dog wagons; placard-bearers of 'Christ Jesus came into the world to save sinners' and 'Flee from the wrath to come'; the famous illuminated signs of Coca-Cola, Wrigley's chewing gum and 'Guinness Time'; the Trocadero, the Quality Inn and Forte's Popular Restaurant; amusement arcades with juke boxes; a nervous young sailor biting his nails.

The filmmakers incidentally documented sights commonplace at the time in the centre of London but now exotic or altogether gone, from peaked-capped commissionaires to displays of 'nude studies' magazines. The camera peers down alleys of sin to a cheerful, innocent soundtrack of the Chas McDevitt Skiffle Group, performing 'My Babe' and 'Greenback Dollar', and Nancy Whiskey (who had recently joined fellow Glaswegian McDevitt's group) singing the Irish ballad 'She Moves Through the Fair'.

Free Cinema films were made outside the mainstream film industry, with low budgets and helped by grants from the British Film Institute's experimental film production fund, or, later, the Ford Motor Company. They had a style (or attitude) of their own: shot in black and white with much use of hand-held cameras, they portrayed the lives and recreations of working-class people with an unpatronising regard for their dignity, and, generally, without the mediation of a narrator.

As Anderson would say thirty years later:

> An unobtrusive, precise camera style. A respect for people as individuals as well as members of a class or an industry. These were the characteristics of Free Cinema. Our films were humanist, not sentimental ... They weren't bland advertisements for the British way of life. They were rough-edged and unpolished ... What we wanted to do was get ordinary, uncelebrated life on the screen. By today's standards, Tony Richardson and Karel Reisz weren't doing anything remarkable when they followed their working-class boys and girls into Chris Barber's jazz club at Wood Green. But in 1956 they were taking British cinema into unexplored territory.

That wasn't strictly true. Journeys of discovery into the hidden world of proletarian life had been taken by John Grierson's cadre of documentary filmmakers in the '30s and '40s. But Anderson and his allies did not feel any particular affinity with them. Indeed, he told an interviewer in 1974:

> The weakness of the traditional documentary movement to me was that their work was essentially social-democratic propaganda of a kind that in the thirties seemed to be progressive; but then during the war their films became totally identified with the Establishment, because they became part of the war effort. So after the war

> the work had no kind of progressive quality; they were simply making rather sentimental, conformist social-democratic pictures ... That was as far as their revolutionary zeal took them. They weren't individually artistically strong enough to strike out on their own.[27]

This is the contempt of the new left for the boring state socialism of their older brothers and sisters, and you find it echoed in all the arguments of 1956, whether about left-wing politics, theatre, literature or cinema. This is a man of the '50s, looking at the progressives of fifteen or twenty years earlier with sophisticated disdain.

There was one filmmaker of the Grierson group whom they did respect: Humphrey Jennings. 'He was the only director for me, of the British documentary movement, who had real poetic quality, perhaps even genius in his own way,' said Anderson. And Reisz agreed: 'Jennnings is the one we admired ... *A Diary for Timothy*, *Fires Were Started* [and] *Listen to Britain* were beautiful films, and we felt we were going on from *them*.'

Although the Free Cinema movement lasted only a few years, its after-effects were considerable. Penelope Houston, who became the editor of the British Film Institute's magazine *Sight and Sound* in 1956, wrote a few years later:

> Free Cinema marked a necessary stage in the particular journey British cinema had to take, and its timing was perfect. As a movement it was (and recognised itself to be) in step with that whole semi-cultural, semi-political wave of protest which dates roughly from the time of Suez and Hungary; which asked, in the voice of Jimmy Porter, why 'there aren't any good causes left' and found

27 Eva Orbanz (ed.), *Journey to a Legend and Back: The British Realistic Film* (Berlin: Edition Volker Spiess, 1977), pp. 41–2, 53.

> its cause in nuclear disarmament; which voiced a political protest through the *New Left Review* and infiltrated the theatre through the Royal Court and Theatre Workshop.[28]

Lindsay Anderson, looking back at the work of the movement, felt that: 'You could feel the inevitable thrust towards drama – towards the feature film.' Some of the most notable New Wave – or, as unfriendly journalists preferred to call them, 'kitchen-sink' – movies of the late '50s and '60s were made by Free Cinema men, such as *Look Back in Anger* (Richardson, 1959), *Saturday Night and Sunday Morning* (Reisz, 1960), *A Taste of Honey* (Richardson, with Walter Lassally, 1961), *The Loneliness of the Long Distance Runner* (Richardson and Lassally, 1962) and *This Sporting Life* (directed by Anderson, produced by Reisz, 1963).

'Free Cinema', Anderson concluded in 1986, 'proved that there is or could be an indigenous film tradition, if we wanted one; that British films can and should be made with British actors rather than American stars; and that a radical spirit is more creative than a conformist one.'[29]

But, for every radical cinéaste at the NFT in 1956, there were 100 conformist picturegoers queuing outside Regals, Ritzes and Essoldos for Alfred Hitchcock's thriller *The Man Who Knew Too Much* – in which Doris Day sang the infuriatingly catchy 'Whatever Will Be, Will Be (*Que Sera, Sera*)' – or *War and Peace*, with Audrey Hepburn and Henry Fonda, or *The King and I*, with Deborah Kerr and Yul Brynner, or Virginia McKenna and Peter Finch in *A Town Like Alice*, based on the book by Nevil Shute – just four from the impressive list of films released in the UK in 1956, many of which are still remembered and esteemed.

Or they went to see war films. Chaps with square jaws, stiff upper

---

28 Penelope Houston, *The Contemporary Cinema* (Harmondsworth: Penguin Books, 1963), p. 115.

29 *Free Cinema 1956 – ?: An Essay on Film by Lindsay Anderson* (Thames TV, 1986).

lips and cut-glass accents may not have been what Lindsay Anderson thought cinema should be about, but, although the war had been over for eleven years, the public, as Robert Muller wrote in *Picture Post*, wanted 'war pictures from here to eternity'. However, as he also pointed out: 'During the last few years, the ... war has been stripped of almost every recorded Allied deed of heroism ... There isn't a submarine mission, a POW camp escape, or an Operation Whatnot that hasn't ended up ... on the Odeon and Gaumont circuits.' He saw only two escape routes: films that showed the enemy being decent chaps as well; or films about the bombing of civilians, nuclear warfare or

> the systematic extermination (by not-so-decent chaps) of racial minorities in concentration camps. Of course, this would mean presenting war, not as a picnic for potential heroes, but as a human indignity. And for the younger generation, who have yet to experience the romance of a world war, this would never do.[30]

The public, however, showed no sign of war-film fatigue. Powell and Pressburger's *The Battle of the River Plate*, which portrayed the captain of the German battleship *Graf Spee* (Peter Finch again) as honourable and humane, was chosen for the Royal Film Performance. Ronald Neame's *The Man Who Never Was* was based on an actual operation by British intelligence. And the Boulting brothers, John and Roy, began their enormously successful career in the British film industry with the comedy *Private's Progress*, starring Ian Carmichael, Richard Attenborough and Terry-Thomas.

Then there was Lewis Gilbert's *Reach for the Sky* – the most popular film of the year. It told the story of RAF pilot Douglas Bader (played – Richard Burton having turned down the part – by Kenneth More),

---

30 Robert Muller, 'It's a Great War for Producers', *Picture Post*, 7 April 1956, p. 27.

who commanded a squadron during the Battle of Britain, despite having lost both legs before the war in a flying accident. Bader was appointed CBE in February 1956. '[His] story', wrote Isabel Quigly in *The Spectator*, 'is one of courage so dogged, so unfaltering as to command not only respect but wonder.'

Naturally. And yet, slowly, the public was shedding its veneration of war heroes, and getting ready to laugh at them. *Reach for the Sky* 'was one of the films we were making fun of in the Aftermyth of War sketch in *Beyond the Fringe*', remembers Alan Bennett. The satirical revue *Beyond the Fringe* opened in 1960, and treated everything with a new irreverence, even the war:

> 'Suddenly Jerry was coming at me out of a bank of cloud. I let him have it, and I think I must have got him in the wing because he spiralled past me out of control. As he did so ... I'll always remember this ... I got a glimpse of his face, and you know ... he smiled. Funny thing, war.' Some nights, greatly daring, I would stump stiff-legged around the stage in imitation of Douglas Bader, feeling priggishly rewarded by the occasional hiss.[31]

In 1956, it wasn't done to mock the war film like that, but attitudes were beginning to shift. In 1957, ITV began showing *The Army Game* – a sitcom that made fun of postwar conscription, what was called 'doing your National Service'. All male Britons aged between eighteen and twenty-six were liable to be 'called up' for two years' full-time service, with an entitlement to be reinstated afterwards in their pre-conscription job, or something equivalent to it. Exciting or threatening, according to one's temperament, this prospect brightened or clouded

31 Alan Bennett, *Writing Home* (London: Faber & Faber, 1994), pp. 200–201 in 1995 paperback edition.

the future of hundreds of thousands of young men in the mid-'50s, only to dissolve in 1960 with the cessation of the call-up.

The Army Game was basically *Private's Progress* (creator Sid Colin's inspiration), but with better jokes and a cast of cunningly differentiated characters like Michael Medwin (later Harry Fowler) as the scheming corporal, Alfie Bass as the ever-complaining 'Excused Boots', and Bill Fraser as the proudly moustachio'd Sergeant Major Snudge, with his catchphrase: 'I've got my beady eye on you.' There were shorter but memorable spells of service by the puzzled Bernard Bresslaw ('I only *arsked*'), the epicene Charles Hawtrey and, in the early episodes, the constitutionally irascible William Hartnell as Snudge's predecessor Sergeant Major Bullimore.

Several of these indefatigable character actors became stalwarts of the *Carry On* films, which began in 1958 with what was, in effect, *The Army Game* extended to movie length. Indeed, in *Carry On Sergeant*, the sergeant in question was played by Hartnell.

The *Army Game* cast also had close parallels in an American TV series of the time that was very popular in Britain. In *The Phil Silvers Show*, Silvers's Sergeant Bilko also led a platoon of dimwits and skivers.

A similar air of disenchantment with what had once seemed heroic – or at least important – permeates one of the best-remembered episodes of *Hancock's Half Hour*. Already established on radio, the comedian's show transferred to TV in July 1956. In 'The Reunion Party', Tony Hancock's character organises a get-together with two of his old army mates, only to discover that they don't share his memories and that the bright sparks he knew in uniform have turned into dim old men in mufti. The hellraiser Smudger is now known by his given Christian name, Cyril; he has a tedious job in a bank, where, after many years, he hopes to get the desk by the window; he doesn't drink any more, and is under the thumb of his ferocious wife.

Set in the '50s, *The Army Game* was safely insulated from the war.

But, in portraying its ordinary soldiers as artful dodgers, continuously engaged in finding ways round regulations and duties, it presented a narrative of army life that was, to say the least, anti-heroic. Young men going for their National Service would perhaps have had a slightly more sceptical attitude to the job they were doing and the officers who were telling them to do it.

Real National Servicemen were learning to find it irksome and ridiculous. David Clark started his National Service in February. Thanks to a detailed diary, his recollections are more reliable than most:

> We were introduced to 'bull', polishing the barrack-room floor and our new boots and uniform buttons and badges, and putting Blanco on our webbing belts and small packs, and so forth. We had our first pay parade, at which, as AC2s (aircraftmen 2nd class), the lowest rank of all, we were paid 4 shillings a day, making a grand weekly total of 28 shillings, from which our National Insurance contribution of 3 shillings and 11 pence was deducted. In modern terms, we earned 20 pence per day, with 1 pound 20 pence per week to put in our pockets after the NI deduction.
>
> These seem ridiculous amounts today, but, for me, entering the RAF straight from school, they represented significantly more than I had ever had before, and, for the first time in my life I felt relatively affluent. For those older fellows who had worked for a few years before being conscripted, it seemed more like penury.

Back at the pictures...

Among the imports, *High Society* was a jazzy update of *The Philadelphia Story*, with Bing Crosby, Frank Sinatra, Grace Kelly and Louis Armstrong; Marilyn Monroe played a hillbilly nightclub singer in the romantic comedy *Bus Stop*; Douglas Sirk directed a harrowing drama of alcoholism and family ties, *Written on the Wind*; and Stanley Kubrick brought out his crime *noir*, *The Killing*. John Ford's *The Searchers*, with John Wayne, is considered by many judges the finest of all Western movies, and is frequently placed in the Top 10s of best films ever.

James Dean made his last film appearance in *Giant* (George Stevens's saga of a Texas ranching dynasty), and Humphrey Bogart made his in *The Harder They Fall* (a movie about fight-rigging in the boxing business), cherished by scriptophiles for corrupt promoter Rod Steiger's lines: 'The people, Eddie, the people! Don't tell me about the people, Eddie. The people sit in front of their little TVs with their bellies full of beer and fall asleep. What do the people know, Eddie?'

Sci-fi enthusiasts could blanch pleasurably at Don Siegel's *Invasion of the Body Snatchers* – with the billing 'Incredible! Invisible! Insatiable!' – in which a small California town finds itself harbouring giant seed-pods that produce alien doubles of its inhabitants, identical in appearance and memory but without human emotion. A doctor, who had been away, returns and muses: 'At first glance, everything looked the same. It wasn't. Something evil had taken possession of the town...' As the film draws to a climax, he tries to warn the townspeople. 'Look, you fools. You're in danger. Can't you see? They're after you. They're after all of us. Our wives, our children, everyone. They're here already. You're next!' Just in time, he gets people to believe him, though that upbeat ending was imposed by the studio and was not what Siegel intended. The film was variously interpreted as some sort of warning: against communist infiltration; against McCarthyism; against bland conformity. In the UK, despite having some scenes cut by the British Board of Film Censors, it was a great success.

Forbidden Planet was a classier production. Filmed in Eastmancolor, it was the first sci-fi movie set on another world and the first film of any kind to employ a wholly electronic soundtrack. It also boasted a plot loosely based on *The Tempest* and a cast including Hollywood grand old man Walter Pidgeon, Leslie Nielsen half a lifetime before *Naked Gun*, and Robby the Robot, a benign forerunner of a Dalek. Acknowledged by Gene Roddenberry as one of the inspirations for *Star Trek*, *Forbidden Planet* has acquired a cult following, with anniversary box sets, a namecheck in *The Rocky Horror Picture Show* and a pastiche in *The Simpsons*.

Filmgoers also halted outside their local picture palaces to stare open-mouthed at posters for *Godzilla, King of the Monsters!* – 'Incredible, unstoppable titan of terror! Civilisation crumbles as its death rays blast a city of 6 million from the face of the earth!' Starring alongside the giant lizard, in this American reconstruction of an earlier Japanese movie, was Raymond Burr, TV's Perry Mason.

Not all the sci-fi was American, though. In *X the Unknown*, Hammer Films followed their success of the previous year, *The Quatermass Xperiment*, with a long, horrified look at the scary phenomenon of radioactivity (a hot topic in the new nuclear age). A monster emerges from a crack in the ground in the Scottish Lowlands, melts anyone who opposes it, and makes its amorphous way to a source of energy – an atomic energy laboratory where there is radioactive cobalt it can feed upon. It becomes visible, a roiling bog of rice pudding, and almost envelops a tiny child. Connoisseurs will perceive an early draft of the idea behind *The Blob*, which came out two years later. The thing detects another food-source and is oozing towards it when a scientist neutralises it with an 'anti-radiation device'. Inverness is saved, but the viewer is left uncertain whether the monster was merely the first in a queue of subterranean something-or-others. The following year, Hammer completed this sort-of-trilogy with *Quatermass 2*.

Later commentators have read the three films as expressions of anxiety about the Cold War, and Britain's declining status as a world power.

For the teenaged filmgoer there was rock 'n' roll. *Love Me Tender* was the first film to feature Elvis Presley ('Mr Rock 'n' Roll in the story he was born to play!'). *The Girl Can't Help It* was an old-fashioned Svengali tale of an agent and a nightclub singer, interspersed with frenetic rock 'n' roll numbers by Little Richard, Gene Vincent, Eddie Cochran and Fats Domino. Richard, Vincent and Domino all penetrated the UK charts in 1956 – Richard with 'Tutti Frutti', Vincent with 'Be-Bop-a-Lula' (derided by the NME as 'a straightforward junior idiot chant'), and Domino with both 'Blueberry Hill' and 'I'm in Love Again'. And for the pre-teens there was the Disney adventure *Davy Crockett, King of the Wild Frontier*, starring Fess Parker in his hugely marketable coonskin cap.

For another segment of the filmgoing public came *...And God Created Woman*, with Brigitte Bardot as a disruptive teenage sex bomb: 'The fast-moving, fascinating story of a demon-driven temptress, who thought the future was invented only to spoil the present.' It was risqué compared with what the postwar years had so far offered, and it earned a magisterial rebuke from the Roman Catholic Church's National Legion of Decency – and a cheer from men in raincoats everywhere – even though today it looks cautious in its sexuality and outdated in its attitudes.

Perhaps we should not be surprised. National Serviceman David Clark's mate Squibs spoke for many young men in 1956: 'After one of our weekends at home, I recall somebody asking Squibs, who had a steady girlfriend at home, if he had "got what he wanted" over the weekend. "Nah," he replied, "and if I had, I'd not still be going out with her."'

One wonders what Squibs – or his girlfriend – made of 'Burn My Candle', the debut record by Shirley Bassey released in February. 'Who wants to help me burn my candle [*boom, boom*] at both ends?' asked the fetchingly innocent-looking nineteen-year-old. 'Surely', said the NME's reviewer Geoffrey Everitt, 'this must be one of the most suggestive songs of all time? Of course it will be greeted with open arms in certain quarters if the censor allows us to have three minutes of fun.' The BBC – no fun at all in matters like this – promptly banned it.

The year 1956 was the first in British history when no life was taken by the judicial system.

This was not the fault of the popular press, which did everything it could to ensure the good old British tradition of hanging people by the neck until they were dead was maintained. Nevertheless, on 16 February, the House of Commons debated the Death Penalty (Abolition) Bill. It was tabled by a dozen MPs, headed by Sydney Silverman (the Labour MP for Nelson & Colne), and stated: 'This House believes that the death penalty for murder no longer accords with the needs or the true interests of a civilised society, and calls upon Her Majesty's Government to introduce forthwith legislation for its abolition or for its suspension for an experimental period.' The motion was carried by 293 votes to 262.

'The large hanging section of the popular press has already shown that it will do all it can to whip up the fears of the public,' reported *The Spectator*:

> It was quite unable to conceal its pleasure that a murder had been committed shortly after the House of Commons vote. 'Murder within three days,' gloated the *Daily Express*. 'First "I cannot hang" murder,' sang the *Daily Mail*. No one thought of pointing out that about 130 murders are committed in this country each year, so that on average there is a murder every three days. Similar tactics were pursued when there was a campaign to bring back flogging.

The *Manchester Guardian* commented the next day:

> Here was high drama ... lifted far above the general run of great conflicts of opinion in the House of Commons by the inescapable sense of individual responsibility before what is, for so many, a challenge to conscience. The pressure on the accommodation of the House both on the floor of the chamber and in the galleries was at its maximum. The two front benches were overloaded.[32]

The bill proceeded through further stages in the Commons, and, on 28 June, was passed on a free vote by 200 votes to ninety-eight – only to be rejected by the Lords on 10 July. 'Lords hang on to rope' was the *Daily Mirror*'s front-page headline the next day, while *The Spectator* commented: 'The abstentionist army was largely composed of hitherto unknown rustics, who thought, perhaps, that abolition was in some way a threat to blood sports.'

During this process, however, and for some time afterwards, the Home Secretary reprieved all persons convicted of murder.

There had always been those who had argued that capital punishment was disgusting or ineffective as a deterrent – or both – but, in the preceding few years, there had been specific causes of disquiet.

One was the Craig–Bentley case of 1952. In the course of a burglary at a south London confectionery warehouse, Christopher Craig, who was sixteen, shot and killed a policeman. His accomplice in the burglary, nineteen-year-old Derek Bentley, had no gun, but was alleged to have shouted to Craig, 'Let him have it!', which was interpreted by the judge as evidence of 'joint enterprise' (common criminal purpose). Craig – being too young to receive the death penalty – was imprisoned, while Bentley – who was rejected for National

32 'Majority of 31 to End Hanging', *Manchester Guardian*, 17 February 1956.

Service as 'mentally substandard' and described by a psychiatrist as 'almost borderline retarded' – was hanged. The outcry led to petitions for mercy signed by 200 MPs, but the Home Secretary Sir David Maxwell Fyfe was unmoved.

Then, in 1955, came the case of Ruth Ellis, a former model and nightclub hostess, who shot her lover David Blakely in the street outside a Hampstead pub. The façade of the Magdala Tavern still bears the mark where one of the shots ricocheted. She immediately gave herself up to police, pleaded guilty at her trial and did not question her conviction. But she had two young children, had recently had a miscarriage after Blakely punched her in the stomach, and was young and attractive, so, for one reason or another, it seemed to many people that there was something particularly offensive about hanging her. A petition for clemency received 50,000 signatures, but was rejected by the new Home Secretary Major Gwilym Lloyd George.

On the day of her execution, the *Daily Mirror* columnist 'Cassandra' (William Connor) wrote:

> It's a fine day for haymaking. A fine day for fishing. A fine day for lolling in the sunshine. And if you feel that way – and I mourn to say that millions of you do – it's a fine day for a hanging.
>
> IF YOU READ THIS BEFORE NINE O'CLOCK THIS MORNING, the last dreadful and obscene preparations for hanging Ruth Ellis will be moving up to their fierce and sickening climax...
>
> IF YOU READ THIS AFTER NINE O'CLOCK, the murderess, Ruth Ellis, will have gone.
>
> The one thing that brings stature and dignity to mankind and raises us above the beasts of the field will have been denied her – pity and the hope of ultimate redemption ...
>
> Two Royal Commissions have protested against these horrible events. Every Home Secretary in recent years has testified to the

> agonies of his task, and the revulsion he has felt towards his duty. None has ever claimed that executions prevent murder.
>
> Yet they go on, and still Parliament has neither the resolve nor the conviction, nor the wit, nor the decency to put an end to these atrocious affairs ...
>
> Yes, it is a fine day.
>
> Oscar Wilde, when he was in Reading Gaol, spoke with melancholy of 'that little tent of blue which prisoners call the sky'.
>
> The tent of blue should be dark and sad at the thing we have done this day.

The American crime novelist Raymond Chandler, who was in London at the time, wrote to the *Evening Standard*:

> I have been tormented for a week at the idea that a highly civilised people should put a rope round the neck of Ruth Ellis and drop her through a trap and break her neck. This was a crime of passion under considerable provocation. No other country in the world would hang this woman.

She was the last woman to be hanged in England.

A Pathé newsreel distributed a few days later carried an unusually weighted commentary:

> Britain's conscience was uneasy ... Millions are asking, 'Is it civilised to kill by law? Does it really act as a deterrent? Is it right to ask any human being to carry out the killing?' ... This was the law of the centuries gone by. Should it remain the law of the twentieth?

While the Ellis case was resonating in the public sphere, a campaign against the death penalty was launched by the publisher Victor

Gollancz, the author Arthur Koestler, and the Anglican canon John Collins, who would later become well known as a founder of the Campaign for Nuclear Disarmament. In the month of Ellis's execution, Koestler began to write *Reflections on Hanging*, published in spring 1956, and, a few years later, he and the *New Statesman* journalist C. H. Rolph co-authored *Hanged by the Neck*, a devastating account of how men and women who were convicted of murder in England were dealt with by the police, the courts and the public hangman.

Speaking of whom, the hangman Albert Pierrepoint, who despatched both Bentley and Ellis, and had rendered that service to hundreds before them, retired in 1956 after disputing a fee. It had been reduced because the man he was due to hang had been reprieved.

A committee under Maxwell Fyfe (by now Viscount Kilmuir) recommended limiting the application of the death penalty. This led, in March 1957, to the introduction of a new Homicide Act that reduced the number of capital crimes. Hangings immediately diminished. In the six years of 1950–55, there had been ninety hangings (twenty-five in 1952 alone); in the nine of 1957–65 there were just twenty-nine. The last hanging in England was in 1964; the next year, Sydney Silverman's Murder (Abolition of Death Penalty) Bill became law, ending capital punishment for murder completely. The few remaining capital offences, such as treason, espionage and arson in a royal dockyard, were removed from the statute books in 1998.

CHAPTER 4

CYPRUS, MONACO AND BOND COUNTRY

On 9 March, Archbishop Makarios, head of the Greek Orthodox Church in Cyprus, and effectively leader of the Greek Cypriot community, was arrested by Special Branch officers at Nicosia Airport on the grounds of 'actively fostering terrorism'. He was deported to Mahe Island in the Seychelles.

The following day, there were riots all over the island, and bombs were thrown at a British military patrol vehicle and at a police station. Further demonstrations were held in Athens and Salonika, and the British consulate in Crete was ransacked. On 21 March, a time bomb was discovered in the bed of the British governor of Cyprus, Field Marshal Sir John Harding.

The 'Cyprus question' had been bothering Britain for some years, particularly as represented by Makarios. Ever since his archiepiscopal election in 1950, he had headed a movement for *enosis* – the union of Cyprus with Greece. In 1954, Greece had raised the Cyprus question at the UN, arguing that the island should be permitted to determine its own future – which, in the eyes of most Greek Cypriots, would almost certainly bring about the desired annexation with what they perceived as the mother country.

The Turkish Cypriot community, then about a fifth of the island's population, naturally saw things rather differently. So did Britain, which regarded Cyprus, a crown colony since 1925, as holding a key strategic position in the Middle East. According to Charles Foley, who founded the English-language *Times of Cyprus* in 1955, a Mercator projection (a cylindrical projection used by sailors, which tends to distort the size of objects as the latitude increases from the equator to the poles) would show the island to be

> a trifling appendage to the mass of Asiatic Turkey from which the Arab states curved downwards, crossed by oil pipelines from Iraq and the Persian Gulf. Egypt's green was severed by the [Suez] Canal, with its British military installations which would be reoccupied in time of war, and the mauve segment of Jordan was another British *place d'armes*. The free and unfettered use of Cyprus was essential in the grand strategic conception, for it was linked up with a network of interests that must 'never' be disturbed.[33]

This principle had been reiterated by the Minister of State for Colonial Affairs, Henry Hopkinson, in Parliament in July 1954, following Eden's announcement that Britain was withdrawing her troops

33 Charles Foley, *Island in Revolt* (London: Longmans, 1962), pp. 66–7.

from Suez to Cyprus. British rule in the island, Hopkinson said, was immutable; Cypriot self-determination was unthinkable. 'I do not', Mr Hopkinson added, 'see any reason to expect any difficulties in Cyprus as a result of this statement.'[34]

In October 1955, Sir John Harding had initiated talks on the island's future, but no agreement had been reached and the talks came to an end in early 1956.

But, even before then, Greek Cypriot hardliners, impatient with Britain's refusal to countenance *enosis*, had created an organisation to fight for it. On 1 April 1955, the people of Cyprus were handed leaflets stating: 'With God's help, with faith in the righteousness of our struggle, with the aid of all Hellenism, WE HEREBY TAKE ON THE STRUGGLE TO RID US OF THE BRITISH YOKE.' It was the manifesto of EOKA, *Ethniki Organosis Kyprion Agoniston* (National Organisation of Cypriot Fighters), led by a mysterious figure known as Dighenis – after Digenes Akritas, a hero in Greek folk poetry. He was unmasked in November 1955 by the *Times of Cyprus* and revealed to be George Grivas, a right-wing ex-soldier and former leader of a nationalist guerrilla group. Among his lieutenants was a young journalist named Nikos Georghiades – originally the Famagusta correspondent of the *Times of Cyprus* – who moved to Nicosia, changed his name to Nikos Sampson and became one of EOKA's hit-men. The organisation's strategy, Grivas wrote later, was to make international news and influence international opinion through 'deeds of heroism and self sacrifice'.

What this amounted to was a series of attacks on British military bases and personnel, and on local sympathisers including the many Turkish Cypriots whom the British had conscripted into the police force to combat EOKA. The EOKA paramilitaries were never numerous, perhaps no more than a few hundred, but they skilfully used

34 Foley, op. cit., p. 11.

familiar terrain, such as the Troodos Mountains in central Cyprus, for planning their strikes and disappearing afterwards. Indeed, a typical report in the *Daily Mail* – 'Dogs lead troops to mountain terror cave' – described British commandos capturing three EOKA fighters, and the weapons they found in their hideout.

Throughout 1956, events in Cyprus frequently made British newspaper headlines. There was a series of shootings of British servicemen, police and civilians around a stretch of Nicosia's main shopping thoroughfare Ledra Street, earning it the nickname 'Murder Mile'. Whether through fear of EOKA reprisals or sympathy with its cause, local residents, when questioned, repeatedly said they had seen nothing. On one occasion, following the shooting of a British policeman, householders were issued with paper and envelopes and instructed to write on the paper everything they knew about EOKA and seal it in the envelope. The envelopes were collected and, as promised, opened in private by the British commissioner of Nicosia. All the papers were blank.[35]

The British response to EOKA provocation was heavy-handed. Curfews became routine.

> [T]he newly arrived Paratroops ... descended on Nicosia like a Wyatt Earp *posse* bent on cleaning up Dodge City ... Throughout Ledra Street hundreds of people were pinned against the wall with arms raised and feet well apart for long-drawn searches ... Startled crowds were ordered out of Sunday cinemas to face a line of troops with Sten guns.[36]

There was a brief and almost comic suspension of hostilities when, on 16 August, leaflets signed by 'Dighenis' announced an immediate

35 Foley, op. cit., p. 68.

36 Foley, op. cit., pp. 74–5.

ceasefire 'to test Britain's sincerity'. A week later, Harding made this ponderous reply:

> It would now be in the public interest to give the terrorists who are still at large in the island the opportunity of extricating themselves from the position into which their action in taking up arms against the established government of the country has led them ... These terrorists will therefore be given the opportunity of surrendering with their arms.

'Are they mad?' asked Foley's colleague Costas Solomonides.

'It seemed that they were,' wrote Foley:

> Eden had sent a cable to Harding, congratulating him on the ceasefire as if there had been some brilliant British victory in the field.
>
> An official in Harding's inner councils told me that the governor's information showed that Eoka [*sic*] was beaten. The ceasefire had been brought about by their increasing losses; moreover, the fraternisation with the troops proved that the people were really on our side all along.
>
> When the inevitable Eoka answer came: 'Victors do not surrender. Come and get us!' no one was disappointed. The British thought it was a matter of delivering the *coup de grâce*, the Turkish leaders were delighted that the British would have no dealings with armed gangsters and crooks, the Greeks seemed rather proud that Harding's 'insulting' demand had been rejected in a properly Spartan way.
>
> An RAF Auster droned over Nicosia ... showering copies of the printed 'Surrender' instructions on amazed heads below ... People in the streets flung their arms up, crying: 'We surrender – now go away.' ... A donkey was let loose in Ledra Street with a placard

> round its neck: 'My Marshal, I surrender!' ... All over Cyprus, 'I surrender' became a comic greeting.[37]

The ceasefire was soon over, and the cycle of killing and chasing resumed once again. It was too much for many Cypriots, especially those who found themselves in minority communities – one of a handful of Greek families in a predominantly Turkish village, or *vice versa* – and, during the four years of conflict, an average of 4,000 Cypriots left the island annually to make their homes in the UK.

Tom Jones, on National Service as a gunner in the Royal Artillery, was sent to Cyprus in August:

> We were transported to a camp in the small village of Stroumbi, in the Paphos area, where EOKA were at their strongest. I was given a new job as an NCO in charge of transport. We had been there about a month when a bomb exploded at the NAAFI of part of our regiment some 20 miles away. Three people were killed and about ten wounded. We knew one or two of them so that was a bit sad. At about the same time one of our lads shot himself in the head and killed himself. It was never known if it was an accident or suicide. Unlike nowadays these men are all buried in Cyprus.
>
> Towards the end of our time in Cyprus, there was a special dispensation. Whereas we had been allowed only beer in our very limited canteen, we could now enjoy wine – but only the local retsina. In later life, I knew some former officers quite well. In hot climates, like Cyprus, they would start early, but at about midday get absolutely legless, every day.
>
> We stayed in Cyprus for a full year; in those days there was no R & R as there is now. At Christmas a few were allowed home if they

37 Foley, op. cit., pp. 96–7.

paid their own airfare, which was damned expensive since this was before packaged holidays and the like.

On 10 March, Britain scored a notable first in aviation, when a Fairey Delta 2 (a supersonic delta-winged research plane), piloted by Peter Twiss, set a world speed record of 1,132mph – more than 300mph faster than the previous (American) record-holder.

'Do you have a sensation of the wind roaring past?' asked the Pathé News interviewer.

'Well, there's no sensation of wind at all,' Twiss patiently explained. 'We're in a pressurised cabin.'

The questioner persisted in scientific enquiry: 'Do you eat a special diet? Or do you eat and smoke and drink like a normal human being?'

'I had a hard-boiled egg at six in the morning.'

Celebrity was a strange bedfellow in the '50s, at least to those who had previously slept undisturbed by it, and the ready answers we would expect today from almost anyone faced with a TV microphone came more hesitantly then. Twiss, wedged between his boss and the Pathé interviewer in case he fainted from the excitement, was asked what his reaction was 'when you woke up this morning and found you were the fastest man'.

'Well, er ... it's very encouraging...'

Imagine how such a Q&A would go nowadays, after the media-training experts had done their stuff.

But Mr Twiss had no such professional assistance, which probably explains his scandalously modest request in the December issue of *Lilliput*. The magazine's journalists had come up with the happy idea of asking 'six men we admire' to name 'the presents most likely to succeed with them this Christmas'. Mr Twiss asked for 'some really hard-wearing trousers' and was rewarded with, and photographed wearing, a pair of '50%-Terylene Sportocrats', priced at 5 guineas.

The new air-speed record stood until December 1957, when it was reclaimed by the United States.

Also in March, the *Daily Mail* Ideal Home Exhibition at London's Olympia was its usual success, attracting more than a million visitors. The most talked-about feature was the 'House of the Future', conceived by the architects Alison and Peter Smithson.

Offering a prediction of how people might live in 1980, it was constructed out of plastic, each room being moulded as a continuous piece. It was equipped with all the latest domestic technology: central heating, air conditioning, colour television, dishwasher, compact cooking appliances and a bathtub and shower that cleaned and dried themselves. Visitors to the exhibition could peer through holes in the walls and watch actors in futuristic costumes 'living' in this new kind of space.

Aggressively forward-looking as it appeared, the Smithsons' structure had echoes of the distant past: the moulded-plastic rooms recalled ancient cave systems, and the patio garden at the centre was inspired by the Roman houses excavated at Pompeii.

This prototype apart, the 'House of the Future', like many of the Smithsons' concepts, was never realised, but more modest attempts to create a living space for the future, or at least the bang-up-to-date present, were made by builder-developers like Taylor Woodrow. The 'Home of Tomorrow' in Crawley New Town was advertised as having 'a dream of a kitchen, which follows the wide-open look ... [a] bright stainless-steel, double-sided sink unit with built-in cupboards above and below', an eye-level refrigerator, and, 'perhaps the most unique of all, a specially made breakfast-table fitment covered with scarlet Formica at working top height with a cascade of drawers – one green baize lined for cutlery – and space for the washing machine'. The house containing all these wonders was priced at £2,195.

Saturday 24 March witnessed a very surprising Grand National. The Queen Mother's horse Devon Loch entered the final straight comfortably leading the field. Its jockey wrote afterwards: 'Never had I felt such power in reserve, such confidence in my mount, such calm in my mind.' Then, just 40 yards from the post, the horse suddenly gave a little jump and slumped to the ground. It hauled itself up again, but was unable to continue the course, and the race was won by ESB.

There was much speculation about the cause of Devon Loch's extraordinary collapse. Did it slip on a wet patch? Shy at the shadow of a fence? The jockey believed that it was frightened by the sound of the crowd. When examined afterwards, the horse appeared perfectly sound, and it won further races.

At the time, the Queen Mother's reaction was much reported: she simply said, 'Oh, that's racing.' Subsequently, 'doing a Devon Loch' passed into the sportswriter's glossary as a pithy way of describing an inexplicable last-minute failure. In August 2012, for example, a *Times* correspondent writing about the Olympic heptathlon described the British runner Jessica Ennis as 'almost there. It would take a Devon Loch-style collapse to deny her the gold medal now.'

The unfortunate jockey came to regard this as the greatest disappointment of his career, and, a year later, he retired from the sport. But we should not feel too sorry for him; his name was Dick Francis and, having exchanged the saddle for a typist's chair, he drew on his experience to write more than forty bestselling novels about the turf.

On 26 March, Jonathan Cape published a new book by their bestselling author: *Diamonds Are Forever*, the latest adventure of Ian Fleming's James Bond. The sequence had begun in 1953 with *Casino Royale*, followed by *Live and Let Die* (1954) and *Moonraker* (1955). *Diamonds Are Forever* was serialised in the *Daily Express* and enthusiastically reviewed by Raymond Chandler in the *Sunday Times*. The first print run of 125,000 quickly sold out.

The twelve novels and two collections of short stories that make up the Bond corpus – the literary corpus, that is to say; the films have taken 007 in directions Fleming could not have conceived – have attracted more critics, analysts and miscellaneous cultural diagnosticians (to say nothing of admirers and list-makers, among them Kingsley Amis, compiler of *The James Bond Dossier*) than perhaps any other group of books published in the second half of the twentieth century. According to Ben Macintyre, in his study *For Your Eyes Only: Ian Fleming and James Bond* (2008), the books provided 'the ideal antidote to Britain's postwar austerity, rationing and the looming premonition of lost power'. Another commentator, William Cook, suggests that: 'Bond pandered to Britain's inflated and increasingly insecure self-image, flattering us with the fantasy that Britannia could still punch above her weight.'

In particular, Fleming is seen as drawing a line beneath – or a knife across the throat of – the thriller writers who had dominated the lending libraries between the wars:

> Sapper, Buchan, Dornford Yates [this roll call is from Alan Bennett's play *Forty Years On*] – practitioners in that school of snobbery with violence that runs like a thread of good-class tweed through twentieth-century literature ... novels of a Europe where history is still a human process, and thrones rise and fall at the behest of international villains.

The Bond books have been held, said Colin Watson in *Snobbery with Violence*, his study of English crime stories and their audience,

> to represent the watershed between the old-style thrillers that people in the first half of the century were happy not to be able to put down, and the escapist literature of the Pop age. Gone, implies this argument, are the cosy, complicated tales of death at the country house party; departed for ever the aristocratic detective ... Arrived is the daring but irresponsible anti-hero, the hireling of realpolitik. He has in his mouth the radioactive ashes of guilt, but because he is an agent in the struggle between 'us' and 'them' instead of the outdated tournament of good and evil, he is enabled to behave ... in a fashion calculated to give readers more piquant vicarious sensations than ever they could have enjoyed in the pages of Edgar Wallace or Dorothy Sayers ... [or] Dornford Yates.

Here Watson is fairly putting the case for Fleming as a genre game-changer. But he is somewhat puzzled. What is it about Bond that fascinates millions of readers?

Is it his role as a pawn – or, at best, a knight – in the Cold War game? He doubts it.

Is it, perhaps, Fleming's brilliance as a writer? Hardly.

Fleming, in his view, is 'a competent storyteller on a journalistic level ... [but] all his villains are monstrous puppets, assembled from the rag-bag of childish imaginings'. Similarly, Bond's sexual conquests 'are distinguishable by name and, in some cases, by slight physical deformities; otherwise they all are standard issue, breast-thrusting lingerie demonstrators that pass for desirable sex-pots in the world of the prep school and, it would seem, British Naval Intelligence'.[38]

---

38 Colin Watson, *Snobbery with Violence* (London: Eyre Methuen, 1979), pp. 233–50 in revised edition.

Fleming's true appeal, Watson suggests, at least to his first generation of readers, was not that he had created a new kind of hero; he had re-outfitted an old one. In his patriotism, his social attitudes and his propensity for violence, Bond is an old boy of much the same school (if not precisely the same class) as E. W. Hornung's Raffles, John Buchan's Richard Hannay, Dornford Yates's Jonathan Mansel or Richard Chandos, and 'Sapper''s Bulldog Drummond. (Fleming is known to have read Buchan and 'Sapper' avidly as a boy.) The incredible villains are merely restyled versions of Edgar Wallace's madmen bent on world domination, or of Sax Rohmer's Fu-Manchu, an obvious model for Fleming's Dr No.

In one respect, however, Fleming did open a window upon the thriller genre and let in the chill air of the Cold War years. His predecessors' improbable plots and outrageous jingoism, Watson argues, actually demonstrated 'the stability and moral health of their society ... such things do not really happen in this well-ordered community of ours: it is only *because* they do not that people find them entertaining as tales'. Fleming, however, insinuated into the hoopla of gunfights and last-minute escapes and fates worse than death 'the proposition that not only were these things happening in very truth, but they were unavoidable, directed to patriotic ends, and approved moreover by ... the Men in the Know'. The Bond books are a cocktail, not newly invented but mixed by Fleming to a new potency

> of equal parts of moral abdication and supra-legal arrogance ... Bond, and all the quasi-Bonds of Fleming's imitators, are depicted as acting entirely without reference to any code other than that curious mixture of bureaucratic nicety and murderous licence whereby, we are assured, the under-cover agents of government everywhere conduct their affairs.[39]

---

39 Ibid.

In the sixty years since, that 'supra-legal arrogance' has become a familiar backdrop in books, movies and TV programmes about spies, secret policemen and licensed-to-kill freelances, from *Defence of the Realm* to the *Bourne* films, *State of Play* to *The X-Files*.

Ian Fleming's Bond, the Bond of *Snobbery with Violence*, really was an early-'50s construct, a product of an age when people of all classes would think more highly of a man because he went to Eton, and Britain still thought of itself as a great power with outposts all over the world. But in 1956 EOKA was making Britain look foolish in Cyprus, while the two Old Etonians Eden and Macmillan, who between them ran British foreign policy (the Foreign Secretary, Selwyn Lloyd, was only nominally in charge), were just about to lead their country into humiliation in Egypt.

Ian Fleming, of course, produced more books about his Bond – *From Russia with Love* (1957), *Dr No* (1958), *Goldfinger* (1959) and so on – at the rate of about one a year, until *Octopussy* in 1966. But the films offered something a little less snobbish, a little less British, a little less imperial, and they constantly changed as new Bonds emerged and the character moved ineluctably downmarket. Just fifty years after 1956, a bartender asked a new and relatively proletarian Bond (Daniel Craig) in the film of *Casino Royale* whether he wanted his vodka martini shaken or stirred, and Bond replied: 'Do I look like I give a damn?' Fleming's Bond could not have said that. The security services in Fleming's day recruited from the best schools, and any spy in the pre-1956 world would have known which vintage claret to order, and whether he wanted his martini shaken or stirred.

In 1956, film stars were not like Daniel Craig. They were polished and impeccable, and, if they were women, married to princes – or at least Hollywood's Grace Kelly was. With the announcement that she was to wed Prince Rainier III of Monaco, the world's press prepared all March for what was billed as 'the wedding of the century'. Alfred

Hitchcock, who had directed Kelly in *Dial M for Murder*, *Rear Window* and *To Catch a Thief*, was quoted as saying he was very happy that she had found herself such a good part.

The couple were required, by the laws of Monaco and the Roman Catholic Church, to have both a civil and a religious wedding. The civil ceremony on 18 April, at which the bride's newly acquired titles were recited – all 142 of them – was followed the next day by a church wedding in St Nicholas Cathedral, televised to an international audience estimated at over thirty million. Among the hundreds of celebrity guests were Cary Grant, Ava Gardner, David Niven and Gloria Swanson, representing art, and the Aga Khan, Aristotle Onassis and Conrad Hilton, representing money. James Bond would have fitted in perfectly.

CHAPTER 5

LOST OPPORTUNITIES: A DIPLOMATIC CAR CRASH INVOLVING BULGE AND KHRUSH

'Thousands mourn as red leaders arrive' screamed the front page of the *Catholic Herald* on 20 April, two days after the Russian cruiser *Orjonikidze* docked at Portsmouth Harbour carrying the Soviet Prime Minister Marshal Nikolai Bulganin and Soviet Communist Party Secretary Nikita Khrushchev.

Thousands may have mourned, but Sir Anthony Eden was not among them. He had worked hard for this. It was the first time since the 1917 revolution that Soviet leaders had visited Britain, and it represented a magnificent opportunity for the still relatively new Prime Minister to put his troubles behind him and score a diplomatic triumph.

And Eden needed it. A couple of weeks earlier, the loyally Conservative *Spectator* had told its readers:

> When, a year ago this week, Sir Anthony Eden took office as Prime Minister, *The Spectator* commented that the Conservative Party existed again for the first time since 1940. This has proved to be dramatically true. The removal of Sir Winston Churchill, whose position and power owed little to any section within the Conservative Party, has enabled the normal play of opinions and forces in the Party to begin again ... Sir Anthony Eden lack[s] both Churchill's prestige and Baldwin's intuitive skill ... His friends do him little service by pretending that his difficulties are merely temporary. Within a mere twelve months the Prime Minister has committed almost every possible mistake, and it is only the loyalty which attaches to any leader and a certain hold on his party born of years of political apprenticeship which have saved him. Both of these can evaporate.

But, whatever else they said of him, everyone thought Eden was a skilful international operator. Sir Anthony now had a golden opportunity to be the Prime Minister to discover that the new Soviet leaders were – as the much later Conservative Prime Minister Margaret Thatcher famously said of the much later Soviet leader Mikhail Gorbachev – men you could do business with.

It was going to be uphill work. Bulganin and Khrushchev were emerging as a successful partnership in the post-Stalin power struggle, but they were not so secure in the Kremlin that they could afford to be seen as an easy touch for Sir Anthony's patrician charm. And the mood at home was not entirely conducive to peacemaking. There were well-attended demonstrations against the visitors, and the Catholic

Church was not alone in seeing them as atheist murderers with whom it would be immoral to do business. The popular press christened them Bulge and Khrush, which seemed to sum up Britain's attitude to the leaders, and sometimes just B and K, as in the *Daily Mirror*'s headline on 19 April, when they visited Downing Street: 'B and K in the Garden of Eden.'

This was Eden's big chance. But the admiralty and the security services had other priorities. For two years, the admiralty had been keen to get to know the noise characteristics of the hulls of Russian cruisers, and what their propellers were capable of – information that was helpful to those who constructed mines and limpets in order to blow them up. The last time a Russian cruiser had put in at Portsmouth (the previous October), the admiralty had secretly sent two divers down to examine it. They claimed the Russians had done the same when one of Britain's cruisers put in at Leningrad.

Of course, the last time they did it, the cruiser was not carrying the Soviet Union's top brass. But this detail did not bother the admiralty; they were pleased with the information they had got the previous time, and could hardly wait for the *Orjonikidze* to dock so as to get some more.

So, in March, somebody from MI6 got in touch with one of the two divers from the previous mission, Commander Lionel 'Buster' Crabb, and asked him if he would kindly go down quietly into Portsmouth Harbour at the dead of night and examine the visitor's hull. Even now, we are not allowed to know who recruited Commander Crabb – the name is redacted from the documents in The National Archives (TNA) – but he was a spy, and he will crop up again in our story, so let's call him Captain Spook.

The plan was codenamed Operation Claret, and Captain Spook, according to a report to the Prime Minister, 'gained the impression' that the Foreign Office approved of it. Just how he gained this impression was to become a matter for earnest enquiry, and all we can say for certain is that it was an impression he had been rather keen on gaining.

However, just before the *Orjonikidze* docked, the Prime Minister got to hear of the plan. 'I am sorry, but we cannot do anything of this kind on this occasion,' he wrote to the admiralty. He was not going to run the risk of anything jeopardising his talks with Bulge and Khrush.

Nobody thought to mention the Prime Minister's view to Commander Crabb, who, on 17 April, the day before the *Orjonikidze* was due to dock, turned up at Portsmouth's Sallyport Hotel, where he met Captain Spook. Both men checked into the hotel, and, the next day, they watched the Russian cruiser sail in. When evening fell, Commander Crabb had a practice go at it, and returned to adjust the weights he was carrying. That evening, he went off to visit some friends who lived at nearby Havant.

Crabb was forty-seven and a massively experienced diver, having done delicate and dangerous diving and bomb-disposal work during the Second World War and, later, in Palestine. But he had been forced into retirement the previous year, and it was known that his heavy drinking and smoking, as well as his age, meant that he was not the diver he had once been. He had been brought back from his civilian job just for this mission.

Bright and early at six o'clock the next morning, Crabb and Spook left their hotel, picked up the naval officer who had been seconded to help them, and went to the dockyard. At 7 a.m., the commander went overboard in his diving gear to take a good look at the *Orjonikidze*'s keel, rudder and screws.

And that's the last anyone ever saw of Commander Crabb.

By 9.15 a.m., Captain Spook and the naval officer were getting seriously alarmed, but nothing strange seemed to be happening on the Russian ship, as far as they could see. They reported that Crabb was missing to someone else whose name we are not allowed to know. A launch was sent out into the harbour to try to look for the commander.

It must have been an odd sight from the Soviet cruiser: the launch constantly going round the area in which the Russians were moored, with those on board no doubt trying hard to look as though they had not a care in the world and were just taking the air.

A full search was briefly considered but judged inadvisable, as the Russians could hardly fail to notice it. They wouldn't find the commander anyway, as he was weighted and his body had probably gone to the bottom of the harbour.

Captain Spook went back to the Sallyport Hotel, paid his bill (and that of Commander Crabb) and took the luggage. What he did for the rest of the day is still an official secret.

The Russians had, of course, noticed the commander. That evening, the Soviet Admiral Orlov was dining with Admiral Burnett and, over the coffee, casually remarked that he had seen a frogman at about 8 a.m.

Over the next few days, admirals and spooks in London whispered the dreadful news to each other, but no one thought to tell the Prime Minister. They were all sure the one thing that mattered was to keep the matter under wraps until the Russians had gone.

But, for the present, the Russians were still there, and they were being given the grand tour. On 21 April, Bulganin and Khrushchev were taken to the atomic energy establishment at Harwell, and to Oxford University, where John Phipps watched with some bemusement their visit to his college (Magdalen), and described it in a talk for the BBC Midland Home Service. It appears the Russians were regarded by many with an almost superstitious dread:

> The two figures, quite short, hatless, in double-breasted suits, were coming down the path ... They passed the waiting undergraduates, raised their hands. Then we knew what we had forgotten. We had not composed our faces. What is the correct way of greeting, as a

> crowd, men whose purposes are unclear, whose smiles are suspect, who are, so they say, despots, tyrants, a species of beast? Especially when they smile, wave, bring gifts, look human.
>
> We clapped or were silent, curious ... Everybody followed [them] all round the college ... An eminent Fellow said, 'Where are the brutes now?' and went to see ... They saw the lawns and the buildings and the blossom. They saw [the historian] A. J. P. Taylor in a window of New Buildings, and he saw them. They even went into the chapel. They signed an autograph book – the ancient history tutor, he whose clear eyes see right through the pretence and propaganda of the Roman Empire, right to its corrupt heart – his son got the signature ... An undergraduate said 'hello' in Russian. Bulganin lightly patted his cheek ... But outside was the crowd, most cheering, some booing, some singing 'Poor Old Joe'. Leaflets were thrown, and over all the evil roar of the Thunderbirds of the motor-cycle police, like a chorus of hell-hounds. Our hate complexes revived.[40]

In Eden's office, Khrushchev saw, to his surprise, what appeared to be a picture of Tsar Nicholas II, the last Tsar of Russia. Eden explained that it was Nicholas's cousin George V. In Scotland, wrote Khrushchev:

> We watched the parade under a tent, which protected us from the light, freezing rain. We had been warned that it always rains in Scotland ... The Scottish military uniforms ... are very unusual – steel grey skirts – and their music is odd too; it's played on special Scottish musical instruments.[41]

---

40 'Did You Hear That?', *The Listener*, 3 May 1956.

41 Nikita Khrushchev et al., *Khrushchev Remembers* (London: Andre Deutsch, 1971).

The Russians finally left on 27 April, whereupon Commander Crabb's mother was told that he was probably dead. The next day, a Captain Sarell was sent to see Crabb's ex-wife, presumably to make sure she kept quiet. Captain Spook went to Crabb's employer and told him to keep his mouth shut too.

Yet, still, ministers were not told. The Secretary to the Admiralty decided, on 30 April, not to tell the First Sea Lord, apparently thinking it was up to the Foreign Office to decide whether ministers should know; Sir Ivone Kirkpatrick, the permanent under-secretary at the Foreign Office (who was personally close to Eden), decided that it was up to the admiralty whether ministers should be told – so both kept their political masters in the dark.

But the news was beginning to leak. Newspapers were starting to ask questions. Journalists found that the relevant pages had been removed from the register of the Sallyport Hotel, and the unfortunate proprietor was unable to explain satisfactorily why Portsmouth police had come in and torn them out. By 4 May, it was abundantly clear that the Prime Minister had to be told – and he was.

Eden was incandescent with rage. The security services had not just undermined him; they had made him look foolish in front of his visitors. Clarissa Eden wrote in her diary: 'The Russians have been very reticent about it. They say they saw him surface but will say no more. Anthony wondered why Khrushchev kept on making jokes about cruisers being so obsolete. They must think us perfect fools.'[42] Khrushchev, judging by his brief reference to the affair in his memoirs, seems to have assumed Eden knew all about it and had authorised it.

Eden demanded a report from Sir Edward Bridges – head of the home civil service, son of the nineteenth-century poet laureate Robert Bridges, and, like Eden, an Old Etonian. Bridges, on the verge of

42 Clarissa Eden, *A Memoir* (London: Orion, 2007), p. 232.

retirement, sifted carefully through the story, interviewed the leading players and produced the report from which we have taken all the above information.

He then gave his opinion. This was, he wrote, a perfectly normal sort of operation – one we did hundreds of times, one the Russians were always doing to us, and one, if properly carried out, that was not especially risky.

But, he said, it was *not* properly carried out; and then there is a page and a half redacted in his report, presumably containing criticism of Captain Spook and his MI6 colleagues, before the words: 'I feel bound to mention this because, had due precautions been observed in carrying out the operation, there is no reason why its failure should have involved the government in any way or caused an embarrassment.'

But what about the fact that the PM had given direct orders that it should not be carried out? Did the PM's word count for nothing? Well, not a lot, it seemed. Sir Edward explained patiently that there seemed to have been a misunderstanding between two officials. A Foreign Office official thought he was being shown the plan for information, and said nothing. An admiralty official thought the Foreign Office official's silence meant consent. As to why no one told the Prime Minister, apparently the admiralty thought that telling ministers was the Foreign Office's job, and the Foreign Office thought it was the admiralty's.

'The attitude of officials in each department', wrote Bridges, 'was that they would tell their minister as soon as the minister in the other department was told – but not before.' The Prime Minister, whose furious annotations pepper the document, wrote beside that sentence: 'Ridiculous.' And it is hard not to agree with him.

However, Sir Edward simply writes with patrician wistfulness: 'Looking back, it is perhaps a pity that the senior officials of the two departments did not have direct discussions on this point.'

When it had all gone horribly wrong, might not the Prime Minister – who was hoping to do business with Bulge and Khrush – have been told? Well, said Sir Edward, in retrospect, perhaps he should. Most of the civil servants involved later agreed 'that it would have been right and prudent to tell ministers what had happened at a considerably earlier stage than was done'. But it was not a very serious mistake, Bridges added, and no one was really at fault.[43]

Sir Anthony did not agree, and neither, one imagines, would the relatives of Commander Crabb have done, had they been given any of this information.

They never knew what happened to him. For years, newspapers enjoyed speculating that he had fallen into Soviet hands, especially after his headless body was washed up a year later, giving rise to all sorts of lurid theories. In fact, after a year in the sea, his headlessness could be explained in entirely natural, if rather indigestible, terms. Almost certainly, he simply got into difficulties and drowned.

Eden's fury was not just directed at those who had commissioned Commander Crabb. The world seemed to conspire to ruin his big diplomatic opportunity. When Foreign Secretary Selwyn Lloyd entertained Bulge and Khrush to lunch, the Foreign Office's usual interpreter was ill and his replacement arrived drunk. Selwyn Lloyd introduced his PPS Lord Lambton, and said he was a man who enjoyed shooting. The interpreter managed to translate this in such a way as to give the impression that Lord Lambton was under sentence of death. Khrushchev was greatly moved and shook hands with him solemnly.

Then, when Khrushchev rose to reply to Lloyd's speech, the interpreter, who was apparently one of those who did not think Eden should be entertaining Bulge and Khrush, decided to embellish what he said: 'He says he is pleased to be here, but whether we are pleased

43 The National Archives, PREM 11, 2077.

to have him is another matter.' Lloyd's expression froze, but Khrushchev did not know anything had gone wrong, and pressed on, saying that Britain and Russia had much in common, to which the interpreter added: 'Don't you believe it – we haven't got eight million prisoners in Siberia.'

At last, Lloyd had the interpreter taken out of the room, and tried to repair the damage through the Russians' own interpreter. But, when the Soviet leader was told what had happened, he burst into gales of laughter. So it looked as though things were OK with Bulge and Khrush, although there was still the irascible Prime Minister to worry about. All the officials were given strict instructions that Eden should not be told. Everyone seemed to be keeping things from the beleaguered and increasingly neurotic Prime Minister that month. The events at that meal stayed under wraps for forty-seven years, until Eden's biographer Richard Thorpe uncovered the relevant documents.[44]

Dinner at Chequers was only marginally better, as Clarissa Eden recorded in her diary:

> Dinner next to Khrushchev. He doesn't eat at all. A lot of jovial shouting across the table to Bulganin. He shouted to Anthony: 'You are an island. You depend for your food and everything on your navy and your ships. We have submarines that can surface and fire rockets inland.'
>
> Anthony replied that England was a porcupine that could send back bombs and rockets to whoever attacked her. Selwyn [Lloyd] told me after that [General] Gruenther [the top American general in Europe] had been trying to find out if the Russians have rocket-firing submarines for ages.

44 D. R. Thorpe, *Eden: The Life and Times of Anthony Eden, First Earl of Avon, 1897–1977* (London: Chatto, 2003), pp. 470–71.

> Anthony told them if anyone attacked the Gulf sheikdoms, we would fight for the oil. Ugly silence. After dinner I leave them to it.[45]

Nothing went as planned. *The Macmillan Diaries* report that 'the public are getting rather upset, esp. about their visit to the Queen'.[46] A dinner with Labour Party leaders at the House of Commons was described in secret CIA reports as

> a fiasco ... Khrushchev antagonised the Labor [*sic*] leaders by repeating charges he made in India that Britain and France had urged Hitler to attack the USSR, and by defending the Stalin–Hitler pact. He further angered them by warning that if the West persisted in re-arming West Germany, the USSR would have no alternative but to seek an alliance with those forces in West Germany who desire an alliance. He added the threat that the USSR had plenty of space to experiment with the hydrogen bomb.

According to Khrushchev, it was all the fault of George Brown, a famously explosive and hard-drinking member of the Labour shadow Cabinet. Khrushchev wrote in his memoirs that Brown had launched into a tirade against the visitors. The diplomat and diarist Harold Nicolson had inside information about this, as he confided in a letter to his wife Vita Sackville-West:

> My Labour friends told me that the dinner ... was a ghastly failure. Khrushchev made a speech saying that it was Russia alone who defeated Germany. George Brown, a Labour front-bench hearty,

---

45 Eden, op. cit., p. 230.

46 *The Macmillan Diaries – The Cabinet Years 1950–57* (London: Macmillan, 2003), p. 552.

> exclaimed, 'May God forgive you.' Khrushchev broke off and asked the interpreter what he had said. It was translated. Khrushchev then banged the table and said, 'What I say is true!' George Brown is not the mild type of Socialist. He replied, 'We lost half a million men while you were Hitler's allies!' *Silence penible* [painful silence].
>
> And, at the Speaker's luncheon yesterday, George Brown went up with an outstretched hand to apologise but Khrushchev put his hand behind his back and said sharply, 'NIET.'[47]

The CIA report's summary was: 'Of all the developments, Khrushchev's clash with the Labor [*sic*] Party may have the most lasting effect in Britain. His abrupt dismissal of demands for the release of social democrats brought a rare degree of unity to the opposition.'[48]

It certainly sounded that way. At Moscow Airport on his return, Khrushchev singled out the Labour leaders for criticism: 'We must tell you, quite frankly, that some of the Labour leaders are definitely anti-Soviet. They spoke about some Social Democrats, alleging they were imprisoned in the Soviet Union and in the People's Democracies. We dismissed this question altogether.' Labour leader Hugh Gaitskell turned down Khrushchev's invitation to visit Moscow.

But Eden fared little better. 'I gather that the negotiations with Eden and For[eign] Sec[retar]y are pretty sticky,' Macmillan confided to his diary.

If Eden had been able to turn the visit round, the events of October and November might have been very different, and he might have carved out a new role for Britain in the world.

As it was, all he achieved was to make it clear that the British government was prepared to defend Middle East oil supplies, by

---

47 Ruth Winstone (ed.), *Events, Dear Boy, Events* (London: Profile Books, 2012), pp. 251–2.

48 http://news.bbc.co.uk/1/hi/england/hampshire/8345951.stm

force if necessary. In doing so, he probably hoped to make force unnecessary. Few diplomatic positions have unravelled so completely, so fast.

CHAPTER 6

A TIDE OF ANGER BURSTS THE THEATRICAL DAM

In 1955, two young theatre directors, Tony Richardson and George Devine, founded a radical new theatre troupe, the English Stage Company, and acquired the rental of the Royal Court Theatre in Sloane Square, London. Devine placed an advertisement in *The Stage* asking for new plays, and John Osborne, then living on a leaky houseboat in Fulham, sent him *Look Back in Anger*.

Devine knew that this was what he had been looking for.

Devine and Richardson's Royal Court opened in April 1956 with a production of Angus Wilson's play *The Mulberry Bush*, and it was not until 8 May that the radical new mission burst on public consciousness. That was the opening night of *Look Back in Anger*, and it was the night that the proletarian spirit of 1956 kicked its way rudely into the genteel upper-middle-class world of English theatre.

In the first half of the twentieth century, the theatre had been the preserve of the well-to-do, with just a few cheap, hard seats high up in the gallery for the rest. Shakespeare's theatre, full of the city's proletarians, was a distant memory. The area of a theatre still called the dress circle was so named because those sitting in it were expected to wear evening dress, like their betters in the stalls – and unlike the commoners in the gallery.

Theatregoers were of the class that was horrified by the election of a Labour government in 1945. West End theatre audiences craved the restoration of what they saw as a proper balance between the classes, and were rewarded in 1948 with William Douglas-Home's *The Chiltern Hundreds*, a vacuous comedy that showed an uppity socialist defeated in an election by a Conservative butler. (Message: real working-class people – the salt of the earth – respect nobility and know their place.) No one could ever have imagined that, within a decade, London theatre would be a place for home-grown literary innovation and radical politics. So far, these had come from overseas – the Royal Court had already produced Bertolt Brecht and Arthur Miller.

J. B. Priestley wrote in 1947:

> Theatre at the moment is not controlled by dramatists, actors, producers or managers, but chiefly by theatre-owners, men of property who may or may not have a taste for the drama ... What I condemn is the property system that allows public amenities and a communal art to be controlled by persons who happen to be rich enough to acquire playhouses.[49]

49 David Pattie, *Modern British Playwriting in the 1950s* (London: Methuen, 2012), p. 29.

Priestley wanted the theatre to be put on the same footing as the new National Health Service. It never was, of course; it continued into the '50s in the same old way, with gentle and unchallenging revues, light comedies (often revivals, like *Charley's Aunt* and *Arsenic and Old Lace*), updates of classics by the trio of theatrical knights – John Gielgud, Laurence Olivier and Ralph Richardson – and a little new work by William Douglas-Home, or the rather better Noël Coward.

The first concession to the new democratic spirit was at the Whitehall Theatre, where actor-manager Brian Rix had discovered that, if he put on laugh-a-minute farces and offered seats in bulk, he could tap into the new coach-party trade. His Whitehall farces filled the theatre most nights, and, in May 1956, he was still presenting the show he had opened nearly two years earlier, *Dry Rot*. It would not close until March 1958.

All of which helps explain why *Look Back in Anger* hit critics and audiences like a torrent of icy water. Theatregoers used to plays that opened in Colonel Bulstrode's library, somewhere in Hampshire, looked on appalled as the curtains parted to reveal the set of *Look Back in Anger*: a cheap, dreary room dominated by an ironing board.

It got worse. Protagonist Jimmy Porter railed against a world that did not care, and shouted the anguished cry of the postwar generation: 'There are no great brave causes left.' He seemed to speak for a generation that could not go and fight for socialism and democracy in Spain, as Jimmy Porter's father had done, nor even for a better and fairer world at home.

Look Back in Anger was Osborne's second go at this idea. His first – written with his friend Anthony Creighton, and, in many ways, a better play – was *Epitaph for George Dillon*, which was a year or two ahead of its time, but has never had the same iconic status. In *Epitaph*, the conflict between the generation that had grown up after the war and the one that was already grown up in the '30s was even starker. One of his slightly older characters, Barney, says: 'Now, you take Hitler – the greatest man that ever lived ... He had the right idea. You've got to be ruthless and it's the same in this business. 'Course, he may have gone a bit too far sometimes.'

George Dillon, a sort of prototype Jimmy Porter, responds ironically: 'Think so?' and Barney says: 'I do. I do think so, most definitely.'

It was, among other things, a clash of generations, and *Look Back in Anger* was the signal for generational war.

To its supporters, it was simply the best thing that had ever happened, not just in the theatre but anywhere. 'I doubt if I could love anyone who did not wish to see *Look Back in Anger*,' wrote Kenneth Tynan in *The Observer*, and he went on to define the two positions:

> 'They are scum' was Mr Maugham's famous verdict on the class of state-aided university students to which Kingsley Amis's *Lucky Jim* belongs; and, since Mr Maugham seldom says anything controversial or uncertain of wide acceptance, his opinion will be that of many. Those who share it better stay away from John Osborne's *Look Back in Anger*, which is all scum and a mile wide.[50]

The story is often told as though Tynan was a voice crying in the wilderness – when, in fact, the play had other vigorous supporters – and as though Osborne represented the political left and his enemies the right – when actually the division was mainly generational rather than political. Indeed, the influential critic for the Conservative magazine *The Spectator*, 31-year-old Anthony Hartley, liked the play as much as Tynan did, and understood it in the same way: 'In the '30s, Jimmy Porter would have been a Communist and fought in Spain, but now there is nothing for him but to work in a sweet

50 Kenneth Tynan, *Theatre Writings* (London: Nick Hern Books, 2007), p. 112.

stall and relive nostalgic memories of the time when there seemed to be something to believe in.' Similarly, John Lahr in the *New York Times Book Review* wrote that the play had 'wiped the smugness off the frivolous face of English theatre'.

Moreover, 'Tynan the political radical' was mostly a figment of fevered popular imagination, and probably of his own as well – though he had certainly moved on since his undergraduate days at Oxford, when, in 1946, he had been a member of a fascist organisation called the Oxford Corporate Club (OCC). The OCC sat at the feet of Sir Oswald Mosley, and Tynan spoke in favour of fascism at the Oxford Union – getting away with it, apparently, by a sort of flippant aesthetic foppery.[51]

The haters of the play were the old men.

The *Daily Mail*'s Cecil Wilson felt aggrieved that so beguiling an actress as Mary Ure should be made to stand at an ironing board: 'Mary Ure's beauty [was] frittered away on the part of a wife who, judging by the time she spends ironing, seems to have taken on the nation's laundry.' Anthony Cookman in *Tatler* could 'only hope that the chronic disease of nagging from which [Jimmy Porter] suffers will abate in course of time'.

On BBC radio's *The Critics*, Ivor Brown railed against the play's setting – a one-room flat in the Midlands – as 'unspeakably dirty and squalid. It is difficult to believe that a colonel's daughter, brought up with some standards, would have stayed in this sty for a day ... I felt angry because it wasted my time.'

Milton Shulman told *Evening Standard* readers: 'Nothing is so comforting to the young as the opportunity to feel sorry for themselves ... It aims at being a despairing cry but achieves only the stature of a self-pitying snivel.' His colleague on the *Evening News* thought it 'putrid

51 Graham Macklin, *Very Deeply Dyed in Black: Sir Oswald Mosley and the Postwar Reconstruction of British Fascism* (London: I. B. Tauris, 2007), p. 37.

bosh', and several hostile critics pointed out that Osborne was only twenty-seven, so, really, what could you expect? The play was 'young, young, young', as John Barber wrote in the *Daily Express*.

The battle lines were clear. Those on age's side manned barricades erected by Somerset Maugham two years previously, in his review of Kingsley Amis's novel *Lucky Jim*, to which Tynan had alluded. In it, Maugham attacked the new sort of undergraduate – the man without wealth, position or public-school education, who nonetheless presumed himself worthy of getting a degree:

> They do not go to the university to acquire culture, but to get a job, and when they have got one, scamp it. They have no manners, and are woefully unable to deal with any social predicament. Their idea of a celebration is to go into a public bar and drink six beers. They are mean, malicious and envious.[52]

On the other side, the barricades of youth were drawn up by Tynan, who wrote that the play represented 'postwar youth as it really is'.

The discontented older members of the audience hurled abuse at the stage and often left as noisily as possible, slamming the door that led directly to the street.[53] Among those who took against the play was the great actor Sir Laurence Olivier, now pushing fifty: 'It stinks, a travesty on England, a lot of bitter rattling on.'[54] He had no idea of the flowering of great brave causes it presaged – from the Campaign for Nuclear Disarmament to anti-apartheid – and would not have thought much of them if he had.

Olivier's old friend and contemporary, the playwright Terence

---

52 Pattie, op. cit., p. 2.

53 Robert Tanitch, *London Stage in the Twentieth Century* (London: Haus Publishing, 2007), p. 166.

54 Jonathan Croall, *John Gielgud* (London: Methuen Drama, 2011), p. 420.

Rattigan, almost walked out after the first act on the first night, and, when he emerged from the theatre, he told waiting journalists that the play should really have been called *Look, Ma, I'm Not Terence Rattigan*. He had earlier urged George Devine not to stage it at all, insisting that it would never work in the theatre. Playwriting, as a formal craft; plays with a set structure, tracing the emotional lives of the upper and middle classes – that was what Rattigan knew well and did perfectly.

Noël Coward appears not to have seen the play on stage, but, months later, he got round to reading it and noted in his diary:

> It is so full of talent and fairly well constructed but I wish I knew why the hero is so dreadfully cross and what about? I should also like to know who, where and why he and his friend run a sweet-stall, and if, considering the hero's unparalleled capacity for invective, they ever manage to sell any sweets? I expect my bewilderment is because I am very old indeed and cannot understand why the younger generation, instead of knocking at the door, should bash the fuck out of it. In this decade there is obviously less and less time for comedy so far as the intelligentsia is concerned.[55]

John Gielgud was also clear that, if this really was the future, it was not *his* future:

> I remember going, not expecting to enjoy it, and enjoying it hugely, and thinking, oh, I see now, this is a whole new lot of people. I remember coming away thinking, now I know how a new sort of class has evolved, politically and socially and everything, and it's very well shown in this play, it's very dramatic, but I don't see there's any place in it for me.

---

55 Ruth Winstone (ed.), *Events, Dear Boy, Events* (London: Profile Books, 2012), p. 260.

And, indeed, in Osborne's theatre, there probably wasn't – though not for the reason Gielgud thought. John Osborne later spoke of 'the blight of buggery, which then dominated the theatre in all its frivolity', adding that 'queer folk were not to be considered' at the Royal Court. This ban would certainly have encompassed Gielgud – as well as Rattigan and Coward – but fortunately that decision was not in Osborne's hands but in those of the rather more enlightened George Devine.[56] Osborne had, as we shall see, equally crass views about the role of women, which, before the end of the year, he would smear over the pages of the *Daily Mail*.

For John Osborne, despite *Look Back in Anger*, was actually not very radical or left-wing at all, either socially or politically – and, ironically, he was considerably less so than Terence Rattigan. Nonetheless, it was Osborne's work that helped open the door for great radical left-wing playwrights like Arnold Wesker and John Arden to emerge in the second half of the '50s.

Elsewhere in London theatre, it was mostly business as usual. William Douglas-Home was bringing the upper middle classes to the Cambridge Theatre to see *The Reluctant Debutante*. There were lots of classics, including Richard Burton and John Neville alternating Othello and Iago at the Old Vic, and Athene Seyler as Mrs Malaprop in *The Rivals* at the Saville. Vivien Leigh and Ronald Lewis starred in Noël Coward's *South Sea Bubble* at the Lyric, and Alec Guinness in a Feydeau farce at the Winter Garden. *Gigi* with Leslie Caron was at the New, and T. S. Eliot's *The Family Reunion*, with Paul Scofield and Sybil Thorndike, played at the Phoenix.[57]

But a new world was stirring, and the Royal Court was not the only place where it made its presence felt, though it was by far the most

56 Croall, op. cit., p. 421.

57 Tanitch, op. cit., pp. 165–7.

important. The Theatre Royal Stratford East was about to open with Brendan Behan's *The Quare Fellow*, and Bertolt Brecht's *Mother Courage and Her Children* was to arrive at the Palace Theatre in August.[58]

And, two months before the opening night of *Look Back in Anger*, the Barry O'Brien Repertory Company, based at the Palace Court, Bournemouth, presented *Jane Eyre*. 'There emerges a characterisation of Samson strength,' said the *Bournemouth Daily Echo* the next day: 'We have never this season seen David Baron in so forthright a performance. His Rochester is a solid achievement in a repertory world so often content with milk and water performances.'

'David Baron' was the 25-year-old Harold Pinter – by then a repertory actor with a couple of years' experience and some decent reviews behind him. He worked with the O'Brien Company until September, when he married fellow repertory actor Vivien Merchant. By October, he had switched to Philip Barrett's New Malvern Company at the Pavilion in Torquay, where he had leading roles in Rattigan's *Separate Tables* and a couple of Agatha Christie thrillers. He had not yet had a play of his own produced, but his first, *The Room* (which he first drafted in November), would be premièred in May 1957, the year in which he also wrote *The Birthday Party* and *The Dumb Waiter*.

Meanwhile, Peter Hall, a 24-year-old Cambridge graduate, got his first big production – *Love's Labour's Lost* at Stratford-upon-Avon – and thus ended the stranglehold of the old actor-managers of the '30s, like Gielgud and Olivier. The previous year, Hall had directed the première of Samuel Beckett's *Waiting for Godot*, and it changed the way people thought. Indeed, Keith Richards, a 25-year-old English teacher at the time, says: 'It seemed to knock for six the idea of a basic play set in the Home Counties when the curtain went up and a butler answered the phone. What does it mean? It means

---

58 Ibid.

what your creative process makes it mean. Nothing has been the same since.'

The new wave had arrived, and the old men had to adjust to it. Rattigan had once described the audience member he thought no playwright would dare upset as 'that nice, respectable, middle-class, middle-aged lady', and, even four years after *Look Back in Anger*, he was still saying: 'I'm pretty sure it won't survive.' But, by then, he knew what he was up against, adding: 'I'm prejudiced because, if it does survive, I know I won't.'

He was partly right. The new wave did survive, and Rattigan's work went into a lengthy, though far from total, eclipse. However, it re-emerged half a century later, when we found, to our surprise, that he was a better and braver playwright than we gave him credit for, and probably more instinctively radical than John Osborne – just older.

His revival, however, came at a price that Rattigan, had he been alive, might not have been keen to pay. Since Osborne had been annexed by the left, Rattigan had to be an icon of the right. As David Hare wrote in *The Guardian* in 2011:

> It has become a commonplace of commentary to turn [Rattigan] into some sort of public school victim whose fall from grace can be put down to nasty goings-on initiated by yobs at the Royal Court and Stratford East in the 1950s. In this seigniorial rewriting of history, the long-delayed opening up of the British stage to working-class voices in two notably small auditoriums on either side of London took place at the expense of a solid craftsman whose skilful celebrations of English middle-class reticence fell unfairly out of favour.

The narrative suited the Thatcher–Major–Blair years, Hare explained:

> Those of us who lived through the Thatcher years will remember how, for the first time, the powerful and successful were encouraged to develop an ugly vein of grievance. To the beaming approval of the Prime Minister, fabulously wealthy business folk took to telling us how little appreciated they were, and how intolerable it was to carry an equal burden of taxation and misunderstanding. With Cameron in charge, this wheedling tone of self-righteous privilege is back in the public discourse.[59]

Laurence Olivier – who, unlike Rattigan, possessed sensitive political antennae – saw the writing on the wall. Having dismissed it the first time, he was persuaded to give *Look Back in Anger* another try in the company of the great American playwright Arthur Miller, who said to him at the interval: 'Larry, you're wrong; this is great stuff.' Indeed, Miller thought that 'the British stage is hermetically sealed against the way that society moves' and that '*Look Back in Anger* seems to me the only modern English play that I have seen'.[60]

Olivier went backstage and found himself surrounded by young actors – often a new sort of actor, for the profession was more open than it had been to those without cut-glass accents. And the great actor suddenly felt old, stuffy, establishment. He ached for something new to happen, for a change from the pattern of his work, which he described as 'a bit deadly – a classical or semi-classical film, a play or two at Stratford, or a nine-month run in the West End'.

So he asked the young playwright if he might think about writing a play with him in mind. Osborne was delighted and flattered, and within what seemed to Olivier to be an amazingly short time the first act of *The Entertainer* arrived. Olivier thought it had been written

59 *The Guardian*, 31 May 2011.

60 Pattie, op. cit., p. 36.

specially for him, though Osborne said the inspiration came from seeing Max Miller on stage, and he only offered it to Olivier afterwards. At all events, Olivier said at once that he would take the part of Archie Rice at the Royal Court. It changed his life.

The Entertainer opened in 1957, but it was a thoroughly up-to-date play set in 1956, with a lot to tell us about the year. Archie Rice is a washed-up stand-up comic in the dusty, depressing, dying days of music hall. Tap-dancing on windswept piers in three-quarters-empty theatres and getting his laughs at his own predicament, he looks sadly skywards after a thin audience reaction and says: 'Don't laugh too loud, it's a very old building.' Olivier, in his usual manner, researched the part carefully, travelling with Osborne to the few remaining musical halls, learning to tap-dance, learning how to deliver stand-up patter perfectly – and then learning to do it badly, for part of the play's tragedy is that Archie is not very good.

Olivier always thought of Archie Rice as his greatest achievement, and he put it down to the fact that 'I know that man – I know him better than he knows himself.' He meant not just that he had met dozens of Archie Rices in dressing rooms during his long career, but that, in a sense, he *was* Archie Rice – a man who had played a part so long that he had forgotten who he was. He knew what Archie meant when he said: 'I'm dead behind those eyes – I don't feel a thing.'

'It's really me, isn't it?' Olivier once said to Osborne. And it was. Archie Rice was everything Olivier would have been without his prodigious talent: a man who never felt quite real except when he was on a stage, a serial adulterer, and as camp as a row of tents.[61]

Osborne, ever up-to-date, set *The Entertainer* during the Suez crisis of October to December 1956, and the play became the most

61 Francis Beckett, *Olivier* (London: Haus Publishing, 2005).

enlightening testament to the event that would, more than anything, define 1956 and its legacy.

Among the critics invited to review the first night of *The Entertainer* was Colin Wilson, whom we shall meet again in Chapter 8. He and Osborne, along with Kingsley Amis, John Wain and others, had been identified by the press as 'angry young men', but for Wilson *The Entertainer* signalled the end of that 'absurd myth': 'Osborne was not angry – just full of sadness and nostalgia for an England that ceased to exist in 1913.' And Wilson had no time for that: 'I hate this British preoccupation with class.' He expected his disenchantment with the play to be echoed by the rest of the press, and was 'staggered' when it wasn't.[62]

It was Osborne's good fortune, as well as his talent and his anger, that made his play a turning point. It could as easily have been Arnold Wesker, who came from the substantial rebellion to the left of the Labour Party and wrote about how they too changed fundamentally in 1956.

Since the demise of the Independent Labour Party in the '30s, the left had been dominated by the Communist Party – a real force in society in a way that is hard to imagine today. The Communist Party had two MPs in 1945, and, in a proportional representation system, would have had a great many more.

Arnold Wesker, from a family of East End Jewish communists (his aunt Sara Wesker was one of Britain's most important communists in the '30s), explained what 1956 meant to the young, the poor and the left, in his trilogy of wonderful, atmospheric plays first performed between 1958 and 1960 at the Royal Court: *Roots*, *I'm Talking About Jerusalem* and *Chicken Soup with Barley*.

As Michael Billington wrote, reviewing the 2005 revival of *Chicken Soup with Barley* in *The Guardian*:

---

62 Colin Wilson, *The Angry Years: The Rise and Fall of the Angry Young Men* (London: Robson Books, 2007), pp. 63–5.

> [Wesker] shows the Kahn family, dominated by the matriarchal communist Sarah, exuberantly celebrating the defeat of Mosley's fascists in Cable Street in 1936. Ten years later, during the Attlee government, the family is already splintering, with daughter Ada abandoning the urban jungle for rural Norfolk.
>
> But the drama comes to a head in 1956, when Ronnie Kahn, distraught by the Soviet invasion of Hungary, returns from Paris to confront his stubbornly idealistic, loyally socialist mother.

Ronnie Kahn tells his mother that Stalin persecuted the Jewish doctors who were falsely accused in 1952 of conspiring to assassinate Soviet leaders, and she says: 'What do you want me to do – move to Hendon and forget who I am?' Wesker told us: 'You can admit the error of an idea, but not the conduct of a whole life.' And, early in June, the dilemma of people like Sara Wesker became acute, when *The Observer* published, for the first time, the full text of Khrushchev's secret speech. There could be no more doubt that, for decades, the Communist Party had persuaded young idealists to support a hideous tyranny.

Almost as significant as what Wesker's plays were saying is the fact that they were performed at all – for they were by, and about, the working class. They were the first, best and most aggressive post-*Look Back in Anger* plays. One of the reasons 1956 matters more than any other year is that:

> It is a sign of how far things had changed in the decade that, alongside Eliot the already established cultural icon, Rattigan the star of the commercial stage, or even the rep-hardened Osborne, a working class Jewish Londoner [Wesker] could have his plays performed on what had become one of the most important stages of the time [the Royal Court].[63]

63 Pattie, op. cit., p. 94.

CHAPTER 7

MASS ENTERTAINMENT CLAIMS ITS INHERITANCE

Just five days before the opening night of *Look Back in Anger*, Granada TV transmitted its first programmes. Two years earlier, the Independent Television Authority (ITA) had given the company the franchise for weekday broadcasting to the north of England. 'The north and London were the two biggest regions,' explained the company's director Sidney Bernstein:

> Granada preferred the north because of its tradition of home-grown culture, and because it offered a chance to start a new creative industry away from the metropolitan atmosphere of London ... and, of course, if you look at a map of the concentration of population in

> the north and a rainfall map, you will see that the North is an ideal place for television.

Studios – the first purpose-built TV studios in the UK – were erected on Quay Street in Manchester. *The Sun* claimed that they stood on the site of a cemetery where tens of thousands of the urban poor had been interred, but there seems to be no historical evidence for that. Sixty years on, the implication is obviously absurd. Programme-makers have no interest in obliterating the urban poor; they prefer to caricature them.

By the end of 1956, partly because of its investment in new studios, Granada was in financial trouble. It was saved by an independent broadcaster in London, Associated-Rediffusion, which guaranteed to underwrite its debts in exchange for a share of its profits. These, thanks to the rapidly growing popularity of independent TV (ITV), were not long in arriving.

After its uncertain start, Granada established itself as a significant broadcaster with programmes like *What the Papers Say* (see Chapter 11), the investigative documentary strand *World in Action*, and *University Challenge*, as well as creating what has become the longest-running TV soap opera in the world, *Coronation Street*.

There was soap before *Coronation Street*, but a very mild brand. In Britain in 1956, viewers every week followed the first-ever TV soap opera, which showed the lives of a lower-middle-class family in Hendon, north London: parents, four children and a live-in granny. It was simply called *The Grove Family*.

In its opening episode in 1954, Bob and Gladys Grove were happy to have paid off their mortgage, with a final month's payment of £13 8s 0d. Now Bob was able to follow his dream and start a building business. (Yes, he was Bob the Builder.) Soon, the BBC was being besieged with letters from viewers who wanted Bob to quote for their own building work (and Gladys to share her slimming tips). In another episode, the Groves worried about making their home burglar-proof. There were no murders, no rapes, no lesbian kisses. To today's TV watcher, it would seem very quaint. To the Queen Mother, visiting the BBC's studios, it was 'so English, so real'.

In 1957, after three years' hard work, the show's writers – Roland and Michael Pertwee, father and brother respectively of the actor Bill Pertwee of the radio sketch programme *Round the Horne* and TV's *Dad's Army* – took a holiday. To their astonishment, the BBC halted the series and never got round to bringing it back. At that point, when fewer than seven million households owned a television, *The Grove Family* had an audience of nine million viewers.

The TV landscape of which Granada had become a part was still reconfiguring itself after the tectonic shift of 1954–55, in which the ITA had been created and ITV had been launched. The BBC might have remained unchallenged in drama, documentary and the coverage of royal events, but ITV had the edge in light entertainment, offering about a dozen such programmes every week to the BBC's average of five. Sunday night was the clash of the Titans, pitting programmes like ITV's new *Sunday Night at the London Palladium*, first seen in September 1955, against the BBC's *What's My Line?*, which had been running since 1951.

What's My Line? invited members of the public who had unusual jobs to be quizzed by a panel of celebrities trying to discover what it was they did. (It was based on a successful American show, in which the quizzee was a celebrity and the panel had to wear blindfolds. This element was reduced to one segment of the British version.) The job-holder was required to sign in, mime his or her work and answer yes-or-no questions. Famously, one early show featured an occupation that sounded as if it was devised by the writers of *Round the Horne* – a saggar maker's bottom knocker. (It's a semi-skilled operative in a pottery kiln. Really.)

The regular panellists were a motley collection of the period's semi-famous. Barbara Kelly was a Canadian actress, and the wife of fellow TV personality and actor Bernard Braden. Comedian Cyril Fletcher was given to reciting 'odd odes'. Lady Isobel Barnett didn't really *do* anything, but was posh and engaging. The magician David Nixon's early onset baldness gave those surreal radio funsters The Goons (whom we shall meet in Chapter 8) one of their best jokes: 'They're flying the skull and crossbones! – No, it's a picture of David Nixon with his arms folded!' And then there was the journalist and broadcaster Gilbert Harding, dubbed by the press 'the rudest man in Britain'. It was claimed that many people watched the programme in the hope that Harding would lose his temper and say something insulting.

Captaining this curious crew was the Dublin-born Eamonn Andrews, a genial presenter whose popularity in this period (he also hosted *This Is Your Life*, and, later, sports and children's programmes) now seems puzzling. Like Russell Harty after him, he was not always ready with an appropriate comment and tended to radiate awkwardness. As 'Seamus Android', he was a regular butt of *Round the Horne*.

Before it was dropped by the BBC in 1963, *What's My Line?* achieved a viewing figure of twelve million.

Sunday Night at the London Palladium was devised by Val Parnell, then managing director of Associated Television (the ITA's London weekend provider), and, in the beginning, much of the show's character was shaped by his earlier experience as boss of the Moss Empires variety circuit. It opened with a dance number featuring showgirls, then a speciality act such as a puppeteer or acrobat, then the gameshow segment 'Beat The Clock', then the headliner, and then an everyone-on-stage finale. An occasional touch of class was added by a ballet dancer like Dame Alicia Markova or Margot Fonteyn.

Most people remember the show being hosted by Bruce Forsyth, or perhaps Norman Vaughan or Jimmy Tarbuck, who, between them, steered it through the late '50s and '60s. But, in its early years, the show's helmsman was the seasoned comedian Tommy Trinder (catchphrase: 'You lucky people!'). Trinder launched it on 25 September 1955 and presented it until 1958, and after him Forsyth seemed somehow too tame, too cuddly. Trinder was always a little dangerous. 'Bob Monkhouse?' he once said of his fellow comedian. 'Now there's a boy who can take a joke. And he doesn't mind whose jokes he takes.' Also: 'I like Bob. I put him on a plane with Shakespeare. No one knows who wrote his stuff either.'

Children would go to school the next day and regale their less fortunate classmates with Trinder's jokes. A lot of them were about Fulham football club, which he part owned. After a 6–0 defeat by Manchester United, he said on the show: 'Not that I like Manchester – got six good reasons to hate the place.'

He talked about the club when he met Field Marshal Montgomery, boasting that star player Johnny Haynes was still only eighteen.

'What about his National Service?' asked the soldier.

'Ah, that's the only sad thing about the lad,' said Trinder, quick as lightning. 'He's a cripple.'[64]

Trinder was fired very suddenly after falling out with Val Parnell and the powerful Lew and Leslie Grade – perhaps because he made merciless fun of them; perhaps because his jokes were too unpredictable; perhaps because he had an affair with Parnell's wife; or perhaps (we cannot be sure) because they thought him anti-Semitic. 'There was some gag he did that seemed seriously to offend the Grades,' says Ronnie Corbett, and Trinder's gags could indeed cause offence. He had once said: 'The army made a man of Liberace – and he sued them.' And then remarked the following morning: 'You couldn't see my desk for protests.'[65]

---

64 Patrick Newley, *You Lucky People – The Tommy Trinder Story* (London: Third Age Press, 2008), pp. 89–90.

65 Newley, op. cit., pp. 82–3.

A partial guestlist of *Sunday Night at the London Palladium* for 1956 makes a useful roster of the public's favourites, and of acts headed that way. Here are Harry Secombe, Norman Wisdom, Morecambe & Wise, Dickie Valentine, Frankie Howerd, Tommy Cooper, Benny Hill, the Beverley Sisters, and Winifred Atwell. And, from the United States, Johnnie Ray, Pat Boone and (twice) Liberace.

Another footballer hit the headlines when the FA Cup Final was held in front of a crowd of 100,000 at Wembley Stadium, and a further five million who were watching it on TV in their living rooms. Manchester City beat Birmingham City 3–1. The game has a special place in Cup Final annals because of the determination of the Manchester City goalie, Bert Trautmann.

He was already an unusual figure in English football. German-born, he served in the Luftwaffe but ended the war as an English prisoner of war. He refused an offer of repatriation, settled in Lancashire and began playing football for St Helens in 1948. His signing for Manchester City was criticised by some supporters, and, when he first played a game in London, he was barracked with shouts of 'Kraut' and 'Nazi' – although he played so well he left the pitch to a standing ovation.

He was on good form again at Wembley in 1956, but, seventeen minutes from the end, was hurt in a diving save. Though he waved away suggestions he should leave the field, from the newsreel footage it is obvious he was in pain, one hand repeatedly pressed to his neck. However, he continued to keep the Birmingham attack at bay until the final whistle.

X-rays later revealed that he had dislocated five vertebrae and cracked one of them too – indeed, the injury had narrowly avoided being fatal.

He was voted Footballer of the Year by the Football Writers' Association, but was out of the game for much of the following season, and took a long time to recover his form.

A week after the Cup Final came the first appearance in a UK pop chart of Elvis Presley, opening the ears of UK listeners by opening the doors of 'Heartbreak Hotel'. It was a gesture that would reverberate through pop music for the rest of the decade.

In the United States, Presley had been making some noise in the music industry for a couple of years with his records for Sun – an adventurous independent label based in Memphis, Tennessee – that audaciously and genre-bendingly fused the twin vernacular idioms of southern black blues and white country music. But the men behind him knew that, in order to attain national rather than merely regional success, he needed to stop remaking old songs. The word went out for new material.

Music publicist Mae Boren Axton and musician Tommy Durden found a song idea in a newspaper story about a Miami hotel guest who had committed suicide and left a note that read: 'I walk a lonely street.' Axton thought of the phrase 'heartbreak hotel', and the two wrote the song in an hour. Presley heard a demo and loved it. When his contract was acquired by major label RCA Victor, and he was put into a Nashville studio in January 1956 for his first session for his new employers, he recorded that same song.

The notion of a guesthouse for the lovelorn, set, as it might be, in an Edward Hopper nightscape, was promising dramatic material, and Presley, with a nod to Johnnie Ray ('the nabob of sob'), turned it into two minutes of distraught *Grand Guignol*. As his biographer Albert Goldman commented: '"Heartbreak Hotel", which is an extravagant and highly exaggerated account of the blues, was more a psychodrama than a musical performance. As such, however, it was an extraordinary novelty and it moved rock music into another imaginative space.'

In Wood Green, north London, twelve-year-old Norman Jopling – a few years away from becoming a keen young reporter on the pop weekly *Record Mirror* – was fascinated. He recalls:

> Like most great pop records, 'Heartbreak Hotel' didn't grab you straightaway. It wasn't like a better sort of Bill Haley. It wasn't fast or frantic, didn't have that Haley swing. It was moody, bluesy, doomy, with a stabbing rock guitar and jazzy piano solo and a voice that went with the looks and went with the name and mumbled words so incoherently to English ears that they slid into each other in an exciting sexy way. Not that I knew what 'sexy' was, having only just learned the 'facts of life' in the [school] playground.[66]

None of this was apparent to Geoffrey Everitt, the pop music reviewer in the UK's leading music paper, the NME. On the record's release in February, he commented:

> If you like gimmick voices, Elvis will slay you, but if you appreciate good singing, I don't suppose you'll manage to hear this disc all through. Of the two sides 'I Was the One' is the better, but this half-brother of Johnnie Ray fails to make any impression on me. If this is singing, then I give up, and furthermore, if this is the stuff that the American record fans are demanding, I'm glad I'm on this side of the Atlantic.

To give you some idea what Everitt *did* approve of, that week he wrote enthusiastically about the new singles by Nat King Cole, bandleader

66 Norman Jopling, *Shake It Up Baby!* (Surrey: RockHistory, 2015), p. 6.

Billy Cotton, the middle-aged Dixieland trombonist Pee Wee Hunt, and a now barely remembered Australian singer named Annette Klooger. Elsewhere in the paper, his colleagues were chiefly excited about the imminent first trip to the UK of the moustachio'd yodeller Slim Whitman.

So HMV Records, RCA Victor's UK licencee, had to look elsewhere for copy for their advertising. They soon found it. Their first ad for 'Heartbreak Hotel', in the NME on 30 March, quoted Patrick Doncaster of the *Daily Mirror*:

> Take a dash of Johnnie Ray, add a sprinkling of Billy Daniels – and what have you got? ELVIS PRESLEY, whom American teenagers are calling the King of Western Bop. He is twenty, single, scorns Western kit for snazzy, jazzy outfits. Now he bids emotionally for recognition in Britain with 'I Was the One' and 'Heartbreak Hotel' (HMV). Will British girls fall for him? I think it's likely.

The characterisation of Presley's music as 'Western Bop', which now seems bizarre, shows us how little the UK music press understood it. A few weeks later, an NME writer described Elvis as a 'young country and western singer' (who was 'destined to emulate Johnnie Ray as the teenagers' delight'). The front-page ad for 'Heartbreak Hotel' on 4 May dispensed with the niceties of musical classification: 'Introducing America's Newest and Greatest Disc Sensation "Rock Age Idol – That's Elvis ... He's Riding The Crest of a Teenage Tidal Wave"' – another excitable bit of copy from the *Daily Mirror*.

Ads made a point of stating that 'Heartbreak Hotel', then retailing for 5s 7d, was available at both 78rpm and 45rpm. By 1956, '45s' were obviously the format of the future: they were smaller (7 inches across rather than 10), lighter and less fragile than '78s', being made of flexible vinyl rather than rigid shellac. But they did need record-players (or gramophones, as they would have been called in 1956) capable of playing them, so, for a time, there was uneven acceptance of the new disc. In early October, the NME published a letter from a reader in Leamington Spa saying that the town's record shops sold one 45 to every hundred 78s. However, less than two months later, a dealer in Nottingham reported that half his sales were of 45s.

The production of 78s had more or less ceased in the US and UK by 1960, but they continued to be manufactured elsewhere, such as the Middle East, for several more years. Machinery capable of pressing 78s still exists, and, over the years, the format has been resuscitated from time to time in small pressing runs and for recherché material. In 1972, for instance, the Beatles not only chose to issue a recording by a little-known Louisiana Cajun band – 'Saturday Night Special' by the Sundown Playboys – on their Apple label, but they even pressed a 78rpm version of it.

There was vigorous debate in the NME's letter columns about the Presley v. Ray issue, and other aspects of the coming of Elvis. 'Letters in hysterical praise or wild revilement of Elvis dominate our "Talking Points" mail to such an extent', the paper reported in June, 'that all the other current topics slung together would make a puny pile in comparison.' E. J. Fuller, of Lower Road, London, SE16, proved himself better informed than Everitt, Doncaster and their kind by making the point that both Presley and Ray copied rhythm & blues singers.

The NME's American correspondent, the jazz writer Nat Hentoff, weighed in with a quote from the celebrated US columnist John Crosby: 'Where do you go from Elvis Presley short of open obscenity, which is against the law? Popular music has been in a tailspin for years now, and I have hopes that with Presley it has touched bottom and will just have to start getting better.' For Crosby, Elvis was 'an unspeakably untalented and vulgar young entertainer'.

Hentoff also quoted an Oakland, California, policeman on Presley's recent performance in that city: 'If he did it in the street, we'd arrest him.' NME writer Rex Morton came up with a witticism: 'Purchasers of Elvis Presley records should be provided with a special dictionary – explaining how to understand the lyrics he sings!'

The menace of rock 'n' roll was the sort of story British newspapers love so much that they can't help improving on the bare facts. In September, *Picture Post* ran a spread headlined: 'Presley fever hits Britain.' Four of the five photographs were of Elvis, and the caption of the fifth ran: 'Presley fever outside Manchester's Gaiety Cinema after a performance of *Rock Around the Clock*.' The brief article was about the 'riots on our own doorstep' provoked by that movie. The sound of the popular press in full cry would certainly have drowned out the pedantic objection that Presley was nowhere to be seen, heard or mentioned in *Rock Around the Clock*.

This now rather innocuous-seeming film did make extraordinary waves. Royston Ellis reported:

> On a single day in September, outbreaks of hooliganism were reported in Lewisham, Glasgow and Liverpool. In Manchester eighteen people were arrested for dancing in the street after the film. Teddies turned fire hoses on audiences whilst from the circle boys threw light bulbs and lighted cigarettes. Police in Liverpool used batons to shepherd a thousand singing screaming and jiving youths for a mile after they had seen the film ... In London cinemas, youths jived in the aisles shouting the incantation 'Rock!' blissfully to themselves. Fireworks were thrown. One boy (quoted in *The Observer*) had this to say: 'Jiving on the stage they were, till the cops came. The cops say, "Get out of it," and you say, "OK, make me!", so they try to make you. It's fun, that's all.'[67]

67 Royston Ellis, *The Big Beat Scene* (London: Four Square Books, 1961), p. 24.

The NME wrote in an editorial:

> This isn't a film for the square, or for the person with any degree of musical taste. Let us not kid ourselves, however, you may find *Rock Around the Clock* horrifying. It may even strike you that the moral of the film – 'it's the percentage that counts' – is the exact opposite of that expressed in *The Benny Goodman Story*. But ... this is a film the young fans are going to turn out in their thousands to see.

The moral message alarmed the clergy of Britain, too. One vicar said in a sermon: 'Rock 'n' roll is a revival of devil dancing, the same sort of thing that is done in black magic rituals. The effect will be to turn young people into devil-worshippers, to stimulate self-expression through sex, to provoke lawlessness and impair nervous stability.'[68]

The Observer offered more thoughtful counsel:

> The jiving craze is best seen as the symptom of a frustrated impulse to do something vigorous and exciting ... The sensible attitude, however, is not to deplore rock 'n' roll but to ask what can be done to give these pent-up energies some healthy and constructive outlets without taming them.[69]

Another calming voice came from an unexpected quarter – Scotland Yard. For a couple of years, the BBC had been showing *Fabian of the Yard*, a police-procedural series based on real-life cases investigated by the Metropolitan Police detective Robert Fabian and recounted in his memoirs. Ex-detective superintendent Fabian had become so public a figure that he had appeared in February on *Desert Island Discs*.

---

68 Ellis, op. cit., p. 23.

69 Ibid.

He wrote in *Empire News*:

> These so-called rock 'n' roll riots are not caused by any sort of rhythm driving 'teenagers crazy. Rock 'n' roll, by its tremendous record sales, has proved that it has gone right into the homes of followers of popular music, and is now part of the musical structure of the nation. What a pity that so basically healthy a form of rhythm and exhilaration should find itself in a position, through no fault of its own, where its very name is immediately associated with Teddy boys and undesirable elements!

Even the NME allowed two views of the matter. Two weeks after their 'horrifying' editorial, the paper printed the opinion of their film reviewer, the movie-director-to-be Michael Winner (then a hustling twenty-year-old showbiz journalist). He wrote that he had witnessed

> a fantastically boisterous public performance ... an audience consisting almost exclusively of youngsters packed the West End cinema and clapped, screamed and cheered at the musical in as raucous a piece of audience participation as I've ever seen in a cinema ... The story of *Rock Around the Clock* is simple. A dance-band manager leaves his old-style band, finds the Comets in a tiny village, and promotes them to world-wide fame ... There is Bill Haley looking just like a rhythmic Georgi Malenkov [until 1955, the Soviet premier] rockin' it and rollin' it for all he is worth.

The NME reported later that the Queen had asked to see *Rock Around the Clock*, and that a print had been rushed by train for delivery to Balmoral.

Further ammunition for the generational war was provided by the NME in a story headed: 'What makes them do this? A psychologist reports on rock 'n' roll.' On 5 July, Dr Ben Walstein, author of *Transference in Psychoanalytic Therapy*, was invited by Art Ford, a disc jockey on station WNEW in New York, to listen to and analyse rock 'n' roll discs, including Elvis Presley's 'Blue Suede Shoes' and 'I'm Left, You're Right, She's Gone', and Little Richard's 'Long Tall Sally'. 'I don't think this is anything that is particularly evil,' Walstein said: 'The emphasis is on the moment of experience ... the return to naturalism, to get away. Well, this is something that all adolescents go for, to get away from the phoniness that the adults are immersed in.' It would be interesting, he added, to look into the 'motivations, perhaps not so much the conscious rationalisation about it, but some of the unconscious motivations, of adults who are so concerned about the fact that kids listen to this kind of music'.

The historian can always discover what the first and fourth estates thought about a social phenomenon. It can be harder to find out what the people responsible for it believed they were doing. But we do have a few indications from the punters themselves:

The *NME*'s 'Talking Points' of 27 July led with a letter from 'Teenager' of Birmingham, who asked the paper not to publish his (or her) name and address, 'as it may affect my work'. 'Teenager' wrote:

> I'm afraid that Miss Kelly [a previous contributor to 'Talking Points'], who hates the hit parade because of 'gimmick' records, would be a real wash-out with my crowd. Every Saturday night, a whole crowd of us 'teenagers gather in sweaters and jeans at my home, where Mum has turned over to me the front room, which she aptly calls the 'Rock-and-Roll Room'.
>
> From 7 p.m. until midnight, the room simply rocks to Bill Haley,

Rusty Draper, Fats Domino, Elvis Presley, The Teenagers, and all the horrible gimmicky records that Miss Kelly refers to. Hot and loud and vulgar music, non-stop for five hours. Luckily, my home is detached, so there is no fear of complaining neighbours.

The room, contemporary in style, hasn't much furniture. Just a gram, record cabinets, studio couch, an assortment of chairs and a soft drinks bar. So we push everything to the sides and just rock-and-roll, and suddenly the whole crazy, mixed-up world seems to be put right, alive and new.

It gives me a feeling that's hard to put in writing. But, on these Saturday nights, when everything is so gay and young, it really feels good to be alive.

In 1956, Terry Hitchen was a seventeen-year-old engineering apprentice in Stoke-on-Trent, earning £2 a week and getting an extra 10 shillings from his parents. He remembers the effect of hearing records like 'Heartbreak Hotel': 'It was a total change. All we had before were sloppy songs like "How Much Is That Doggie in the Window?" ... Youth had never been heard of.'

For live entertainment, he and his friends, mostly workers in the potteries and coal mines, attended the Saturday-night dances at the town hall, where, if they were lucky, they might hear a jazz band like Chris Barber's. Terry remembered:

> Everybody put a suit on, and a tie. The girls tended towards the twin set and pearls, a bit like mother. Though shorter skirts were coming in. And what they called 'whirlpool bras', which gave a girl a bit of uplift. With a tight jumper or a nice tight white blouse, they looked very pretty.

He also recalled going to the first rock 'n' roll movies, like *Rock Around the Clock* and *The Girl Can't Help It*: 'There was no rioting, as such, just people getting up and dancing. It was unheard-of to stand up in a cinema and dance. And the ushers would come along and eject them. But no police. It was all good-natured, really.'

Wendy Simms grew up in Merthyr Vale in south Wales:

> Teenagers would gather along Aberfan Road on a Sunday night, calling in Manueli's café for a glass of hot Vimto, and then parade up and down the road between Aberfan and Troedyrhiw. It was what was known as the 'monkey parade' – boys looking to meet girls and girls looking to meet boys, all dressed up in their Sunday best. The local dance hall opened in my teenage years. It was underneath the cinema. No alcohol was sold, only soft drinks. If you went on the Friday you would get a free pass for Wednesday. A live band would play and the popular dance was the jive.[70]

Beryl Hinde was twenty-three in 1956. Born in Enfield in north London, she left school at fifteen and went to work. 'The '50s were wonderful years,' she remembered:

> There was plenty of work and plenty of enjoyment. People were happy. People by then had started to earn money because there was so much work about that you could have two or three jobs.

70 David Hall, *Working Lives* (London: Bantam Press, 2012), p. 48.

> I had two jobs … I worked in a factory in the day and in a canteen at night.

Beryl gives us some clues as to what Wendy's friends' 'Sunday best' might have looked like:

> You couldn't afford to buy much because, although there were clothes around then, they were very expensive. We used to curl our hair up in iron curlers, which left your hair rusty. Everybody had curls. You wore sweatshirts because of the American influence in the pictures. You wore skirts with lots of layers of lace because they bounced when you did the dancing. The boys were very smart in their Teddy boy clothes. It was an era of clothes. Everybody dressed up and wanted to look good. I had the pickle, the beauty spot that we made with blacking. We used to blacken our eyebrows by putting a stick up the chimney. We had sugar water in our hair to be like a lacquer. We had lots of tricks. We used to mix cocoa with flour to have powder on our faces. It used to go on the boys' shirts when you danced with them.[71]

Royston Ellis wrote:

> At this time, young people were emerging disgustedly from the dearth and darkness which had been the lot of previous generations of teenagers. After [the] deprived years of the Second World War, a rebellious streak was showing in young people.
>
> The streak revealed itself startlingly with the beginning of the

71 Sarah Ryle, *The Making of Tesco: A Story of British Shopping* (London: Bantam Press, 2013), pp. 34–5.

> Teddy Boy era. In an effort to bring a little gaiety to their lives, young people started spending money on a fashion that really belonged to them ... Basically, the Teddy Boy's garb consisted of tightly tapered high-waisted stove-pipe trousers, with thick-soled square-toed shoes. The jacket was a long drape coat to almost knee-length, with velvet lapels and padded shoulders. The favourite colour was black. Often there was a double-breasted waistcoat to set off the suit, together with a bootlace in place of a tie. These bootlace ties were clipped at the neck with a brooch bearing initials, a skull, or similar motif.
>
> The Teddy Boy's hair was worn long. Sometimes it flopped forward on the forehead in a jumble of greasy curls, or it was delicately blow-waved to stick out in front like an elephant's trunk ... Alternatively the hair would be brushed back in various styles, such as the 'Boston'. Another much-worn style was the 'D.A.' so called because the hair was brushed back to resemble a Duck's 'Arse'.[72]

It was not a look that went down well in the Cotswolds. 'The sight of the frowzy, slouching Teds sneering under the Co-op clock was like a breath of slum air across a spring field,' huffed a Gloucestershire newspaper.

Nor did it appeal to Anthony Burgess. The novelist and his wife Lynne returned to England in 1956 after a couple of years in Malaya and it was not the country they remembered. Instead of new Elizabethans, they found new Edwardians:

> There was a new laxness about. The memory of wartime and postwar deprivation was still strong in me, to say nothing of the ascetic aspirations of Crippsian socialism, and I did not like this hedonistic

72 Ellis, op. cit., p. 19.

> Britain. Everybody had a television set, and a constant question in pubs, when Lynne and I apologised for our ignorance of the new world and explained our tropical truculence, was 'What kind of television do you have out there?' ... We had seen a little of BBC television before sailing, and that had been genteel and leisurely, but now there was a commercial channel full of banal urgencies. The British seemed to be giving nothing to the world but consuming much.
>
> There was a new cult of youth, and the young were being encouraged to do most of the consuming. I had heard of Teddy Boys, and now I saw them on street corners and in coffee bars. They had originally called themselves Edwardian Strutters, and they wore a kind of costume that evoked a period of chauvinism and imperial expansion. This was a curious anachronism in an age when I and others were presiding over the collapse of the Empire. There was clearly a vague nostalgia for an old Britain which the new one contradicted. The collective aggression of the imperial epoch had transformed itself into a debased violence of which youth had the monopoly. The more articulate of the young were angry, and John Osborne was telling them why. It was anger at the consumerist vacuum which the young were themselves condoning.[73]

As rock 'n' roll made its gestures of defiance, an academic in Hull was composing a trenchant criticism of the entire rock 'n' roll lifestyle, represented for him by the 'juke-box boys ... who spend their evening listening in harshly lighted milk-bars to the "nickelodeons"'. (A nickelodeon and a juke box were the same thing – the former so called because, in its original American form, it cost a nickel to play a disc.) In *The Uses of Literacy*, published in 1957, Richard Hoggart wrote:

73 Anthony Burgess, *Little Wilson and Big God* (London: Heinemann, 1987), pp. 417–18 in 1988 Penguin edition.

> The milk bars indicate at once, in the nastiness of their modernistic knick-knacks, their glaring showiness, an aesthetic breakdown so complete that, in comparison with them, the layout of the living-rooms in some of the poor homes from which the customers come seems to speak of a tradition as balanced and civilised as an eighteenth-century town-house ... Most of the customers are boys aged between fifteen and twenty, with drape-suits, picture ties and an American slouch. Most of them cannot afford a succession of milk-shakes, and make cups of tea serve for an hour or two, whilst – and this is their main reason for coming – they put copper after copper into the mechanical record-player ... The records ... almost all are American; almost all are 'vocals' and the styles of singing much advanced beyond what is normally heard on the Light Programme of the BBC. Some of the tunes are catchy; all have been doctored for presentation so that they have the kind of beat which is currently popular; much use is made of the 'hollow-cosmos' effect which echo-chamber recording gives ... The young men waggle one shoulder or stare, as desperately as Humphrey Bogart, across the tubular chairs.
>
> Compared even with the pub around the corner, this is all a peculiarly thin and pallid form of dissipation, a sort of spiritual dry-rot amid the odour of boiled milk. Many of the customers – their clothes, their hair-styles, their facial expressions all indicate – are living to a large extent in a myth-world compounded of a few simple elements which they take to be those of American life.[74]

Hoggart even scorned the lyrics of the songs the 'juke-box boys' might have been listening to, comparing them unfavourably with 'Any Old Iron' and 'My Old Man Said "Foller the Van"' – relics of the Edwardian music-hall stage.[75]

---

74 Richard Hoggart, *The Uses of Literacy* (London: Chatto & Windus, 1957), pp. 203–204.

75 Hoggart, op. cit., p. 187.

It is difficult to read these jeremiads today without incredulous laughter. Hoggart's disapproval fell like a sledgehammer upon the harmless nut of a side-street café in Egham or Edgehill where a few kids drank frothy coffee and put threepenny pieces in the juke box. Difficult not to feel irritation, too, since he refused, throughout the book, to be specific, to move from the vague to the concrete, to *identify* the singers and songs – or books, magazines and films – that he was damning.

Hoggart was in his mid-forties when he wrote *The Uses of Literacy*, and probably temperamentally resistant to the appeal of milk bars (and the coffee bars that were beginning to supplant them). Those who were teenagers in the '50s may remember the bars rather differently: warm, brightly lit and generally fight-free havens for boys or girls who wanted to get out of the house and meet their friends, but were bored by the youth club and too young or nervous to go to a pub. In their own way, the bars were exciting places, with the gleaming chrome of the Gaggia coffee machines, the tentative exoticism of Formica-topped tables, bullfight posters and candles in Chianti bottles. The very coffee was thrilling, tasting nothing like what you made at home from powdered Nescafé or Camp coffee essence.

The coffee bar was an essentially Italian idea. As social historian Arthur Marwick commented:

> Apart from American rock, the other important foreign influence on Britain of the fifties was Italian. As with rock, the Italian idiom was populist, accessible: Italian *couture* very definitely was not *haut*... In addition, most British cities already had something of an Italian population, mainly engaged in some branch of the catering trade.[76]

But not everyone wanted to measure out their life in coffee spoons.

---

76 Arthur Marwick, *Britain in Our Century* (London: Thames & Hudson, 1984), p. 160.

A 25-year-old designer and printer from London's East End, Lionel Bart, bewailed the Italianisation of the traditional caff in 'Oh, For a Cup of Tea' – the first song he managed to sell, bought by bandleader Billy Cotton in 1956 for 25 guineas: 'Oh, for a cup of tea / Instead of a cuppuchini! ... Oh, for a Rosie Lee / Instead of a black depresso!'[77]

In an otherwise sympathetic review of *The Uses of Literacy*, Kingsley Amis observed that Hoggart

> sees his 'mass publications and entertainments' from the outside. He tells us in a note that ballroom dancing is the second largest entertainment industry in the country with its 500-odd ballrooms, but he might never have been in one of them for any sign he gives of understanding the part they play in their patrons' world. His account of modern popular songs is evidently based upon an exiguous, ill-chosen sample and is riddled with precarious intuitions about such imponderables as the kind and degree of self-consciousness displayed.[78]

For a more clued-up explanation than Hoggart's of what was going on among teenagers, we can turn to another analyst of popular culture, George Melly – singer, critic and much else. (But by no means *parti pris*: 'Aesthetically and morally,' he wrote in *Revolt into Style*, 'rock rates pretty low in my book.') Only eight years younger than Hoggart, Melly had the immense advantage of being *involved* in popular music, as a singer in a jazz band at a time when jazz bands had a genuinely popular following. Even so, he would write later that 'a whole new world was in the process of being born, and we were entirely unaware of it'.

He and his jazz friends

77 David and Caroline Stafford, *Fings Ain't What They Used t' Be: The Lionel Bart Story* (London: Omnibus, 2011), pp. 42–3.

78 Kingsley Amis, 'From Aspidistra to Juke Box' in *What Became of Jane Austen? And Other Questions* (London: Jonathan Cape, 1970), p. 92 in 1972 Panther edition.

> had heard ... 'Rock Around The Clock', and decided that it was a drag. I can remember asking who was the white blues singer someone had put on the gramophone at a party, and learning with some surprise that it was Elvis Presley ... Hit records were a fact. We never bought them, but we knew they existed. What we failed to understand was the age of the new audience. Dickie Valentine's fans were between eighteen and twenty-five. The records of ... 'Winnie' Atwell were bought by Mums and Dads, but the new audience, the multitude outside, the secret society preparing a revolution in 'the Two I's', Old Compton Street, were sixteen or less ... Everything they did and said, everything they liked or rejected, was useful in that it identified them *as a group*. At that time the boys were faced with conscription. This meant that they knew their 'real life' as adults was not in question. Between leaving school and going into the army, they could live out a fantasy life, their pockets full of money from a dead-end job. Circling round them and quick to move in were various interested adults: agents, record companies, clothing manufacturers, concert promoters, but the invention of the teenage thing was initially the work of the teenagers themselves. It was they who chose Haley and Presley as their heroes, and it was from their ranks that they threw up and deified their first British idol, Tommy Steele.[79]

Steele, who was discovered in the 2i's in 1956, was the first British artist to establish himself through rock 'n' roll. It was a trick that took some skill to pull off. Royston Ellis reminds us:

> One must remember the reputation rock 'n' roll had gained for itself in 1956. It was hooligans['] music, and as such no one but the yobs wanted anything to do with it. [John] Kennedy [Steele's manager]

79 George Melly, *Owning Up* (London: Weidenfeld & Nicolson, 1965), pp. 163–7 in 1970 Penguin edition.

> hit on the idea of making rock respectable. Out of his imagination came stories of Tommy Steele playing for debs and dukes.[80]

In October, the young ex-seaman, 'currently resident in cabaret at London's Stork Club', made his TV debut on the BBC's *Off the Record*. Soon afterwards, he broke into the Top 30 with his first release, 'Rock with the Caveman', co-written with Lionel Bart. A week later, the NME ran a story under the headline: 'Six weeks to stardom! The amazing rise to fame of Britain's rock 'n' roll sensation – TOMMY STEELE!'

'Amazing rise' seems a bit much: 'Caveman' that week stood at number thirteen and never climbed any higher, and his next single didn't even chart. But his third record, 'Singing the Blues', justified the hype, entering the Top 30 in December and, in January 1957, reaching number one. Keith Fordyce, who had taken over as the NME's pop reviewer, caught Steele's act at the Finsbury Park Empire in December, and decided that he was 'the greatest of all the British rock 'n' rollers!' After just a few months in show business, he was given the leading role in a film called, with fantastic chutzpah, *The Tommy Steele Story*.

Another BBC show that featured Steele was *Six-Five Special*, which was being plotted in the latter part of 1956, and arrived in the nation's living rooms in February 1957 – the first nationally transmitted TV programme made exclusively for teenagers. It was dreamed up by Jack Good, a 25-year-old producer fresh out of the BBC trainee programme. He was a former president of the Oxford University Dramatic Society and, a few years later, a sharp and opinionated commentator on pop music in the pages of the weekly music paper *Disc*.

Old rock 'n' rollers' memories of *Six-Five Special* tend to focus on Don Lang & his Frantic Five or Wee Willie Harris (a small, frenzied

---

80 Ellis, op. cit., p. 48.

singer from Bermondsey), as they offered eccentric and very English types of rock 'n' roll, but were at least in the target area. In fact, because of the BBC's ignorance or distrust of what teenagers were listening to, much of the show's airtime was consigned to exponents of the music rock 'n' roll was meant to displace: the King Brothers, the Mike Sammes Singers, Ronnie Hilton, Lita 'How Much Is That Doggie in the Window?' Roza, Dickie Valentine (*again*).

Presiding over this farrago as presenters were figures like the boxer Freddie Mills, the comedians Mike and Bernie Winters, Jim Dale (before he signed up to the *Carry On* franchise), and – for a change, someone actually involved in the music business, working as a disc jockey – Pete Murray.

Pop historian Alan Clayson adds:

> Into the bargain, Jack Good was obliged to balance even this anodyne pop with comedy, string quartets, interviews with U-certificate film stars, pre-recorded shorts about career opportunities in, say, the aircraft industry, and slots about sport, purposeful hobbies, the Great Outdoors and further hearty pastimes intended to distract young minds from what was described in *Scouting for Boys* as 'the secret vice of beastliness'. Thus *Six-Five Special*'s general ambiance wasn't far removed from that of a youth club, where soft drinks, a presiding pipe-smoking vicar in a cardigan, and a wholesome, self-improving reek were the norm, and Teddy Boys got themselves barred for letting slip a 'bloody' or brandishing a cigarette.[81]

We're reminded of Jonathan Miller's upbeat clergyman in *Beyond the Fringe*: 'Don't call me Vicar – call me Dick – that's the sort of Vicar I am!'

---

81 Alan Clayson, *Vintage Rock* 15 (January/February 2015), pp. 62–7.

Unable to realise his vision for the programme, Good resigned and went to ITV, where he developed the much less compromised pop music show *Oh Boy!*, which went out on Saturday evenings against *Six-Five Special* but started five minutes earlier. *Oh Boy!* lasted only two years, but Good had made his point, and his work directly influenced the much longer-running *Ready Steady Go!* – and, arguably, all of its successors.

Tommy Steele and George Melly met a couple of times in 1956. They were on the same record label (Decca), and found themselves on a TV show in which, as was the practice then (and for a long time afterwards), they would be miming to their new singles. It's possible to detect the first stirrings of a tectonic shift in pop music simply in the titles of the songs they were plugging. Steele's was 'Rock with the Caveman'; Melly's was a novelty song from 1931 called 'My Canary Has Circles Under His Eyes'.

Steele, Melly wrote later, 'was a very big deal indeed. The only thing was I'd never heard of him ... He, in his turn, hadn't heard of me. I don't know which of us was the more surprised.'

Not long afterwards, the two men ran into each other again at a concert. Melly and his jazz friends, going on first, elicited 'no more than token applause. The audience was not hostile. It was just that we didn't seem to be there.' For Steele, after the interval, however:

> The moment the curtain went up a high-pitched squeaking and shrieking started. I was absolutely amazed. After a couple of numbers I left and went back to the pub. The band was playing darts and Frank Parr [the trombonist] was getting quite drunk. The orgiastic cries of worship inside the cinema were perfectly audible, and this moved him to prophesy.
>
> 'You hear that!' he announced as he swayed about, 'that's the death of jazz. We've had it. In six months we'll all be in the bread line!'[82]

82 Melly, op. cit., pp. 166–7.

In fact, jazz was not even moribund. In May, Louis Armstrong played his first concert in London in twenty-one years; in June, his EP *Take It Satch* became the first extended-play release to reach the UK pop chart. (The first LPs to do so, in the same month, were Frank Sinatra's *Songs for Swinging Lovers* and the soundtrack of the movie musical *Carousel*. 'Long-playing discs have created a revolution in the hit parade,' commented the excited NME.)

In July, the pop chart embraced Humphrey Lyttelton's 'Bad Penny Blues', accurately described by the NME's Mike Butcher as 'an ungimmicked twelve-bar blues, with slicked-up Cripple Clarence Loften [*sic*] piano figures and a preaching muted trumpet'. What he meant by 'slicked-up' was that this fairly straightforward jazz performance had been turned clanging and odd by its engineer Joe Meek, who radically compressed the band's sound and pushed Johnny Parker's boogie-woogie piano to the front. Meek was a creative if eccentric figure who went on to work with many pop artists of the '60s.

Soon, the traditional jazz played by Melly and his colleagues would be moulded (and abbreviated) by promoters into 'Trad', and would give lucrative careers to Acker Bilk, Kenny Ball, Chris Barber and other showman leaders. Meanwhile, the intelligentsia dinner-partied to the cool, cerebral jazz of Dave Brubeck or the Modern Jazz Quartet.

'It was about this time', according to the historian Eric Hobsbawm, 'that the London cultural establishment, stung by the challenge of the so-called "angry young men" of the 1950s, thought it advisable to pay attention to jazz, for which they advertised their passion.' *The Observer* took on Kingsley Amis as its jazz critic, and the *Daily Telegraph* riposted by engaging his friend Philip Larkin in the same role. 'It seemed to me', said Hobsbawm, 'that I understood at least as much about the subject as Kingsley Amis and had been familiar with it much longer' – so he landed his own critical column in the

New Statesman and occupied it for a decade, writing under the name Francis Newton, 'after [trumpeter] Frankie Newton, one of the few jazz players known to have been a communist'.[83]

For years, jazz enthusiasts had been divided by a verbal battle between the traditionalists and modernists – those who liked Louis and Sidney Bechet (who, like Louis Armstrong, toured the UK in 1956), say, as against those who liked Stan Kenton (another 1956 visitor to the UK) and Miles Davis. A spokesman for the traditionalists was the French critic Hugues Panassié, who roundly declared in the September issue of *Jazz Journal*: 'The so-called modern jazz is a music for those who walk on their heads.'

It was Panassié's own head he should have been worried about. As the subsequent history of jazz has shown, he had it buried in the sand. Another Frenchman, André Hodeir, expressed a more modernist view in *Jazz: Its Evolution and Essence*, published in 1956. The English men's magazine *Lilliput* praised it for 'providing a brilliant and beautifully balanced survey of the whole floor-shaking phenomenon', and added: 'If your girl friend never reads another book, make sure she reads this one.' People really did say things like that in 1956.

But in fact the relationships between the two styles of jazz and between jazz and rock 'n' roll were not straightforwardly adversarial. Respectable older jazz bandleaders, like Lionel Hampton (yet another 1956 visitor to the UK) and Count Basie, unapologetically extended their big-band-swing approach to rock 'n' roll numbers. And it was a jazz drummer who made the first serious British response to rock 'n' roll.

Early in August, when Tommy Steele was still a speculative gleam

83 Eric Hobsbawm, *Interesting Times* (London: Allen Lane, 2002), pp. 225–7 in 2003 Abacus edition.

in his backers' eyes, Tony Crombie launched what the NME called 'Britain's first full-time rock 'n' roll band'. (Their manager was Pete King, sometime jazz saxophonist and, for many years, co-proprietor with Ronnie Scott of London's most famous jazz club.) Six weeks later, The Rockets opened in Portsmouth. The NME reviewer said:

> The powerful rhythmic beat previously heard only on American records was being effectively reproduced for the first time on a British stage, and even the Mums and Dads of the family variety audience joined in good-humouredly. Obviously modelled on Bill Haley's Comets and including several of their numbers, Tony Crombie's Rockets have superb drive.

The band continued to draw crowds on its countrywide tour. After giving a rave review to its show at London's Finsbury Park Empire, the NME quoted Crombie as saying:

> I had a band two years ago with more concentrated jazz talent and potential than any other group in the country ... And it lost me everything I had. Perhaps rock 'n' roll will introduce a whole lot of kids to real jazz. Maybe they'll prefer to keep hearing it the way it is. Anyway, it's a swinging kind of music we enjoy playing.

Royston Ellis, documenting this period in *The Big Beat Scene*, identified 'one of the symbols of the younger generation' as 'the popularity of Big Beat music – be it rock 'n' roll or knock-about jazz'. At Britain's first Jazz Weekend, held at Butlin's holiday camp in Clacton in autumn 1956, modernists like Ronnie Scott and Joe Harriott entertained a crowd of 'jazz fans and Teddy Boys'. This may be puzzling to those who see jazz and rock 'n' roll as mutually unharmonious, even discordant idioms. The fact is that many teenagers would have gone *anywhere* rather than listen to their mums' and dads' music, and – given that anywheres weren't easy to find in 1956 – a jazz weekend would do as well as a rock 'n' roll hop. Either way, you wouldn't run into Dickie Valentine.

'The jazz people were by no means teenagers,' Hobsbawm wrote, reflecting on skiffle and Trad:

> And yet ... what the music they made inspired was essentially a somewhat older children's crusade. They were part of the youth culture that was by then becoming sufficiently visible for those of us who roamed on its outskirts for whatever reason to recognise its existence ... Much of what symbolised the youth counter-culture of the 1960s was ... taken over from the old jazz scene.[84]

However, as a long-term prophet, that drunken trombonist had been right: rock 'n' roll and its descendants would take up permanent residence in the grand hotel of popular culture, while jazz shuffled off glumly to find rooms in the suburbs.

In the meantime, neither genre gave a damn about the very first Eurovision Song Contest, held in May at the Teatro Kursaal in Lugano, Switzerland, with a Swiss TV presenter named Lohengrin Filippello. The concept had been devised the year before by the European Broadcasting Union as 'a pan-European competition for light music'. These days, the contest is a major TV event, but in the mid-'50s relatively few Europeans owned a television and, for the first few years, the show was chiefly for a radio audience. In 1956, there were entrants from seven countries, but not from the UK, which had missed the deadline for applying and would not feature in the contest until the following year. The first Eurovision Song Contest

84 Hobsbawm, op. cit., pp. 226–7.

winner was a number called, boringly enough, 'Refrain', sung by Lys Assia from, surprisingly enough, Switzerland. Neither jazz nor rock were anywhere to be heard.

CHAPTER 8

THE ALIENATED NOVELIST, AND WHAT THE LITERARY ESTABLISHMENT DID TO HIM

One of the most remarkable books of 1956, published by Gollancz on 28 May, was the first work of an intermittently employed 24-year-old who spent many of his days in the British Museum Reading Room and his nights in a sleeping bag on Hampstead Heath. Colin Wilson had begun writing *The Outsider* over Christmas 1954, when the thought came to him:

> I was in the position of so many of my favourite characters in fiction: Dostoevsky's Raskolnikov, Rilke's Malte Laurids Brigge, the young writer in

> Hamsun's *Hunger* ... alone in my room, feeling totally cut off from the rest of society. It was not a position I relished ... I began writing about it in my journal, trying to pin it down. And then, quite suddenly, I saw that I had the makings of a book. I turned to the back of my journal and wrote at the head of the page: 'Notes for a book *The Outsider in Literature*.'[85]

Wilson's theme was social alienation, as described by twentieth-century writers. He had plenty to work with. As Kingsley Amis wrote in his review for *The Spectator*:

> Here they come – tramp, tramp, tramp – all those characters you thought were discredited, or had never read, or (if you are like me) had never heard of: Barbusse, Sartre, Camus, Kierkegaard, Nietzsche, Herman Hesse ... The Legion of the Lost are we, as the old song has it. Marching on to hell with the drum playing – pick up the step there!

Having had some fun with this ragged platoon of continental misfits, Amis set about expressing the ordinary chap's attitude to Wilson's cosmic dissatisfaction:

> A lot of people get a bit fed up from time to time ... but they do not on this account go round considering themselves as, or behaving like, Stephen Dedalus; at least they try not to, and rightly. At the risk of being written off as a spiritual wakey-wakey man, it is worth asserting that to tear one's fascinated gaze away from the raree-show of one's own dilemmas, to value Mr Pickwick higher than Raskolnikov, to try to be a bit pleasant occasionally, are aims worth making an effort for.[86]

---

85 Colin Wilson, introduction to a reprint of *The Outsider* (London: Picador, 1978).

86 Kingsley Amis, 'The Legion of the Lost' in *What Became of Jane Austen? And Other Questions* (London: Jonathan Cape, 1970), pp. 93–5 in 1972 Panther edition.

But between these slices of characteristic low-browism Amis spread a thin layer of approval, praising the author's 'admirable clarity and unpretentiousness'. Other reviewers, including such heavyweights as Philip Toynbee in *The Observer* and Cyril Connolly in the *Sunday Times*, were much more impressed by Wilson's 'inquiry into the nature of the sickness of mankind in the mid-twentieth century'. Toynbee called it 'truly astounding ... exhaustive and luminously intelligent'. 'His is the philosophy of a rebel,' explained the *Daily Mail*'s F. G. Prince-White, 'and he expresses it with immense vigour and the full assurance of youth.' Victor Gollancz, after taking Wilson to lunch and giving him an advance of £25, told him 'gravely': 'I think it possible you may be a man of genius.'

Altogether, the young sage was taken very seriously indeed. But not for long.

Perhaps fearing that it had been too easily seduced by this swashbuckling polymath, the critical establishment rounded like a disenchanted ex-lover on his next book, *Religion and the Rebel* (1957), and boxed its ears.

Wilson had been enlisted into the ranks of the supposedly 'angry young men', but the publicity value of this badge had, he later wrote:

> thoroughly outstayed its welcome, and created in the British press an atmosphere of irritable hostility like an approaching storm. Before long, almost every reference to Angry Young Men was dyspeptically hostile.
>
> Where *The Outsider* was concerned, this usually took the form of dismissing it ... as an anthology of quotations ... Gollancz watched with dismay my plunge within months from intellectual stardom to relegation as some kind of imposter.[87]

87 Colin Wilson, *The Angry Years: The Rise and Fall of the Angry Young Men* (London: Robson Books, 2007), p. 61.

The playwright Arnold Wesker asserted that, at the launch party for *Declaration* (a 1957 collection of essays by Wilson, John Wain, John Osborne, Kenneth Tynan, Doris Lessing, Lindsay Anderson and other 'opinion-moulders of the day'), 'a sack (or was it a bag) of flour was dropped from the balcony upon Colin Wilson, who was thought by many to be oppressively arrogant'.[88] Wilson himself denied that he was present – 'which may have been just as well, for ... there was a plot to tar and feather me'.[89]

What with these indignities – whether real or rumoured – and the bad reviews, Wilson's reputation never recovered, and he took himself off to Cornwall to edit true-crime anthologies, write about UFOs, contribute to the Cthulhu Mythos created by the American fantasy writer H. P. Lovecraft, and eulogise the spoon-bender Uri Geller. His fate can be read as a moral lesson – or, at least, a cautionary tale – about the dangers of literary fashion. John Ezard wrote after Wilson died in 2013: 'He was greatly gifted ... [but with] an imperfect analytical ability and a protective conceit that left him virtually impervious to the rational or intuitive arguments of others. Yet the literary establishment's handling of his first books remains one of the more memorable intellectual disgraces of our time.'[90]

The Outsider had been dedicated to Angus Wilson, who, as a librarian in the Reading Room, had been kind to the young author. 'He was the first published novelist I had ever clapped eyes on,' Colin Wilson would recall, 'and I stared at him with fascination.' By the time *The Outsider* was published, Angus Wilson had left the British Museum to become a full-time writer, encouraged by the success, among both critics and readers, of his short-story collections *The*

88 Arnold Wesker, *As Much As I Dare: An Autobiography (1932–1959)* (London: Century, 1994), p. 459.

89 Wilson, op. cit., p. 129.

90 John Ezard, obituary of Colin Wilson, *The Guardian*, 9 December 2013.

Wrong Set (1949) and *Such Darling Dodos* (1950) and his novel *Hemlock and After* (1952), which were distinguished by their mordant wit at the expense of family sensitivities and social pretensions. His novel *Anglo-Saxon Attitudes*, published in the same month as *The Outsider*, is regarded by some as his best, though others have preferred such later works as *The Old Men at the Zoo* (1961), *Late Call* (1964) or *No Laughing Matter* (1967).

Thirty years later, in an admiring essay, Malcolm Bradbury wrote:

> [Angus] Wilson has much to say here about the relationship between public and private morality, and about the ambiguity of the puritanical sense of British virtue. The moral theme that so much concerned the 1950s is itself heavily tested. 'You take up something where somebody's in the wrong and make an arbitrary decision about the goats and the sheep, and then start making moral noises,' says Elvira Portway. 'It's just an English parlour game.'

Bradbury roundly declared Angus Wilson

> the most developed and impressive novel-writer of his generation, the generation that ... made its mark after World War Two – a writer who carries enormous substance in his work, has produced some of our bulkiest and most socially solid fictions ... [and has become] a novelist of extended historical and human scope.[91]

Yet his appeal to the common reader faded – albeit more gradually than Colin Wilson's – and, for years, titles that had once been bestsellers for Penguin were invisible on bookshop shelves. In 2008, when *The*

91 Malcolm Bradbury, *No, Not Bloomsbury* (London: André Deutsch, 1987), pp. 220, 231 in 1989 Arena edition.

Guardian asked a number of writers what books they would most like to see back in print, Margaret Drabble chose three of Angus Wilson's, including *Anglo-Saxon Attitudes*, which, she said, 'analyses a wide range of British society in a complicated plot that offers all the pleasures of detective fiction combined with a steady and humane insight. Each time I reread it, I find a new nuance, another accurate guess about the world we were about to inhabit.' Faber duly made it available again.

Piercing and painful analyses of British society were a feature of the literature of 1956. Britain's place in the world was being questioned as never before, and so, it seemed, was the place of Britons in Britain:

> Most people nowadays take it for granted that the aristocracy is utterly impoverished, a view carefully fostered by the lords themselves ... There are still many enormous fortunes in the English aristocracy, into which income tax and death duties have made no appreciable inroads. Arundel, Petworth, Hatfield, Woburn, Hardwicke, Blenheim, Haddon, Drumlanrig, Alnwick, Stratfield Saye, Harewood, Knole, Knowsley, Wilton, Holkham, Glamis, Cullen, Cliveden, Highclere, Althorp, Mentmore – all vast houses – are still inhabited by lords who have inherited them, or by members of their families.[92]

The speaker is Nancy Mitford, whose novels *The Pursuit of Love* and *Love in a Cold Climate* have been described as 'evok[ing] a lost world of English upper class elegance and endearing eccentricity', though they are rather subtler – and sharper – than that. Here, however, she was not engaged in fiction. Her essay 'The English Aristocracy' was first published in the magazine *Encounter* in September 1955, but was much more widely read when she included it in a collection she edited

---

92 Nancy Mitford (ed.), *Noblesse Oblige* (London: Hamish Hamilton, 1956).

a year later under the title *Noblesse Oblige: An Enquiry into the Identifiable Characteristics of the English Aristocracy*. Among other contributions to this valuable sociological study of the toff were John Betjeman's poem 'How to Get on in Society' (which, rather unkindly and snobbishly, put the aspiring middle classes in their place: 'Phone for the fish-knives, Norman' ... 'Are the requisites all in the toilet?' ... 'I must have things daintily served'), and Professor Alan Ross of Birmingham University's tour de force of sociolinguistics 'U and Non-U' (which meticulously listed such class-defining usages as the pronunciation of 'medicine' and 'venison': 'U – two syllables; Non-U – three syllables').

Mitford's 'little list' ('a mere fraction of the whole') named twenty-one great houses. Six decades on, has this catalogue of halls, castles and granges become a litany of loss? Not a bit of it. All the houses stand; seventeen of them are still owned, and at least partly occupied, by the families who had them in 1956. The grindstone of taxes and death duties that their owners so bemoaned may have continued to erode those once enormous fortunes, but the owners have been ingenious in finding ways to alleviate their poverty: Alnwick makes a wizard income by playing Hogwarts in the *Harry Potter* films, while Highclere is viewed by millions every week in its role as Downton Abbey. They stand as assertions, in bricks and mortar, that however Colin Wilson and John Osborne might have railed, and however Nancy Mitford and John Betjeman might have lampooned, the old rich hang on. And, as if to assert the fact that old literary values were (and still are) capable of defying their detractors, July 1956 saw the twenty-first birthday of Penguin Books.

The ten titles first offered to the public in July 1935, a wayward selection that embraced Hemingway, Agatha Christie and Mary Webb, had expanded into a catalogue of more than a thousand, and the company's original *raison d'être* – reprinting for sixpence what others had previously published between boards at several times that price – had been so far modified that now more than half of the books it published were originals.

Among those that had already come out in 1956 were the five-volume *Pelican Book of English Prose* (edited by Kenneth Allott, spanning more than three centuries) and *The Penguin Book of English Verse*. Reprints included Angus Wilson's *Hemlock and After*, C. P. Snow's *The Masters*, Nicholas Monsarratt's *The Cruel Sea* (a story of small ships in the Battle of the Atlantic in the Second World War), sets of novels by C. S. Forester and John Buchan, and Sir Kenneth Clark's *Landscape into Art*. In 1956, the Penguin catalogue was a largely risk-free zone.

'In a sense the freelance phase of Penguin is over,' wrote Sir William Emrys Williams, Penguin's editor-in-chief. 'The adventurous sallies have given way to the solid responsibility of building up a comprehensive Popular Educator.'[93] This was presumably intended to sound marmoreal, but today seems merely pompous – a balloon of complacency that any ambitious young editor at Penguin HQ would have itched to puncture. Within five years, the list would look very different, with reprints of 'angry young men' novels like John Braine's *Room at the Top*, John Wain's *Hurry On Down* and Kingsley Amis's *Lucky Jim*, the publication of the *New English Dramatists* series (Osborne, Wesker, Arden, Pinter), and the bold gesture that was the first paperback edition of *Lady Chatterley's Lover*.

Back in 1956, though, one of Penguin's bestselling lines was detective fiction of the kind that would come to be called 'classic' – stories from the interwar or early postwar years, almost invariably about murder, very often in financially and socially reassuring circumstances: the vicarage; the big house; the private school; the university common room; the gentleman's club. The leading practitioners, after the perennially popular Agatha Christie, were Ngaio Marsh, Gladys Mitchell,

93 *The Penguin Story* (Harmondsworth: Penguin Books, 1956), p. 60.

Dorothy Sayers and Margery Allingham – in the '50s, crime fiction was a rare literary genre in which women led the pack – together with the donnish Michael Innes, John Dickson Carr (doyen of the locked-room puzzle) and Freeman Wills Crofts (a prolific deviser of somewhat plodding police procedurals). According to a Penguin historian, during the '50s these green-jacketed volumes accounted for a quarter of the company's sales.[94]

But there were other jackets on the decade's paperback shelves besides Penguin's austere greens and oranges. They were vivid, sometimes lurid full-colour covers, befitting a more realistic sort of reading than the least-likely-person mysteries and body-in-the-library melodramas of detective fiction. But they, too, belonged firmly to the world before 1956. As the cultural historian Ken Worpole wrote:

> It is likely that in the 1950s the most widely read books in Britain were books that dealt with the experiences of male combatants in the Second World War ... In total we are talking about not many more than twenty paperback books, all published in the 1950s, yet between them they were sold to millions and read in even larger numbers. As a secondary school student in this period, I would have to say that they were the staple reading diet of myself and all my school peers.[95]

Anyone of Worpole's generation (he was born in 1944) will echo that, and will instantly recognise the titles he goes on to cite: *The Dam Busters* (Paul Brickhill); *The Bridge over the River Kwai* (Pierre Boulle); *The Colditz Story* (P. R. Reid); *The White Rabbit* (Bruce Marshall); and *The Naked Island* (Russell Braddon). All of those, and many others like them,

94 *Fifty Penguin Years* (Harmondsworth: Penguin Books, 1985), pp. 61, 65–7.

95 Ken Worpole, *Dockers and Detectives* (London: Verso, 1983), p. 50.

were published by Pan Books, a paperback imprint jointly owned by Macmillan, Collins and Heinemann. Pan was Penguin's chief rival in the soft-cover marketplace, and, so far as war stories were concerned, the market leader, because Allen Lane, Penguin's founder, disliked books about the war, and seldom agreed to publish them. (He made an exception for Edward Young's *One of Our Submarines*, which appeared in 1954 as the 1,000th Penguin – but only because Young had been Penguin's first designer, and had drawn the little penguin that became the company's logo.)

Escape narratives like *The Colditz Story* and Brickhill's *The Great Escape* and *Escape – Or Die* dealt exclusively, as did almost all the bestselling war books, with the experiences of officer-class, ex-public-school prisoners, who implicitly felt, in Reid's words, that there is 'no other sport that is the peer of escape'.

'Sport'! We might be listening to Bulldog Drummond or Raffles.

Alan Bennett catches the buoyant tone of these stories precisely in *Forty Years On*. A soldier writes home:

> I don't mind being a prisoner of war. It's not half as bad as school really and the food slightly better. There are seven Old Marlburians in my hut, which is rather a bore. They display to the full a disgusting capacity for making the best of a bad job.

Even more numerous than the escape stories, but similar in their social and ethical positioning, were the heroic tales of RAF pilots, secret agents and other lone operators, which, according to Worpole, 'took on the forms and narrative styles of the popular genres of adventure stories'. These included books like *The Dam Busters*, *Reach for the Sky* (Brickhill again), *Enemy Coast Ahead* (by the Dambusters' pilot Guy Gibson), *Boldness Be My Friend* (Richard Pape), *Two Eggs on My Plate* (Oluf Reef Olsen) or *Ill Met by Moonlight* (W. Stanley Moss).

These, and the escape stories, argued Worpole,

> provided two of the most important images of the Britain ... that had to be preserved after the war was over. The first was the evocation of a rural England of country houses, village pubs, public schools, Oxbridge and expensive sports cars. The second was the representation of Britain at war as a second Elizabethan era ... [This] is in no way to denigrate the courage and achievements of these pilots and their crews; this was the England they had been brought up in and wished to preserve. But it was certainly not everybody's England, or Britain ... None of the writers registered that there were many versions of Britain, of which theirs was only one, and there were simply no accounts by servicemen or women in the ranks of the other Britain. The Britain of mass unemployment, large urban slums, rickets, TB, relieving officers [local officials who received and investigated poor people's applications for relief], tied cottages, game-keepers and the various other manifestations of a deeply divided class society, simply didn't exist.[96]

But there were alternative voices – a few. The one that speaks most clearly to us across the years is that of Alexander Baron, in *From the City, From the Plough*. Baron was from London's East End, a working-class, Jewish Labour youth organiser. His rank-and-file soldier characters in the D-Day invasion 'comfort each other, sort out squabbles, try to learn to live communally – and wait'. Worpole summarises:

> The battle scenes that follow the final landing are horrendous ... and only a handful survive. The values that emanate from Baron's

96 Worpole, op. cit., pp. 57–9.

> book are not those of some mythologised 'England' or specious nationalism, but of a class that puts the welfare of others, mutual support and solidarity, above the values of individualism and self-interest. Whereas the heroes of much popular war literature are always shown to be fighting in order to preserve the past, the men in *From the City, From the Plough* are shown to be fighting for a different future.[97]

The distinguished reviewer V. S. Pritchett called it 'the only war book that has conveyed any sense of reality to me'. It has the reputation of a fugitive, half-forgotten document, though in fact it came out in Pan Books in the early '50s and other paperback editions in subsequent decades. But we can be sure that, in 1956, its tale of life and death in the ranks did not strike the correct 'new Elizabethan' note of optimism curbed by respect.

If more proof were needed that the old literary preoccupations held good in 1956, *The Spectator* competition on 29 June provided it. Three months after the death of the writer E. C. Bentley, the magazine asked for topical examples of his most famous poetic invention – the clerihew. R. Kennard Davis offered:

> *To me the first of October*
> *Merely suggests that summer is over.*
> *It conveys a nuance far less pleasant*
> *To the pheasant.*

97 Worpole, op. cit., pp. 66–7.

Fellow competition winner R. J. Hirst was thinking thoughts no less traditionally British, though with a wistful recognition that things might change:

The 24th of May
Is still known as Empire Day.
Might we not celebrate our shrunken power
With an Empire Hour?

But Mr Hirst (we are guessing it was 'Mr' because it generally was, though initials were still sometimes used in 1956 to disguise female authorship) could not have known just how fast that change would happen.

Contemporary verse of more substance was presented in the anthology *New Lines*, published in July. Its nine contributors – among them Philip Larkin, Kingsley Amis, John Wain, Elizabeth Jennings and D. J. Enright – were all in their early or mid-thirties, except Thom Gunn (then twenty-seven) and the somewhat older editor Robert Conquest. Earlier in 1956, Enright had edited the collection *Poets of the 1950s*, which mustered the same cast of contributors, with the exception of Gunn. These poets – 'anti-phoney ... sceptical, robust, ironic', as Anthony Hartley had described them in *The Spectator* a couple of years earlier – were seen as belonging to some kind of movement, helpfully called 'The Movement'.

In his introduction, Conquest attempted to distinguish the poetry of this younger set from that of their predecessors: 'It is free from both mystical and logical compulsions and – like modern philosophy – is empirical in its attitude to all that comes ... [It refuses] to abandon a rational structure and comprehensible language, even when the verse is most highly charged with sensuous or emotional intent.'[98]

Larkin, according to his most recent biographer James Booth, was 'uncomfortable with [Conquest's] polemical tone', and wrote to him: 'No doubt I shall come in for a good deal of anti-Movement sniping' – though Conquest had been careful not to use the term 'Movement' in his introduction. Larkin had, in fact, few bonds, personal or poetic, with most of his co-anthologees. He had known Amis well, and the younger Wain somewhat, since their time at Oxford, and Conquest was a newly acquired friend, who shared, as Amis did, his taste for girlie magazines; but he remarked in an interview years later: 'Bob Conquest's *New Lines* in 1956 put us all between the same covers. But it certainly never occurred to me that I had anything in common with Thom Gunn, or Donald Davie, for instance.'[99]

Reviewing *New Lines* in *The Spectator*, Anthony Hartley saw it as 'a fairly impressive testimony to the fact that there are quite a large number of young poets around who are producing work of a reasonable standard of competence'. As praise goes, this would probably have seemed to the poets concerned – in Peter Cook's words a few years later in *Beyond the Fringe* – 'not quite the conflagration we'd been banking on', but Hartley's point was to distinguish this 'competent' verse from the 'obscurantism' and 'incantatory rubbish' of the '40s:

> After 1948, it was no longer possible for a young poet to base his work on the prone and speechless dialect of the psychiatrist's couch ... In 1956 it is possible for the first time in many years for the poet

98 Robert Conquest (ed.), *New Lines* (London: Macmillan, 1956), p. xv.

99 James Booth, *Philip Larkin: Life, Art and Love* (London: Bloomsbury, 2014), pp. 204–8.

to write directly about the world around him, to celebrate it in the real sense of the word.[100]

The end of June and the beginning of July saw early skirmishes in what were to become two of the great battlefields of the second half of the twentieth century: the environment, and the intellectual development of children.

On 5 July, Parliament passed the Clean Air Act, a belated response to the Great Smog of December 1952. This had not been just any old thick fog. A combination of factors – smoke from coal fires, emissions from factory chimneys, anticyclonic weather conditions – led to London being enveloped for five days in a pungent, yellow-brown fog, permeated with pollutants including hundreds of tonnes of sulphuric and hydrochloric acid. Around 4,000 people are estimated to have died from respiratory infections within a few days, and the long-term toll may have been as high as 12,000.

Londoners had long been familiar with heavy fogs – like the 'pea soupers' that lurk in the city of Sherlock Holmes and Jack the Ripper – but the 1952 smog was much more threatening. Afterwards, the Conservative government tried to avoid a public enquiry by claiming that the death toll was due to a flu epidemic, but it eventually had to appoint a select committee to report on air pollution. This, and a private members' bill, brought about the introduction of 'smoke control areas' in certain towns and cities, where only smokeless fuels could be burned, as well as the relocation of future power stations away from cities. The 1956 Clean Air Act is seen now as an early moment in the environmental movement.

100 Anthony Hartley, 'Poets of the '50s', *The Spectator*, 20 July 1956, pp. 100–101.

At the same time, *The Guardian*, under the headline 'Higher IQ in children of the atomic age', reported:

> Intelligence tests recently carried out among more than a thousand children in Wolverhampton schools appear to show a striking and quite unexpected increase in the mental capacity of children born since 1945. A psychiatrist concerned in the tests has suggested that the most probable hypothesis to account for this change is the effect on the brain of the increase in 'background radio-activity'.
>
> The tests were carried out under the direction of Dr J. Ford Thomson, consultant children's psychiatrist to the Wolverhampton and Shrewsbury group of hospitals. They were begun after several children ... had been found to show quite unexpected abilities. A child of seven and a half, described as a problem child in the 'C' stream at school, was found to be exceedingly clever and well informed on astronomy, and was given an intelligence quotient of 142.

Excited by such results, Dr Thomson ransacked Wolverhampton for more prodigies – and found that *all* the children of the relevant age group were extraordinarily advanced. He concluded that the effect of the radiation they had absorbed – both natural and man-made – had been 'to speed up the development of their brain structure'. But he struck a warning note: although increased radiation might be stimulating to children now, what might be its longer-term effect?

Dr Thomson's field was child guidance, and it may be that his radiation hypothesis was no more than an offhand speculation. At any rate, it does not appear to have aroused any support, and his optimism about the supposedly beneficial effects of exposure to radiation is not shared by present-day scientists. A 2014 scientific journal paper suggests that the radiation from mobile phones, laptops and tablets is absorbed more quickly by children than by adults, and, since it is generally acknowledged to be carcinogenic, they are more likely to be harmed by it.[101]

It was three more weeks before the launch, on 9 July, of something that certainly *did* affect the intellectual development of most of us who were children in 1956: one of the iconic playthings of the post-war era – the small die-cast model vehicles called Corgi Toys. Their name was a nod to their manufacturer Mettoy's new factory at Fforestfach, Swansea, where the line was produced. Situating the plant in south Wales provided jobs for many of those who had lost theirs in the scaling-down of local coal mining.

The models released in 1956 were mainly family saloon cars familiar on British roads (the Ford Consul, Austin Cambridge, Morris Cowley, Vauxhall Velox, Rover 90, Riley Pathfinder and Hillman Husky) and a couple of sports cars (the Austin-Healey 100 and Triumph TR2). To distinguish them from Dinky Toys, a rival line produced by Meccano, Corgis were individually packaged in blue and black boxes (changed in 1959 to the better-known blue and yellow design).

Corgi Toys were produced in enormous numbers for two decades: family cars; Grand Prix and Formula One racing cars; commercial, agricultural and military vehicles; and tie-in models linked to TV programmes and films, such as James Bond's Aston Martin DB5 from *Goldfinger* – the all-time Corgi bestseller.

By the early '80s, however, the market for toy cars, already slowed by rising costs and competition from computer games, had run out of gas. Dinky Toys closed down in 1980, and Lesney, who made Matchbox Toys, followed in 1982. Corgi went into receivership in 1983, but was saved by a management buy-out, and continued to manufacture toy cars. After other changes of ownership, it was acquired in 2008 by Hornby.

---

101 L. Lloyd Morgan, Santosh Kesari and Devra Lee Davis, 'Why Children Absorb More Microwave Radiation Than Adults: The Consequences', *Journal of Microscopy & Ultrastructure*, 2:4 (December 2014), pp. 197–204.

Corgis from the Mettoy period of 1956–83 are now established collectables, regularly seen at auction houses and on eBay. One of those first Consuls or Cowleys, originally sold for shillings, can now be worth £200 or more – but only if they belonged to a child so finicky, or farsighted, as to keep both toy and box in pristine condition.

Less of a collector's item – in fact, to be blunt, not one at all – is a single that came out in June and charted in July, rising as high as number two: the two-part 'All Star Hit Parade', in which six acts from the Decca label – Dickie Valentine, Winifred Atwell, David Whitfield, Lita Roza, Joan Regan and Dave King – performed versions of current hits. Yet this is a historic item: the first-ever charity disc, anticipating Bob Geldof and Band Aid by almost thirty years. It was sponsored by the cricket charity The Lord's Taverners, and all profits went to the National Playing Fields Association, which, in due course, received a cheque for £10,000.

June was also the perverse release date of 'I'm Walking Backwards for Christmas', the first record by The Goons. Spike Milligan, Peter Sellers and Harry Secombe had been entrancing those who were clued in to their humour – and mystifying those who weren't (including many BBC high-ups) – on the BBC Home Service since 1951. By 1956, they were into their sixth (and, towards the end of the year, seventh) series of *The Goon Show*, their adventures including 'The Raid of the International Christmas Pudding', 'The Jet-Propelled Guided NAAFI', 'The Great Tuscan Salami Scandal' and 'The Nasty Affair at the Burami Oasis'. They had seven million listeners, an audience today's BBC producers can only dream of. Michael Foot declared that Spike Milligan had displaced Proudhon and Kropotkin as his favourite anarchist, and being able to imitate *Goon Show* characters was a small patch of common ground between John Lennon and Prince Charles.[102]

Other 1956 *Goon Show* spinoffs included the short film *The Case of the Mukkinese Battle Horn* and another Top 10 single, 'Bloodnok's Rock 'n' Roll'/'Ying Tong Song'. These are treasured chiefly by Goonatics, but *The Goon Show* itself was a model for the next generation of radio and TV funsters. *Monty Python's Flying Circus* and *The Hitchhiker's Guide to the Galaxy* are just two of many shows that were deeply imbued with its brilliant idiocy.

Also part of the legacy was the generation of Goonstruck young men (somehow it was always young men) who went around saying, 'You can't get the wood, you know,' and calling each other 'Neddy' or 'my *capitaine*'. 'The disciples were always the problem,' Alan Bennett reflected. '*The Goon Show* was very funny, the people who liked it (and knew it by heart) less so.'[103] Bennett's own work was to suffer a similar fate, with young men loudly declaiming his famous sermon – 'And my brother Esau is an hairy man, but I am a smooth man' – becoming a positive menace in the '60s and '70s.

---

102 Graham McCann, *Spike & Co.: Inside the House of Fun with Milligan, Sykes, Galton & Simpson* (London: Hodder, 2006), p. 206.

103 Alan Bennett, *Untold Stories* (London: Faber & Faber/Profile Books, 2005), p. 307.

CHAPTER 9

OFF-SPIN, OLIVE OIL, OUTINGS AND OTHER SUMMER DISTRACTIONS

On the last day of July, a record was set during the fourth Ashes Test at Old Trafford. There might have been little more to say about it than that – sporting records are set and broken, and the broken ones go into the historical wastepaper basket – except for the fact that this one has not been broken. Perhaps it never will be.

When the Test began on Thursday 26 July, the two teams were level at a match each. The previous evening, England's 34-year-old off-spinner Jim Laker had walked out on to the pitch to take a look at it, and had met the great Australian batsman Don Bradman, who was retired from Test cricket but attended the matches as a journalist. 'Flat and slow,' commented Bradman. 'Plenty of runs on it.'

England proved him right: by lunch on the second day, they had scored 459, with Peter Richardson and the Rev. David Sheppard hitting centuries. Australia went in to bat and, for a time, did well enough. England's crack spinning team of Laker and Tony Lock had made Surrey the most feared side in the County Championship, which they won every year from 1952 to 1958. 'Ashes to ashes, dust to dust,' people would say, 'if Laker doesn't get you, Lockie must.' But they made no headway. Then, just before tea, the England captain Peter May switched them around, so that Laker was bowling from the Stretford End. He promptly took two wickets, and, after the interval, seven of the remaining eight. Lock took the other. Australia were all out for 84. Laker's figures for the innings were 9 for 37.

Following on, Australia lost another wicket to Laker, but most of the next two playing days were lost to bad weather – it had been the wettest July in 100 years – and Laker took just one more wicket.

On Tuesday (31 July), Australia survived until lunch without further loss. Then the sun came out, the pitch went sticky, Laker proved unplayable and Australia were all out for 205. Laker took all ten wickets for 53, achieving match figures of 19 for 90. No one had ever taken that many wickets in a Test, and, almost sixty years later, no one has again. In that summer's Tests, Laker took forty-six wickets – the highest total ever in an Ashes series.

There were complaints afterwards that the pitch had been overwatered to favour the England spinners. 'It was a terrible pitch,' agreed the Australian all-rounder Richie Benaud. 'But a terrible pitch on which England made 459.'

Not the least extraordinary fact about Laker's second-innings clean sweep is that he had done it before, just two months earlier, taking 10 for 88 when Australia played Surrey. The odds against his repeating such a feat in a Test match 'would be incalculable', wrote his biographer Don Mosey. 'No one, no matter how fertile his imagination, how burning his ambition, how iron-clad his confidence, could possibly visualise such a double. But Jim Laker did it.'

It was a summer of wonders. Just nine days after Jim Laker achieved the seemingly miraculous, an art exhibition was opened by Robby the Robot from the movie *Forbidden Planet* (see Chapter 3). It was at the Whitechapel Art Gallery, and presented collaborations between architects, painters, sculptors and other artists, embodying their visions of contemporary art. Each of the dozen teams worked independently of the rest, but the exhibition was envisaged as a single environment.

It had been conceived two years before by the architect and critic Theo Crosby, editor of the magazine *Architectural Design*. It ran for a month and was visited by almost 1,000 people a day. Today, it is considered the forerunner of the British pop art movement.

As the artist Richard Hamilton explained in a 2003 interview:

> The idea was that there were certain things that were new in our visual environment, such as cinema, the juke box, Marilyn Monroe and comics. All these images from popular culture contrasted with the way we saw things that could be informed by straightforward optical experience. The visual illusions were taken from books. They weren't decoration, they were just enlargements of images, and you felt them on that scale. So these things were put together and presented in as exciting a way as possible. The juke box ran continuously, and people could make a choice without putting money in; but this resulted in such constant use that you

> never got what you wanted, because your choice would play an hour later. There were all these games with sound, optical illusion and imagery. One chamber in the fun house was even a kind of space capsule. There were portholes from science fiction which showed aliens looking through the windows.

The exhibit that has impressed itself most upon cultural memory was the room created by Group 2, in which Hamilton showed his pop art poster *Just what is it that makes today's homes so different, so appealing?* alongside other pop and op art posters, dazzle panels and a carpet that smelled of strawberries.

Group 6, consisting of architects Alison and Peter Smithson and artists Eduardo Paolozzi and Nigel Henderson, offered *Patio and Pavilion*, a walled structure with a corrugated plastic roof. The installation was scattered with found objects such as bicycle parts, a battered bugle and a handless clock. Other groups included figures like the graphic designer Germano Facetti (who led the design department at Penguin Books for most of the '60s), the artist and architect Victor Pasmore, artists Adrian Heath and Toni del Renzio, and architects Ernö Goldfinger and James Stirling.

On 17 August, detective superintendent Henry Hannam and detective sergeant Charles Hewett of the Metropolitan Police murder squad took over from their colleagues in Eastbourne the case of a local doctor and the allegedly suspicious deaths of some of his patients. What their investigations uncovered would lead to a notable trial, and to important modifications of the English legal system.

John Bodkin Adams, then fifty-seven, was a plump Irishman who had been raised in a family of Plymouth Brethren. He had been in general practice in Eastbourne since 1922. There had been talk about him since 1935, when one of his patients died and left him more than £7,000 – about two-thirds of her estate. In an interview later, he stated that he had received a number of anonymous postcards accusing him of 'bumping off' his patients. Many others, however, remembered him gratefully when making their wills, and by 1956 he had been mentioned in at least 132 of them. He was one of the wealthiest GPs in the country and the chosen physician of many distinguished people who lived in and around Eastbourne. It was one of them, the musical-comedy star Leslie Henson, who had taken the matter beyond rumour. After his friend Gertrude Hullett, a patient of Adams, died on 23 July, of what appeared to be a barbiturate overdose, he made an anonymous phone call to the Eastbourne police.

Hannam and Hewett decided to investigate the previous ten years of Adams's practice, and, with the help of the Home Office pathologist Francis Camps, they decided that more than half of the 310 death certificates Adams had signed during the period gave grounds for suspicion. In particular, he had a habit of giving his patients injections without revealing the contents of the shots to the attending nurses, whom he generally sent out of the room. He also failed to keep a register of the dangerous drugs he handled. After an investigation plagued by delays, he was charged on 19 December with the murder of Edith Alice Morell, a wealthy widow whom he had turned into a heroin addict. Upon his arrest, he is reported to have said: 'Can you prove it was murder? ... I didn't think you could prove it was murder. She was dying in any event.'

At the trial in April 1957 – thanks, probably, to conflicting expert testimonies and discrepancies between witnesses' statements – Adams was found not guilty. There were suggestions that important people had 'interfered' in the trial. It was known to police, for example, that Adams was rumoured to have homosexual connections with both the mayor and the deputy chief constable of Eastbourne. It has also been suggested that a special interest in the case might have been taken by the Prime Minister Harold Macmillan – his brother-in-law the 10th Duke of Devonshire had died in 1950 and had been attended to the end by Adams – or by the Attorney General Sir Reginald Manningham-Buller, who, after Adams was acquitted of murdering Morell, inexplicably declined to prosecute him for the murder of Gertrude Hullett (which many observers considered a stronger case).

A possible reason for high-level watchfulness was that, if Adams were found guilty, disaffected doctors (who were then numerous) might desert the profession for fear of being similarly arraigned for fallible prescription – a result that could endanger the future both of the NHS and of the new and vulnerable government.

Subsequent commentators, especially since the police and DPP files were made available in 2003, have generally agreed on Adams's guilt. According to the historian Pamela Cullen, he 'may have had more victims than Shipman – and he had a far more successful career as a serial killer'. (Harold Shipman was accused in 2000 of murdering his patients, and became the first British doctor to be found guilty of that charge.)

The case was the first to establish the principle of double effect. If a doctor gives treatment to a seriously ill patient with the aim of relieving pain or distress (which, the defence had argued, was what Adams had been doing), and, as a result, the patient's life is inadvertently shortened, the doctor is not guilty of murder. It also led to changes to the Dangerous Drugs Regulations, with Schedule 4 poisons henceforth requiring a signed and dated record of the patient's details and the total dose administered.

Though acquitted, Adams resigned from the NHS. In July 1957, he was found guilty of forging prescriptions, falsifying cremation forms and committing offences under the Dangerous Drugs Act. He was fined £2,400, and in November he was struck off the Medical Register, although he regained his licence four years later. Throughout, he continued to practise privately, with many friends and patients stoutly maintaining his innocence.

Kingsley Amis in his *Memoirs* describes a meeting with Melford Stevenson. Stevenson had been one of the prosecution team at Adams's trial, and had always maintained that, had he been given the opportunity to lead it, he would have prosecuted Adams on six counts of murder and secured a conviction: 'He was incredibly lucky to have literally got away with murder.' Adams, Stevenson recalled,

> took a house in Hove, not very far from where I live. I happened to be passing one day and saw he had installed a brass plate outside his door that read: 'John Bodkin Adams, MD, etc. At home 5 p.m. to 7 p.m.' As if he were inviting the world in general in for a glass of sherry.[104]

Adams died in 1983, leaving an estate of over £400,000.

While the police were looking into Dr Adams, William Connor – 'Cassandra' of the *Daily Mirror* – was looking into an icon of the time, and not liking what he found. His findings, and their denouement, throw an interesting and disturbing light on mid-'50s Britain and its attitudes.

The American pianist Liberace – an entertainer to whom the word 'flamboyant' could not begin to do justice – arrived at London's Waterloo station on 27 September, on a train labelled 'Liberace Special',

104 Kingsley Amis, *Memoirs* (London: Hutchinson, 1991), pp. 303–4.

to begin his European tour. He would perform at the Royal Festival Hall, twice on *Sunday Night at the London Palladium*, and in Manchester.

The following day, Connor devoted the whole of his immensely popular column to the man the Pathé newsreel commentator had called 'the well-known American leader of fashion':

> I have to report that Mr. Liberace ... is about the most that man can take ... He is the summit of sex – the pinnacle of Masculine, Feminine and Neuter. Everything that He, She and It can ever want ... this deadly, winking, sniggering, snuggling, chromium-plated, scent-impregnated, luminous, quivering, giggling, fruit-flavoured, mincing, ice-covered heap of mother love ... He reeks with emetic language that can only make grown men long for a quiet corner, an aspidistra, a handkerchief and the old heave-ho. Without doubt, he is the biggest sentimental vomit of all time ...
>
> Nobody since Aimee Semple MacPherson [a ballyhooed American evangelist of the '20s] has purveyed a bigger, richer and more varied slag-heap of lilac-covered hokum. Nobody anywhere ever made so much money out of high-speed piano playing with the ghost of Chopin gibbering at every note. There must be something wrong with us that our teenagers longing for sex and our middle-aged matrons fed up with sex alike should fall for such a sugary mountain of jingling claptrap wrapped up in such a preposterous clown.

Even without hints like 'fruit-flavoured' and 'mincing', it was perfectly clear to many readers what Connor was implying. American magazines like *Hollywood Confidential* had been hinting for a couple of years that Liberace was not – to use a phrase of the time – 'as other men are'. The entertainer was reported to have sent them telegrams saying: 'What you said hurt me very much. I cried all the way to the bank.'

A month after the *Mirror* piece appeared, Liberace sued both the paper and Connor for libel. According to one witness, this was exactly what Connor had hoped would happen: 'He laughed about it and said it was going to be a bit of fun.' Connor admitted that it was libellous and said that Liberace 'would get a lot of money from the *Daily Mirror*'.[105]

The case came to court in 1959 – delayed by the pianist's packed engagement diary – and Liberace returned to Britain to respond to 'the most improper article that has ever been written about me'.

'Are you a homosexual?' asked his counsel Gilbert Beyfus QC.

'No, sir.'

'Have you ever indulged in homosexual practices?'

'No, sir, never in my life. I am against the practice because it offends convention and it offends society.'[106]

Nobody emerges from this case with honour. Liberace denied what many Americans in show business knew to be true; the *Mirror* denied implying it, when every intelligent reader knew they had. Liberace's lawyers seemed, at times, not so much to be arguing for their client as attacking the popular press. Indeed, Roy Greenslade, writing about the trial fifty years later, noted that the questions put to the *Mirror*'s editor Hugh Cudlipp, by both Beyfus and the judge Mr Justice Salmon, 'reek[ed] with middle class distaste for popular journalism'.[107]

The jury found in Liberace's favour, and he was awarded £8,000 in damages and £27,000 in costs – at that date, the largest libel settlement in British legal history. Connor, whose long career in journalism was chiefly spent examining more substantial figures, was knighted in 1965. Władziu Valentino Liberace died in 1987 of AIDS-related cytomegalovirus pneumonia.

---

105 Darden Asbury Pyron, *Liberace: An American Boy* (Chicago: University of Chicago Press, 2000), pp. 223–9, 233–4.

106 Ibid.

107 Roy Greenslade, 'The meaning of "fruit": how the Daily Mirror libelled Liberace', *The Guardian*, 26 May 2009.

Reading Connor's diatribe with more than ordinary curiosity would have been the fifteen members of the Departmental Committee on Homosexual Offences and Prostitution, which had been meeting at intervals since 1954, and was discussing its findings throughout 1956.

Homosexuality was a toxic subject in Britain in this period. The Earl of Dudley would not have been thought intemperate when he said in the House of Lords: 'I cannot stand homosexuals. They are the most disgusting people in the world. I loathe them. Prison is much too good a place for them.' Homosexual men were routinely entrapped and arrested by the police, and, in many cases, their lives would be ruined. The cryptanalyst Alan Turing, a leader of the Bletchley Park codebreaking team during the Second World War, was prosecuted for homosexual acts and agreed to chemical castration. He died in 1954 of probably intentional cyanide poisoning.

According to a survey, 93 per cent of the country at the time believed homosexuality to be a medical condition that could be cured. The Home Secretary Sir David Maxwell Fyfe had undertaken to rid the nation of 'this plague', with a 'new drive against male vice'.

The Departmental Committee was created in the wake of the 1954 trial of the Conservative politician Edward John Barrington Douglas-Scott-Montagu, 3rd Baron Montagu of Beaulieu, and his friends Michael Pitt-Rivers and Peter Wildeblood, for illegal offences involving young servicemen. The trial had prompted much public debate, and some thoughtful, not illiberal leaders in the quality press. The committee was chaired by John Wolfenden (a former headmaster), and consisted of politicians, doctors and lawyers, who heard evidence from police officers, psychiatrists and churchmen – as well as from a few homosexual men prepared to be questioned about their lives, including the journalist Wildeblood, and Patrick Trevor-Roper, brother of the historian Hugh.

Three of the committee were women – Mrs Kathleen Lovibond, of

Uxbridge juvenile Magistrates' Court; Lady Stopford, also a magistrate; and Mrs Mary Cohen, of the Glasgow Girl Guides – and it was judged that their feelings should be spared by some use of euphemism. Wolfenden proposed that for the word 'homosexuals' they should substitute 'Huntleys', and for 'prostitutes', 'Palmers'. The biscuit manufacturer Huntley & Palmers was a major donor to the University of Reading, of which Wolfenden was then the vice-chancellor.

The committee's report recommended (with only one dissenting member) that homosexual behaviour between consenting adults in private should no longer be a criminal offence: 'It is not, in our view, the function of the law to intervene in the private life of citizens, or to seek to enforce any particular pattern of behaviour.'

It was an important public statement, but the battle for what would come to be called gay rights would be fought for another decade. As G. Rattray Taylor wrote in 1959: 'The proposals of the Wolfenden report as regards homosexuality ... have been accepted by public opinion with a notable lack of fuss: but ... the Conservative government has not been willing to introduce this change because of the known opposition of its more extreme supporters.'[108] Homosexual acts between consenting adult males were finally decriminalised in 1967 by the Sexual Offences Act. The age of homosexual consent, then twenty-one, was lowered to eighteen in 1994 and sixteen in 2001.

No doubt the *Daily Mirror* was carefully kept out of the hands of the nation's schoolchildren, in case they started asking each other in the playground just what exactly Liberace was supposed to have *done*, although many of them were too young to know their Liberace from their Archie Andrews.

In any event, they would more likely have been absorbed in the novelty of school itself, given that, in 1956, beating even the youngest

---

108 G. Rattray Taylor, *Sex in History* (London: Panther Books, 1965), p. 287.

schoolchildren with canes was commonplace in most schools – and that tended to concentrate the mind.

'My first day at school, Mum was anxious, I was just "lost",' remembers one of the 1956 school intake:

> It was my first real interaction with other children – the first [realisation] that the world is made up of all sorts of people ... something I don't think had ever occurred to me before then, as I lay cocooned in the new semi-detached council house in which I had been born and was to spend the next eighteen years of my life ... The new knowledge of different sorts of people at that particular school helped me more than anything to prepare for 'looking after' myself physically and mentally, then and in later life, and gave me insights I might never have otherwise had.
>
> It was a poor school, built in Victorian times, poor standard of education, generally poor kids from poor backgrounds ... Discipline was rigid: the headmaster roamed the corridors and classrooms with a cane hidden up the sleeve of his jacket – and we all felt its sting on bruised hands, whether for talking, eating a sweet or perhaps giving a 'funny' glance.[109]

Another pupil, Marian Cox, entered her small village school for the first time in 1956, aged four:

> As I walked through the classroom door, it was a place of wonderment to me: pictures and numbers adorned every wall and in the centre of the polished wooden floor a large cream-coloured encaged stove was warming the room. There were only thirty-two of us in the whole school, with three teachers, who were obeyed and

109 http://memoriesneverdie.co.uk/12.html

> respected. The youngest used the girls' playground – from the age of seven the boys had a separate one, with a high wall. The school garden was tended by the older boys. The earth toilets were at the end of the playground; we had running water but no mains drainage. In winter the crates of small bottles of milk were brought in frozen and left by the stove until break time.

Everyone who went to school in 1956 remembers those little bottles. The 1945 Labour government had decreed that all schoolchildren were to be given a third of a pint of milk every day at the nation's expense, and so crates of small bottles were delivered to every school in the country, from Eton to the local secondary modern, every morning. Marian Cox continues:

> At lunchtime, whatever the weather, we walked about a mile up a narrow lane to the wooden village hall, where two very nice ladies cooked us a much appreciated dinner (that's lunch to posh folk). Every morning we sang a hymn before classes began, and, at 3.30 we sang again before we left. Life was carefree and innocent and our playtimes were always outside. We heard tales of the war and rationing, but that was the past and a brave new world was evolving.

And with this new, unrationed world came new food and new ways of eating it – but gradually: Britons would not lightly say farewell to spam fritters, mulligatawny soup or Heinz Salad Cream. In 1956, shocking though it will be for today's sophisticated shopper to hear, garlic was chiefly used to prevent colds, olive oil, sold in tiny bottles in chemists' shops, was for clearing blocked ears, and basil, as the food writer Jane Grigson noted, 'was no more than the name of bachelor uncles'.

Grigson's forerunner, the great Elizabeth David, remembered

that you had to go to London's Soho to find 'such things as Italian *pasta*, and Parmesan cheese, olive oil, *salame*, and occasionally Parma ham', as well as 'southern vegetables such as aubergines, red and green peppers, fennel, [and] the tiny marrows called by the French *courgettes* and in Italy *zucchini*'. (It's eloquent of the period that the now commonplace courgette had to be both defined and italicised.)

In the first half of the '50s, David published four pioneering cookbooks: *Mediterranean Food* (1950), *French Country Cooking* (1951), *Italian Food* (1954) and *Summer Cooking* (1955). She continued to educate her readers about food – not only how to buy, cook and eat it, but also its cultural history – for a further twenty-odd years, building an unassailable reputation as the woman who, according to her biographer Artemis Cooper, 'inspired a whole generation not only to cook, but to think about food in an entirely different way'.

For the novelist Anthony Burgess, who returned to England in 1956, 'the days of austerity were over. The British were tearing into beef and lapping up cream ices ... We ate in Rule's [reputedly London's oldest restaurant, opened in 1798] and were shocked to see scampi cooked in butter.'[110]

To get some idea of what Elizabeth David was up against, we must try to imagine what shopping was like in the Britain of 1956. During the first postwar decade, product rationing, shortage of building materials and other factors had slowed the development of the retail landscape. The typical high street was, as it had been in the '30s, a mixture of independent shops and ones owned by multiples and cooperative societies.

But the concept of *self-service* shopping – familiar in the United States since 1916, when Clarence Saunders opened his first Piggly Wiggly

110 Anthony Burgess, *Little Wilson and Big God* (London: Heinemann, 1987), p. 417 in 1988 Penguin edition.

store in Memphis, Tennessee – was viewed with suspicion by the British public and its retailers alike. The London Co-operative Society opened its first self-service store in 1942, but by 1947 there were reportedly still no more than ten self-service shops in the whole of Britain. The trade magazine *The Grocer* spoke for many when it wrote: 'The people of this country have long been accustomed to counter-service, and it is doubtful whether they would be content to wander round a store hunting for goods.'

Eight years later, the trade was still sceptical. A conference on self-service shopping, held at the College for Distributive Trades in London in April 1955, asked itself: 'Are self-service shops becoming so streamlined, so clinically efficient, that there is a danger of customers staying away from them because they miss the social side of shopping? Quite a few delegates – themselves disciples of the self-service creed – seemed to think that this was a real threat.' The Postmaster General, Dr Charles Hill, said that:

> Self-service is still on trial at the bar of public opinion, and even its keenest advocates must recognise that there is an unreasoning obstinate trait in human nature that makes people hanker after such old-fashioned, unproductive, inefficient aspects of shopping as gossiping with the grocer and the friends they meet in his shop.

'The customers hated it,' recalled a unnamed woman, who was interviewed by researchers about her work in an early self-service store:

> They wouldn't pick up a basket. They were very suspicious. They didn't want to buy much, and they felt belittled, I think, at having a basket with perhaps two Oxos in, and a small loaf ... People hated the way there was nobody to talk to them. People didn't feel that

> they'd done a proper morning's shopping if they hadn't had all these conversations which took up the assistant's time.

Shoppers valued not only the affability of their local stores – 'everybody knew everybody else' – but their lack of hustle: 'You could always have a sit-down in the grocer's shop,' said another interviewee. 'There was always a stool or something so it was a pleasure shopping rather than a chore.' And there was always something to watch, too: portions of butter being chopped from a huge block and shaped by wooden paddles; spices being poured from large canisters, or dried fruit from wooden drawers; loose tea and sugar being weighed out into paper bags; the fresh slicing of bacon or ham; the wire-cutting of cheese.

But against such fond vignettes of shopping the old-time way, we must set accounts like the following, from a resident of Abbey Wood in south-east London (which had only counter-service shops until the late '50s):

> In the small shops, there was a slightly condescending air ... [and] a more mature person behind the counter. And ... they thought that someone of twenty [or] twenty-one, who was married, you know, wasn't going to know anything ... I can remember going to the butcher's and I asked for a quarter of a pound of mince because I only wanted a small amount cos I was just ... stuffing something, you see. And he looked at me very condescending and he said, 'Oh, having a dinner party, madam?'

There were other pressures involved in a trip to the shops. A further interviewee, a man who was taken shopping with his mother in Guildford in the '50s, recalled that 'women did make an effort to look their best when they went to the shop because they felt that the shopkeeper must see that they've made an effort'. Any adventurousness in a woman's shopping – an exotic or unusually expensive purchase, say – could be noted and commented on behind her back. Shoppers intimidated by such pitfalls might indeed have welcomed the busy impersonality of a larger store. They would soon be offered it.

Over the preceding half-century, the American retail industry had run with the self-service idea, and it had scored a spectacular goal with the supermarket – a self-service store, with separate product departments, that routinely offered high volumes of goods at discounted prices. The first American example was opened in 1930, but it took more than twenty years for Britain to follow, when Express Dairies opened the first of their Premier Supermarkets in 1951 in Streatham, south London. In 1955, they were joined by Waitrose. Within a decade, the country had more than 500 such stores, the majority of them operated by Premier, Victor Value and Fine Fare – soon to be joined by Tesco, which opened its first supermarket in a disused cinema in Maldon, Essex, in 1956.

Along with their eating and shopping habits, Britons were reshaping the character of their holidaymaking. In the summer of 1956, many working-class people were still faithful to the annual coach outing, whether to Blackpool or Morecambe Bay, Torquay or Paignton, or any of dozens of other seaside resorts. But there was more competition for their custom. By the mid-'50s, over 20,000 coaches would move in and out of Victoria Coach Station every year – many of them following routes first defined by eighteenth- and nineteenth-century stagecoaches.

Motor coaches were hot, journeys long, roadside facilities scanty, yet many people loved this kind of holiday travel, because it created a communal atmosphere impossible in the compartments of a train.

Trips would be enlivened by sing-songs, and travellers with a bit of go – or a drink inside them – would entertain fellow passengers with jokes or impersonations. Long before they reached the 'Las Vegas of the north', they would have heard about George Formby and his little stick of Blackpool rock.

Such was the camaraderie of the charabanc that, if the trippers didn't know each other when they got on, they surely would by the time they got off. 'We were all very friendly,' remembered Barbara Flin, a former tour guide for the Wallace Arnold coach line, 'and it was quite an emotional time when we all said goodbye.'[111]

But, by the summer of 1956, more and more people were not only taking holidays at the seaside but driving there in their own cars. Seaside resorts, neglected or repurposed during the Second World War, smartened themselves up and made vigorous pitches for a share of the new market. Their customers were no longer content to settle for a boarding house, a deckchair on the beach, a stroll on the pier and a fish supper. Before them were dangled the temptations of golf, bowling (on greens, of course, not the ten-pin variety), dance orchestras, the 'finest coastline and beaches in Europe' at Newquay, the 'sub-tropical climate' of St Austell and the 'champagne air' of Scarborough.

'Everything is in full swing from June to September at sunny Rhyl,' shrilled an advert, above a sketch of a young woman on a swing in a swimsuit that, frankly, shows her bottom. By a curious coincidence, an illustrated guide – to Rhyl, that is – could be obtained, for a sixpenny postal order, from a Mr Frank Bottom.[112]

A review of 'Holidays in Britain' for the *Daily Mail Year Book* did its clumsy best to crank up the enthusiasm for the emerging trend,

111 *The Golden Age of Coach Travel* (*Timeshift* series 10:6), BBC-TV, first transmitted 5 January 2012.

112 *Daily Mail Year Book 1956* (London: Associated Newspapers, 1956), p. 296.

though it sounds dreadfully as though an aristocrat is talking down to the proletariat:

> The time-honoured habit of visiting the same resort year after year has also been challenged, and more and more is it being realised that a holiday affords an opportunity of seeing more of the beauty of the countryside and some historical places ... Shall it be to some well-known resort, inland or on the coast, from which it will be possible to make a series of visits to many of the interesting places in a large area, or shall it be a sort of progressive tour of some part of the country, resting each evening at a different spot? ... Having decided where to go, another primary consideration is as to the most satisfactory method of reaching it. Those who possess a motor car or motorcycle will naturally wish to avail themselves of it.[113]

It's amazing that anyone, after trudging through this mire of leaden and patronising prose, should still feel like going on holiday at all. But they did – and, very often, to a holiday camp.

We think of holiday camps as an invention of the interwar years, connected with the fresh-air movement, rambling and the like, but there were seaside camps as early as the first decade of the twentieth century. One such was the Socialist Camp at Caister, instigated in 1906 by J. Fletcher Dodd, a founder member of the Independent Labour Party. Working-class people unable to afford conventional holidays were accommodated in tents on the gusty Norfolk shore, where they were approvingly inspected by visitors like Keir Hardie and George Lansbury.

In the '30s, Caister could house several hundred guests in wooden chalets (if you booked early) or tents (if you didn't), offering them, as one patron remembered, 'lively times and times of great exchange

---

113 *Daily Mail Year Book 1957* (London: Associated Newspapers), p. 292.

of ideas'. But not *too* lively. Mr Dodd had a rulebook: 'Bathers must wear regulation costume ... Intoxicants, gambling, rowdy conduct and improper language prohibited. All lights out after 11.30 p.m.'[114] 'The highlight of the week', said Betty Rose, who stayed at Caister as a child in 1947, 'was a Sunday afternoon lecture on the labour movement.'[115]

By the '50s, Caister had many competitors – few of them primarily dedicated to lectures or great exchanges of ideas. It was a boom time for the home of hi-de-hi. Not only were there the multiple branches of Billy Butlin's enterprise at Skegness, Clacton, Filey, Pwllheli, Saltdean, Blackpool and Cliftonville (as well as those of the rival chains forged by Fred Pontin and Harry Warner), but there were also scores of independent ventures, such as Chesil Beach at Weymouth, Great Tree at Looe in Cornwall, Sunshine at Hayling Island ('Four meals served daily'), The Denes near Lowestoft ('Interior sprung mattresses') and the Constitutional Holiday Camp at Hopton-on-Sea, near Great Yarmouth ('Established 1928 ... 6000ft dance floor ... resident band').

What the holiday camp offered that the traditional seaside holiday couldn't was a site where there was always something to do, whatever the weather: 'Three whole hours of varied entertainment from immediately after breakfast until lunchtime ... an equally fun-packed afternoon ... one continuous round of attractions follow dinner until midnight ... and everything happens within a few minutes' stroll of your chalet or dining hall.'[116] And everything was covered by the all-in tariff. There might be clouds over Clacton, it might be pouring in Pwllheli, but Butlin's campers would be cosy and dry at the rep theatre, the all-star variety show or the knobbly-knees competition.

The most profound change in British holidaymaking, though,

---

114 *Holiday Camps: No Loud Talking After 11*, BBC East, 1979.

115 http://www.qlhs.org.uk/oracle/first-holidays/first-holidays.htm

116 *Daily Mail Year Book* 1957 (London: Associated Newspapers, 1956), p. 1.

was the development of the overseas package tour, which began in the early '50s. In 1952, according to a survey published by the *Daily Herald*, only 50 per cent of Britons took holidays at all, and, of those, only 3 per cent went abroad.[117] But, during that same year, cheaper tourist-class fares were introduced and foreign exchange allowances were raised. In 1954, amendments to the Convention on International Civil Aviation created a surge in mass tourism using charter planes, and then, in 1955, a new short-haul terminal opened at Heathrow (what became Terminal 2).

'There were lots of aeroplanes left over from the war,' explains Professor Graham Miller of the University of Surrey, which 'led to a reduction in the prices of flights. Then Spain and southern Europe were trying to rebuild their economies. They had to consider what they had to sell; they had sun, they had beaches – so they put up hotels and there was an industry.' Adventurous Britons began to contemplate swapping Torquay for Torremolinos, the Cornish Riviera for the Costa del Sol. Air travel in the UK increased by 18 per cent in 1956, and the passenger shipping companies began to take out insurance by acquiring or creating airlines.

But people still needed to be prodded. At a 1955 convention of travel agents, James Maxwell, president of the Association of British Travel Agents, complained about the millions of Britons who stubbornly resisted foreign travel. 'What on earth's the matter with them?' he expostulated:

> Are they afraid of leaving their homes behind them for a fortnight or so? Are they completely devoid of interest in what goes on outside their daily ken? Do they not realise that a holiday, in these

117 Roger Bray and Vladimir Raitz, *Flight to the Sun: The Story of the Holiday Revolution* (London: Continuum, 2001), p. 34.

> hard-working days, is virtually an essential? Whatever the reason for their shyness, something must be done about them.[118]

What did Mr Maxwell have in mind? Garlic at gunpoint? Compulsory calamari? But, as it turned out, suspicion of foreign travel was fast evaporating as people tried it and reported back glowingly to their friends and workmates. Favourite destinations in these early days of the package tour were Mallorca, Sardinia, Corsica, the Costa Brava and another Spanish region to which the tourist industry gave the name of the Costa Blanca – a long stretch of Mediterranean coastline, including 'a once quiet fishing village' named Benidorm.[119]

But not yet Ibiza. When a British airline proposed the idea of conveying tourists to the island by flying boat, the Spanish authorities refused. Within a few years, however, Ibiza became accessible by air, whereupon it was advertised in brochures as 'a very small island where nothing exciting is expected to happen'.[120]

A fortnight's holiday in the Costa Brava in high season in the '50s cost £35 per person – estimated as one-fifth of a typical annual salary – but that was mostly for travel and accommodation; food and drink were, for a British pocket, laughably cheap, with a bottle of Spanish wine costing something like ninepence.

Vladimir Raitz, whose Horizon Holidays pioneered package deals in Europe in the '50s, reckoned that he didn't just offer people beaches and cheap booze, though:

> Providing a fortnight in the Mediterranean sun to a wide segment of the British public, hereto the prerogative of well-to-do members

118 Bray and Raitz, op. cit., p. 48.

119 Bray and Raitz, op. cit., p. 49.

120 Horizon ad reproduced in Bray and Raitz, op. cit., p. 71.

> of the bourgeoisie, brought with it what can only be described as a social revolution; the man in the street acquired a taste for wine, for foreign food, started to learn French, Spanish or Italian, made friends in the foreign lands he had visited – in fact, became more 'cosmopolitan', with all that that entailed.

Naturally, there was opposition from the representatives of British holidaymaking. In December, Harry Lund, president of the Scarborough Hotels Association, let fly at what he called 'the garlic and olive oil gang':

> I mean those writers, usually women, who happily accept on the Continent the sort of carpetless room with iron bedstead, flock mattress and early Victorian plumbing which they would raise all hell about over here. Imagine what they would say if instead of bacon and eggs and the incomparable meats and vegetables of England we were to give them starch-loaded Continental breakfasts ... If they are willing to put up with that sort of thing over there it's their own look-out. What we do object to is that they should then be given good space in journals and valuable time on the air in which to drool about how much better and cheaper foreign hotels are than our own.[121]

Back in the UK, the music press was beginning to realise that rock 'n' roll was more than a craze. On 21 September, Bill Haley had five discs in the pop chart – even 'Rock Around the Clock' had made a reappearance – and Elvis Presley, already represented by 'Heartbreak

121 '"Garlic and Olive Oil" Holidays', *Manchester Guardian*, 11 December 1956.

Hotel' and 'I Want You, I Need You, I Love You', had just added 'Hound Dog'. The following week, Gene Vincent's 'Be-Bop-a-Lula' joined them, at which point almost half the records in the Top 30 could have been classed as rock 'n' roll.

So, rock 'n' roll was in for the present, and whether it had a future only the charts would reveal. But did it have a past?

The *New Musical Express* answered that question with a four-page 'Rock 'n' Roll Supplement'. Jazz critic Mike Butcher sketched a brief history of rock 'n' roll's ancestry in blues and rhythm & blues, dropping names like Bessie Smith and Louis Jordan. There was an article by the New York disc jockey Alan Freed – one of rock 'n' roll's first promoters and exploiters. A feature called 'Spotlight on the Rock 'n' Roll Stars' focused not only on Haley, Presley and Vincent but on black artists like Ruth Brown, Dinah Washington and Clyde McPhatter, sometime lead singer with The Drifters. These were people hardly ever written about in the music papers or heard on radio.

Delving even further into the subculture, the feature 'Rock 'n' Roll on Record' listed discs by Chuck Berry, Bo Diddley, LaVern Baker, Wynonie Harris and others. Such hardline rhythm & blues was, even in the United States, often hard to find – other than in record stores in black sections – but a little of it (a very little of it) was becoming available in the UK: a 78 or 45 here, an EP there. And yet this wasn't a jump-on-the-bandwagon response to Haley and Presley, nor did it have anything to do with the teenagers who listened to them. So for whom were such recordings issued? A possible (partial) answer is Britain's West Indian communities.

The Caribbean had been listening closely to black American rhythm & blues since the '40s. The effervescent singer and bandleader Louis Jordan, of 'Five Guys Named Moe' and 'Choo Choo Ch'Boogie' fame, toured there in 1950–51, making a great impression, and the shuffle-beat blues and boogies of singer/pianists like Fats Domino, Amos

Milburn and Rosco Gordon had a formative influence on ska (the predecessor of reggae). 'In the '50s,' ska artist Laurel Aitken remembered:

> We used to listen to American rhythm & blues from New Orleans. Everybody used to dance to that music in Jamaica ... men like Smiley Lewis, Joe Turner, Rosco Gordon ... I was influenced by him [Gordon]. Not only me, but other guys during that time was influenced by him because it was very popular – the boogie-woogie stuff.

Producer Bunny Lee confirmed: 'The three biggest R&B artists in Jamaica [were] Fats Domino, Rosco Gordon and Lloyd Price.'[122]

During the '50s, many thousands of West Indians exchanged their island homes for the grey streets of Birmingham, Manchester and London: 'According to figures published by the British Caribbean Welfare Service in February, 1957, there were about 78,000 British West Indians living in the United Kingdom. Immigration from the West Indies amounted to over 26,000 in 1956, compared with 24,000 in 1955.'[123] These figures may well have been underestimates: by 1961, the 1957 total had more than doubled.

These new British communities became a new market, catered for by record stores like The Diskery in Birmingham's Hurst Street, or Foxley's by Kilburn station in north London. Ray Foxley, a pianist who played with Ken Colyer and Chris Barber, opened the shop in 1955 and found so much interest in rhythm & blues records among Jamaican customers that he commissioned a friend who worked on transatlantic passenger ships to bring back new R&B discs from New York.

Since the early '50s, record labels like Vogue, London and Melodisc had been releasing examples of the hot new sounds coming out

---

122 Phil Etgart, notes to CD set *Jump Blues Jamaica Way: Jamaica Sound System Classics 1945–1960* (Fantastic Voyage FVTD 185), 2014.

123 *Daily Mail Year Book 1958* (London: Associated Newspapers, 1957), p. 289.

of the Caribbean and the United States. Melodisc's musical director from 1953 was the Trinidadian Rupert Nurse, a musician who had been playing round London since the '40s with fellow Trinidadians such as Lord Kitchener and Winifred Atwell. 'Kitch' was a respected calypsonian who had come to Britain in 1948 on the *Empire Windrush* with Lord Beginner, who himself would be famed for his recording of 'Victory Test Match' ('cricket, lovely cricket').

The effervescent honkytonk pianist Winifred Atwell was already here, studying at the Royal Academy of Music, but she moonlighted playing ragtime and boogie woogie in nightclubs. She would have a dozen Top 20 hits between 1952 and 1957, reaching number one in 1954 with 'Let's Have Another Party', and again in 1956 with 'The Poor People of Paris'.

In 1954, Nurse led the band at the Sunset club in Carnaby Street – one of a handful of central London venues in the '50s that were hospitable to Caribbean immigrants and black American servicemen. Another was the Flamingo in the West End's Coventry Street (it later moved to Wardour Street), which would become important in the history of UK rhythm & blues, and, later, mod music. For Melodisc, Nurse made a pitch for the Afro-Caribbean market by recording calypsonians like Kitchener – who became a mainstay of the catalogue – and jazz players such as the Jamaican alto saxophonist Joe Harriott.

Another producer who freelanced for Melodisc was Denis Preston – in the '50s, the go-to man for almost any kind of exotic music. He supervised Lord Beginner's cricket calypso in 1950 and many of Kitchener's sessions, and, in 1956, produced Humphrey Lyttelton's 'Bad Penny Blues' (see Chapter 7). In the same year, he opened his Lansdowne Studios in Holland Park, west London, where one of his first productions was Lonnie Donegan's skiffle version of another venerable American folk song, 'Cumberland Gap'. A few years later came Acker Bilk's dreamy clarinet feature 'Stranger on the Shore', and, subsequently, sessions with John Lennon and Yoko Ono, Rod Stewart, and the Sex Pistols. Over more than two decades, Preston produced innumerable recordings of jazz, folk, blues and what would now be called world music, and, in a quiet and under-acknowledged way, he was a pioneer documenter of non-mainstream musical idioms.

Following close behind these men was a Jamaican-born twenty-something named Chris Blackwell, who created Island Records. He would go on to promote the work of Bob Marley, Toots & the Maytals and Jimmy Cliff, before turning Island into a leading indie label for rock acts as diverse as Roxy Music and U2.

The journey to that point had begun back at the beginning of the decade, when Caribbean radio sets were tuned to American stations playing swing and jive, and the island traditions of calypso and mento began to make room for American-inspired rhythm & blues. It would continue, on two continents, through ska, blue beat, rock steady and other musical transformations, and eventually lead to reggae – the first music from the Caribbean to influence the sound of the world.

CHAPTER 10

THE LAST FEW SECONDS OF THE IMPERIAL DELUSION

At Archbishop Tenison's Grammar School in Croydon, south London, in October 1956, fifteen-year-old Richard Rawles faced a troubling ideological dilemma: should he refuse to join the school's Air Training Corps (ATC)?

As a young communist, his grounds for refusal were based on the fact that the British Army would be used against the forces of progress and socialism – as it had been in Korea, and might again be in Suez. However, joining the ATC would provide some useful small-arms training for when the revolution came. So what should he do?

He consulted the Communist Party elders and they told him to join. However, while the Communist Party had decided not to call for an end to National Service in 1956 – believing that the revolution was near at hand and that Soviet Britain would need a people's army – it had compromised with its younger members by demanding the call-up be reduced to eighteen months. And so, as a disciplined young communist, Richard had scrawled 'Cut the call-up' on a wall near the school – whereupon some wag added an extra line to the first 'c', altering the slogan to read 'Gut the call-up'.

On the other side of the ideological divide at Archbishop Tenison's lay fellow pupil Trevor Grundy, who at sixteen was a year older than Richard. His father Sidney Grundy, a member of Sir Oswald Mosley's British Union of Fascists in the '30s, had spent most of the war in prison under Regulation 18B. This was a regulation that allowed the government to imprison, without trial, people whom the security services considered a danger to the war effort. Sidney had heroically refused to plead for his release, telling a tribunal in 1940: 'As long as my leader [Mosley] is in prison without trial, I will stay in prison without trial' – and Trevor was fiercely proud of his father. Indeed, in 1956, both were members of Mosley's Union Movement.

Young Trevor regularly sat at the feet of Bob Row, the editor of Mosley's journal *Union*, and Row's wisdom came direct from the Leader (it always had an upper-case 'L' in Mosley circles). Row, a frequent visitor to the Grundy home (he lusted after Trevor's older sister), had told young Trevor that 1956 would see Mosley's big comeback, as the Jews were going to overthrow Nasser in Egypt:

> They'll go to war against Nasser, Mrs G [Trevor's mother], and Britain will go in with them because of that chinless wonder Anthony Eden. We'll all be dragged into another Jewish war and British lives

> will be lost in the Middle East and the Arabs will turn away from Britain and look to the Soviet Union.[124]

Today, most people imagine that the Holocaust immediately made anti-Semitism untenable everywhere, and that even the Mosleyites had moved on from blaming Jews to blaming black Africans and West Indians. But the Holocaust was not yet fully a part of the British consciousness, and casual anti-Semitism was still almost respectable in 1956. John Osborne's character Barney in the play *Epitaph for George Dillon* – 'Hitler may have gone a bit too far sometimes' – was perfectly believable to 1956 theatre audiences. The League of Empire Loyalists' journal *Candour* – the Union Movement's rival for the neo-fascist vote, generally at the time considered eccentric but harmless, certainly compared to Mosley's lot – could still say:

> That minority groups, particularly Jewish groups, which have been constantly at odds with the world in general, should be attracted by the idea of an international organisation existing for the protection of human rights is very understandable, and it is hardly surprising that Jewish periodicals should devote some attention to the findings of the United Nations and its specialised agencies.

Richard and Trevor, from their opposed ideological standpoints, had reached the same prediction, and events moved swiftly to prove them right. Before they returned to Archbishop Tenison's school after their summer break, the drums of war could already be heard: on 26 July, Colonel Gamal Abdel Nasser nationalised the Suez Canal.

Egypt had been virtually under British administration since 1882, though never actually a colony. Nationalist feeling had always been

124 Trevor Grundy, *Memoir of a Fascist Childhood* (London: Heinemann, 1998), pp. 91–2.

strong, but Britain was determined not to cede control of the Suez Canal – a vitally important trade route – to 'the natives', upon whom, naturally, no reliance could be placed.

In 1936, the young, brilliant Foreign Secretary Anthony Eden, the fast-rising star of British politics, agreed that the British would withdraw but keep a specified number of troops on Egyptian soil, mainly to protect the canal.

This treaty was up for renewal in 1956.

Come the '50s, however, Britain was governed by men who still thought of Egypt as some sort of colony. As one Eden biographer put it: 'The British ambassador still drove through Cairo with motorcyclists blowing whistles before him, and behaved more like a colonial governor than a diplomatic representative.'[125]

The imagined innate superiority of the British character and culture, which most British people still took for granted, allowed the troops in Egypt to behave with an imperial arrogance that naturally infuriated the locals.

No British soldier ever referred to 'Egyptians'; they were always the 'wogs'. An officer once found on his desk a driver's report of a traffic accident between a British Army vehicle and a Rolls-Royce that read: 'Two wogs were inside, and their names were King Farouk and Ali Ismail.' The officer told the driver to rewrite it; he could not refer to the King of Egypt as a 'wog'. The report came back: 'I asked them their names ... they were King Farouk and another wog called Ali Ismail.'[126]

It never occurred to the British that they wouldn't be welcome – but they weren't. The year 1952 saw the start of violent confrontation between Egyptians and British troops. Egyptians were killed by British bullets, and a nationalistic military regime headed by General

---

125 Peter Wilby, *Eden* (London: Haus Publishing, 2006).

126 Dominic Sandbrook, *Never Had It So Good* (London: Little, Brown, 2005), p. 3.

Muhammad Naguib took power in Egypt. Eden, once again Foreign Secretary, agreed to talk to him. This, to the harrumph tendency that always lurks on the Conservative Party's back benches, looked suspiciously like selling out Britain's imperial destiny to the great unwashed. And Eden's boss, Prime Minister Winston Churchill, had rather a lot of sympathy with the harrumph tendency when it came to matters of empire.

So the dread word 'appeasement' was once again heard in the land. Churchill was said to be 'in a rage against AE, speaking of "appeasement" and saying that he never knew before that Munich was situated on the Nile'.[127]

This was really dangerous for Eden. He got his way, but at the expense of a near breach of his relationship with Churchill, and a near revolt from the back benches. In 1954, when 36-year-old Colonel Nasser ousted, imprisoned and replaced General Naguib, Eden agreed a treaty under which British troops were to be withdrawn from Egypt by June 1956. But Eden refused to allow arms sales to Nasser, and Nasser instead turned to the Soviet Union to equip his army.

Relations were further strained when the US and Britain pulled out of the massive Aswan Dam project, designed to make the Nile – always, from the time of the pharaohs, the natural resource upon which Egypt has depended – provide both energy and irrigation. The dam, Nasser believed, would lift his people out of abject poverty, and nationalising the Suez Canal would go some way to providing an alternative income – as well as telling the West who was in charge on Egyptian territory.

So, on 26 July, in a broadcast speech in Alexandria, Nasser pronounced the name of Ferdinand de Lesseps, the designer of the Suez Canal. The name was the secret signal for his troops to enter

---

127 Wilby, op. cit.

the canal offices and take them over. He seems to have feared his army commanders might not hear the signal, for, after saying de Lesseps's name once, he found ways of returning to it two or three more times in the speech.

Years later, in 2006, engineer Ezzat Adel – one of only thirty men entrusted with the secret before Nasser's speech – told the BBC that keeping the mission such a closely guarded secret was the reason it succeeded:

> The first thing to do was to inform [the staff]: 'We guarantee your safety, your family's safety and we also guarantee all your salaries, premiums and everything and we moreover request you to continue working for the Suez Canal; nobody will be fired.'
>
> Everything went smoothly for a period of time, less than two weeks ... until we noticed that some of the employees that were on summer holidays did not return. Some foreigners, also staff, [were] selling their cars, their furniture, so we anticipated that there [was] a move to leave the Egyptians alone to run the Suez Canal.

As newly appointed under-secretary general of the Suez Canal Authority, Mr Adel had to move fast. If the canal was to remain open, he needed experienced pilots to guide the ships through the narrow shipping lanes. But new pilots were found and trained, and, ultimately, the nationalisation of the canal proved a success.

Mr Adel – who became chairman of the Suez Canal Company in the mid-'80s – never doubted that Nasser was right to nationalise the canal:

> Egypt lost 120,000 people digging the Suez Canal, by shovels and carrying cases of sand under almost slavery conditions, very little health care, very few wages. Against this very high sacrifice Egypt did not get a fair share of the profits of the Suez Canal.

> Egypt paid all the head shareholders of the Suez Canal Company the full value of their shares in the money market in Paris the day before nationalisation.

So, today, it's hard to see what the British got so indignant about. But in 1956 nationalising the canal seemed like an affront to Britain's imperial pretensions, as well as a threat to her oil supplies, and Eden was under fierce pressure to respond. The Middle East was providing 70 per cent of the West's oil, and half of Europe's supply came through the Suez Canal.

On 27 July, *The Spectator* commented:

> The dangerous nature of the international game Egypt has been playing under the guidance of Colonel Nasser has been sharply underlined in the past week ... the refusal of America and Britain to support the Aswan Dam for reasons stated to be primarily economic ... certainly [has] a great deal to do with Egypt's behaviour in the international field in the past year or so ... The Russian Foreign Minister Mr Shepilov evidently made it clear on his recent visit to Cairo that his government would not support Egypt in a war against Israel, and it is clear that Col. Nasser has sustained a number of considerable diplomatic defeats. At the time of writing, it is not clear whether, in fact, Egypt will get Russian support for the Aswan Dam.

The LEL wanted Britain to go in 'like a lion' to put the Egyptians in their place, and seemed willing to overlook the awkward fact that this meant supporting the Israelis. The LEL had its own internal problems that month. At its AGM in October, the Leamington delegate, one Colin Jordan, had proposed that membership be restricted to 'white Gentile British subjects'. Mr Jordan was soon to become disillusioned with the LEL's moderation and start to call himself a Nazi, but in October 1956 LEL leader A. K. Chesterton defused the awkward moment by saying that, if he had looked around the room and seen serried rows of black and Jewish faces, he might have shared Mr Jordan's concern, but, as it was, it was scarcely a problem.

Macmillan thought Nasser 'an Asiatic Mussolini' and wrote: 'The unanimous view of the Cabinet was in favour of strong and resolute action.'[128] Eden appointed an 'Egypt Committee' – himself, Salisbury, Lord Home and Macmillan – and it became the real power in the Suez crisis, bypassing the Cabinet.

Pressure on the Prime Minister to treat Nasser like a Middle Eastern Mussolini chimed with Sir Anthony's own instincts. Only two years had elapsed since Eden had battled Churchill to be allowed to negotiate with Egypt, but it seemed a lifetime away.

The following week, *The Spectator*'s editorial poured petrol on the flames, and showed the Prime Minister – if he did not already know it – that there was no shortage of Conservatives ready to accuse him of appeasement:

> Colonel Nasser's seizure of the Suez Canal provides a fitting climax to the disasters that have recently overtaken British policy in the Middle East. It is not the nationalisation itself that is serious – the concession would in any case have lapsed in 1968 – but, judging by the colonel's speeches and the Egyptian press and radio, it seems that the present Egyptian government has decided to ride the storm of hatred and xenophobia, which were always potentially present in the fanatical and under-nourished Egyptian masses ... Those who, like the Prime Minister, believed that a deal could be done with him have been decisively proved wrong. Great Britain is now in the position of having the main artery of her oil supplies dominated by an irresponsible government

128 *The Macmillan Diaries* (London: Pan Macmillan, 2003), pp. 578–9.

> which has shown itself indifferent to international agreements and which is at the mercy of a rabidly nationalist public opinion. It is not a situation which any power could tolerate.

It did not escape Eden and Macmillan that 1956 was the twentieth anniversary of Hitler's occupation of the Rhineland – indeed, they were almost mesmerised by the shadow of the Führer.

The Spectator noted that US Secretary of State John Foster Dulles had suddenly flown to London, assuming that he wanted to make sure Britain and France were not about to do anything that might embarrass President Eisenhower just a few weeks ahead of what he hoped would be his re-election for a second term.

That assumption was correct. Eisenhower's London ambassador had told him the British were determined 'to drive Nasser out of Egypt', and the President had written privately to Eden: 'I hope that you will consent to reviewing the matter once more in its broadest aspects. It is for this reason that I have asked Foster [Dulles] to leave this afternoon to meet your people tomorrow in London.'

But, opined *The Spectator*, Sir Anthony must not allow the Americans to push him around: 'The American government should be made to understand that, even in an election year, the vital interests of Britain and France should be given at least as much consideration as, say, those of the Formosa government.' Reading those words now is like hearing the dying grunt of a long-extinct mammal. Within weeks, reality struck with a dull thud, and no one in London would ever again suggest that an American government be 'made to understand' anything it did not have a mind to understand.

Chancellor of the Exchequer Harold Macmillan was delighted at Dulles's visit. Macmillan, whose real love was foreign affairs, was the leading Cabinet hawk over Suez. With a Foreign Secretary who knew he was not suited to the job – and was being used as a cipher by a sick, tense and overstretched Prime Minister – Macmillan was emerging as the government's chief Suez strategist.

'The chief problem', he wrote in his diary on 31 July, 'is how to fill up the time while our striking force can be got ready.'[129]

On 1 August, Macmillan saw Dulles:

> I told Foster, as plainly as I could, that we just could not afford to lose this game. It was a question not of honour, but of survival. We must either get Nasser out by diplomacy or by force ... I think he was quite alarmed; for he had hoped to find me less extreme, I think. We must keep the Americans really frightened ... Then they will help us to get what we want, without the necessity for force. But we must have (a) international control of the canal (b) humiliation and collapse of Nasser.[130]

Before the end of the year, Macmillan was to understand that Britain would have neither of these requirements, and trying to keep the Americans frightened was one of the rottenest ideas he had ever had. But, in the summer of 1956, even Macmillan – with his excellent American contacts (he and Eisenhower had bonded in north Africa during the war), his sophisticated grasp of history and his sensitive political antennae – simply didn't get it. The British government was going to have to get used to the idea that when Uncle Sam said no, that was that.

By the time he became Prime Minister just six months later, Macmillan got it, and it governed the conduct of his premiership, and that of almost all his successors to this day. That's the measure of the change that 1956 wrought.

Throughout August and September, Macmillan's diaries are full

---

129 *The Macmillan Diaries*, p. 580.

130 Ibid.

of the Suez crisis, and, by October, he was getting very restive. 'The Suez situation is beginning to slip out of our hands,' he wrote in his diary on 4 October:

> I try not to think that we have 'missed the bus' – if we have, it is really due to the long time it has taken to get military arrangements into shape. But we must, by one means or another, win this struggle. Nasser may well try to preach Holy War in the Middle East and (even to their own loss) the mob and the demagogues may create a ruinous position for us. Without oil and without the profits from oil, neither UK nor western Europe can survive.[131]

The government's mind was made up, though ministers already knew they would be leading a divided nation into war. New opposition leader Hugh Gaitskell could hardly have been clearer when he wrote to Eden on 8 August: 'I could not regard an armed attack on Egypt by ourselves and the French as justified by anything Nasser has done so far or as consistent with the Charter of the United Nations.'

Preparing the army for war had to be done somewhat discreetly – the government did not want people to think it had already decided upon war – but they could not disguise the fact that army vehicles were being repainted in desert colours, and that a good few lives were already being disrupted by the drumbeats of war. These were some of them.

Keith Richards had finished his National Service in 1955 and gone to work in his chosen profession, as a teacher at Hendon County Grammar School in north London. But, in the summer of 1956, when

131 Ruth Winstone (ed.), *Events, Dear Boy, Events* (London: Profile Books, 2012), p. 256.

he had planned to take a long summer holiday and congratulate himself on a successful first year in the classroom, he was suddenly recalled, and instead spent the season in uniform in Sussex, being trained for desert combat.

He was allowed to return to school at the end of the summer, and watched resentfully as his colleagues came back relaxed and, in some cases, tanned after a leisurely summer: 'I had been attending terribly dull lectures. They told us it would be hot and sandy. It was a weird feeling of still having the tentacles of the army creeping towards me.'

Donald MacLean (not the spy) had a ruined summer too. Nine years after being released from the wartime Royal Electrical and Mechanical Engineers, he was recalled as a reservist captain:

> I had just three days to delegate work and buy some tropical gear, then say goodbye to my anxious wife and baby. The long hot summer was spent in a camp near the racing stables at Ogbourne St George, doing the fatuous things that armies invent when there is nothing purposeful to do, and listening to reports of the ebb and flow of political posturing.[132]

Stuart Smith was coming to the end of his two-year National Service stint and looking forward to a return to 'civvie street'. A university graduate, he had been offered a promising opening with a Manchester engineering firm and had wedding plans for early 1957.

132 Donald MacLean's blog autobiography, www.the-life-of-me.

Just before he was due to be demobbed, a rumour ran round the camp that the government was considering an extension of National Service because of the crisis. As if to confirm it, his squad was told that they had to prepare 200 lorries for shipment to the Middle East. In the army vehicle depot near Derby, where Stuart was stationed, several thousand army vehicles – the majority of which had been repatriated from Europe and north Africa at the end of hostilities – were parked along the old runways:

> Most of the squad had completed apprenticeships prior to National Service and had good jobs waiting for them; several, like myself, had planned early marriages. None of us wanted to remain in the army [even though] there was a general belief that 'Nasser needed putting in his place' and there was concern that a serious economic crisis would occur if the Suez Canal were permanently blocked. [However,] in the event, National Service was not extended, and in a few short weeks,we had all gone our separate ways, never to meet again.

John Tween was less lucky. He received his call-up papers on the morning of his wedding on Saturday 11 August, telling him to report at once, that very day.

He made some telephone calls, explained to several representatives of officialdom that it was his wedding day, and was eventually given grudging permission to report on Monday. He and his fiancée cancelled their honeymoon in Jersey, married at George Street Congregational Church in Croydon and spent one night together in the Selsdon Park Hotel (which was to become famous fourteen years later, in 1970, as the place where Edward Heath and his shadow Cabinet hammered out the manifesto identified ever after as the product of a hard-faced individual known as 'Selsdon Man'). Then John left for the Middle East.

Still, said Mrs Tween, John got back at Christmas, and the couple 'had nearly fifty-six years of very happy marriage until he sadly passed away in 2012'.

Jenny Field had an even more rushed wedding. Her fiancé was a reservist in the army, and was recalled for service when the threat of a crisis in Suez arose – which looked like the end of their plans for an October wedding.

Then, suddenly, on 15 August, there he was, standing in her office – when she thought he was well on his way to the Middle East. He told her he had just three hours, so could they please get married straightaway?

The senior partner in Jenny's law firm let her have a few hours off work, a local vicar agreed to get her a special licence, Jenny's mother found some papers that were needed because Jenny's surname had been changed by deed poll after her parents' divorce, and she rushed home on a London bus to change into the suit her mother had bought her for the wedding. Jenny's husband-to-be asked her if she had her Post Office savings book with her, so that she could buy her ring until he could repay her.

Jenny takes up the story:

> We literally ran to the church; the vicar was waiting for us; within minutes, my mother arrived with the deed poll certificate and flowers. About half an hour later we were man and wife, with a strict sermon from our vicar that just because we married in haste, the

serious vows we made to each other meant exactly the same as a well-planned wedding.

From the church, we boarded another bus to take us to my husband's home, 6 miles away. His mother was ironing; he laid our marriage certificate on her ironing board and said: 'We've done it, Mum, we got married.' I don't think it pleased her, but she said nothing, not wanting to upset my husband on his embarkation – he had to return to army barracks in just ninety minutes. Bless her, times were very hard, but she made us salmon sandwiches, and opened a bottle of sherry as a toast to us. He flew to Libya that late afternoon and did not return until late December.

'We will be celebrating our fifty-ninth wedding anniversary this August,' wrote Jenny in April 2015.

Oddly, when all these men were being recalled to service and shipped out to the Middle East at enormous expense, the British Army, by some bureaucratic oversight, was sending home men it already had out there. Recently transferred from the canal zone to Tripoli, Lieutenant John Izbicki – just about to fly home at the end of his National Service – listened gloomily to Eden's announcement. 'It looks like I won't be going home after all,' he said to anyone who would listen. 'They're bound to want every soldier who can carry a rifle up front. And I thought I had left Egypt.'

But, he continues: 'I had miscalculated the British Army's unflagging resolve to stick to protocol and procedure. My tickets to fly back to London on 30 October were prepared; my seat booked. There was no question of my staying behind. It was in breach of protocol.' So, while his old comrades were fighting for Port Said, Izbicki was flying home through an electric storm; and the day of the ceasefire was the day he started his journalistic career on the *Manchester Evening Chronicle*.[133]

It's an ill wind that blows nobody any good, and Anne Black remembers that autumn with affection. She was sailing to Australia on board SS *Orion* with her husband of four days so that he could take up a contract with the Australian Navy:

> Everything about shipboard life was exciting and new and very different for a young girl from a Glasgow suburb who'd never been out of Scotland before. Gibraltar and Naples were amazing to me: the sun, the colour of the sea, orange trees, olive trees, and Pompeii to visit. Next stop was to be Port Said, then the Suez Canal; desert and palm trees and warnings of immense heat – how exotic could life get?

But rumours of trouble at Suez meant a change of direction, and the ship received orders to sail for Malta and await further orders there. The canal had been closed: 'The Grand Harbour at Valletta was full of ships, frigates, destroyers, aircraft carriers, passenger ships and cruisers. We were lucky to get ashore and feel the buzz and excitement in the port, as shore leave was stopped for everybody later in the day.'

The captain was told to head for Australia by way of South Africa and the Cape of Good Hope:

> It took six weeks to sail to Sydney instead of the customary three but as it was our honeymoon we just thought we were lucky to be in the wrong place at the right time ... As they sailed out of Valletta harbour, the naval ships had the sailors in their whites, lined up along the decks with military music playing over the tannoys, and

133 John Izbicki, *Life Between the Lines* (London: Umbria Press, 2012), pp. 111–12.

> it felt very moving as those ships sailed past with the young men heading for the unknown.

Preparing an army for a modern war is bound to involve some end-of-an-era moments. During the Second World War, the Lancaster had been Britain's primary bomber, conducting more than 150,000 sorties. Lancasters flew in the Dambusters' raids; Lancasters sank the *Tirpitz*; Lancasters bombed the U-Boat pens of Kiel, Brest, Lorient and Bordeaux in the summer of 1944. Over 7,000 were built, of which more than 3,200 were lost in action. The Lancaster, in the words of Arthur 'Bomber' Harris, head of Bomber Command, was 'the shining sword' of the RAF.

In peacetime, Lancasters had been repurposed as tankers, carriers of freight or mail, and even civilian passenger flights. Some later models were refitted to play their forerunners in the 1955 film *The Dam Busters*. Many were broken up in the late '50s, and, today, fewer than twenty are known to exist – just two of them capable of being flown. The British one, a 1945 model that never took part in any serious action, is part of the Battle of Britain Memorial Flight aerial display team.

On 15 October 1956, the RAF said farewell when D-Delta – the last Lancaster in the service – took her final flight before being sent to the breaker's yard.

Two days later, on 17 October, the world's first power station to generate industrial-scale electricity from nuclear energy was connected to the UK national grid. It made sense if Britain was to go to war over oil: it must have seemed like a way of starting to look after our energy needs in other ways, as well as to place ourselves at the front in the arms race. Located at Calder Hall in Cumbria, adjoining the Windscale nuclear reactors on the site now known as Sellafield, the station was formally switched on by the Queen.

'This new power, which has proved itself to be such a terrifying weapon of destruction,' she said, 'is harnessed for the first time for the common good of our community.' Minutes later, Workington, 15 miles up the coast, became the first town in the world to be supplied with light, heat and power from nuclear energy. Within four hours, the first nuclear electricity had reached London. Britain, people said, was entering upon a new 'atomic age'.

This was a buzz-phrase of the time, applied to everything from architecture and product design to movies like *Forbidden Planet*. There were atomic-age comics, atomic-age typefaces, atomic-age furniture, atomic-age wallpaper – the term even found its way into an English school story. In *Whizz for Atomms* (see Chapter 1), Nigel Molesworth – now described as 'the atomic-age cynic' – hurrahed the nuclear future: '"I think, peason," sa prof. molesworth, gravely, "that we may now conect the cyclotron to the reactor. We shall then be ready for the plutonium –" ... Above them tower the huge atommic PILE which they hav constructed in the MUSICK room.'[134]

Writer Geoffrey Willans may have been more in the know than his readers realised. Although it would be five years before anyone admitted it in public, Calder Hall's primary purpose was not to create electricity for civil use. Its four Magnox reactors (of which two began operating in 1956, the others following in 1958–59) were, at first, chiefly employed in the production of weapons-grade plutonium.

At its peak, Calder Hall delivered four times as much electricity as in 1956, though it remained a relatively small supplier. Originally designed to last twenty years, it operated for more than twice as long, and, before its closure in 2003, was the oldest Magnox power station in the world. Thanks to its four giant cooling towers, it was a landmark along that section of the Irish Sea coast. After the station's closure, and an unsuccessful campaign to preserve them, the towers were demolished

134 Geoffrey Willans and Ronald Searle, *The Compleet Molesworth* (London: Max Parrish, 1958), p. 241.

in 2007. The Calder Hall site is presently being decommissioned – a process that, it is estimated, will continue until the next century.

Real schools in 1956 bore more resemblance to Molesworth's St Custard's than you might imagine. They were often brutal and sometimes primitive, in a way we associate with much longer ago – but, at Archbishop Tenison's, the politics were bang up to date. Richard Rawles was caricaturing Trevor Grundy's fascist group as the Roundheads, while Trevor Grundy was teaching the school's Mosleyites a derisive takeoff of 'The Red Flag' that he had learned from his father:

The red flag is turning pink,
It's not so red as people think.
With gallons of beer and gallons of blood,
We'll drag the red flag through the mud.

Trevor was soon appointed to run Mosley's youth movement, and he took his young protégés from Archbishop Tenison's to the Union Movement's annual dinner above a pub in Victoria. There they met the guest of honour Hans-Ulrich Rudel, one of Hitler's most decorated pilots, who had shot down hundreds of Russian planes on the Eastern Front, and lost both his legs in the process.[135]

In Parliament, the young Labour MP Tony Benn was looking with satisfaction at a hideously frustrated government, desperate to attack Egypt, being told by its military advisers that the army was still not ready. Benn wrote in his diary on 22 October:

> The government are in a terrible mess and they have lost confidence in Eden. The specific problems that confront them are Suez, the

135 Grundy, op. cit., p. 95.

> muddle over defence, the economic crisis and the awful bloodshed in Cyprus. The Labour Party on the other hand is in better shape than it has been since I have been an MP. Hugh Gaitskell has done very well as Leader despite the serious error he made at the start of the Suez crisis. Nye Bevan is Treasurer and has a real chance to make his contribution to the unity of the Party.[136]

Far more significant than what we can read of what Benn wrote that day is what we cannot read of what Macmillan wrote. Macmillan destroyed his diaries from 5 October 1956 to 3 February 1957 – apparently at the request of Anthony Eden.[137]

We shall probably never know the full story they were hiding, but it does not look as though either Eden or Macmillan did much in the next few months that they could later be proud of. October's secret diplomatic activity culminated on 24 October with the signing of the Protocol of Sèvres, a secret agreement between the UK, France and Israel, allowing Israel to invade Sinai with the support of the other two governments.

The plot was this: Israel would attack Egypt across the Sinai; Britain and France would call on both sides to withdraw from the canal; Nasser was sure to refuse, and this would then enable Britain and France to place their armies, supposedly as a peacemaking force, between the Egyptian and Israeli forces – taking control of the canal and humiliating Nasser.

It was hare-brained and dishonest, and ministers acted a little as though they knew it. Meetings were held at which secretaries were asked to withdraw or take no minutes, or at which the minutes were destroyed. When word got out, Eden lied and said the agreement did not exist.

---

136 Winstone (ed.), op. cit., pp. 256–7.

137 *The Macmillan Diaries*, p. 607.

Sèvres must have seemed like a lifeline, for nothing else was going right in the government's Suez planning. Military chiefs were warning that Egypt, with its Soviet and Czech weapons, was far from being a negligible military force. Egypt had shown that it did not intend to close the canal and that Egyptian pilots were quite capable of guiding ships through it – thus removing part of the excuse for attacking the country. There were also increasing expert doubts about the legality of using force against Egypt, and the Labour Party was now firmly opposed to war – as were the Liberals and the Archbishop of Canterbury. Plus, Eisenhower had to face re-election in November and was expected to win, so he was not likely to welcome an international crisis a day or two before polling.

Yet, at the end of September, Macmillan, having been in Washington for a meeting of the International Monetary Fund, came home seemingly convinced he had squared the President. As an old wartime friend and colleague of President Eisenhower, he had the rare privilege of a private audience in the Oval Office.

Eisenhower was very cordial: 'It was just like talking to him in the old days at the St George's Hotel in Algiers.' They reminisced about old times, and talked a little about Suez. Macmillan also met Dulles, who seems to have said that he wanted peace to be kept until the presidential election on 6 November – and emphasised this point by reminding Macmillan that the Americans had helped the Tories at the general election the previous year.

Somehow, Macmillan managed to come away convinced that the Americans would support military action over Suez, and encouraged his Prime Minister's natural propensity to believe the same thing. Roger Makins, ambassador in Washington, was present at the meeting with Eisenhower, and he said later that there was no basis for Macmillan's optimism. The missing section of Macmillan's diaries begins almost immediately after his return to London.

Britain's position was crumbling, but none of those in charge of British policy seemed to have realised it. Even when, towards the end of October, the task force sailed from Malta to Port Said and found itself harassed by the US Sixth Fleet permanently based in the Mediterranean – which shone its searchlights on the British and French vessels and interfered with their radar – the penny seemed not to have dropped. And the legal case for war, as the Cabinet knew, was thin. The government's law officers doubted the legality of the proposed invasion, and a Cabinet minute spelled out the problem:

> The Cabinet agreed that we should be on weak ground in basing our resistance on the narrow argument that Colonel Nasser had acted illegally. The Suez Canal Company was registered as an Egyptian company under Egyptian law; and Colonel Nasser had indicated that he intended to compensate the shareholders at ruling market prices. From a narrow legal point of view, his action amounted to no more than a decision to buy out the shareholders. Our case must be presented on wider international grounds.[138]

And thus it was, at the culmination of President Eisenhower's whistle-stop campaign for re-election, on 27 October, with just ten days to go before polling day, that he heard of Israel's full-scale mobilisation and sent a telegram to Prime Minister Ben-Gurion urging him to 'do nothing to endanger the peace'. Israel invaded Sinai two days later.

The next day, Britain and France issued their ultimatum to Israel and Egypt. Israel accepted it, but advanced nonetheless – and an eager young colonel called Ariel Sharon exceeded his orders, taking all his objectives at once. No one had explained to Colonel Sharon that he was depriving Britain and France of their flimsy excuse to invade by

138 Peter Hennessy, *Having It So Good: Britain in the Fifties* (London: Penguin Books, 2006), p. 426.

completing his mission and ensuring there was no further fighting the European powers could step in and put a stop to.

Egypt, of course, rejected the Anglo-French ultimatum. On 31 October, Britain bombed Egyptian airfields and defence installations.

CHAPTER 11

THE SOVIET UNION: JUST ANOTHER IMPERIALIST

On the day that Colonel Sharon began leading his forces deep into Egyptian territory, journalists at the *Daily Worker*, Britain's communist daily newspaper, were doing something that, just a week earlier, would have seemed unthinkable. They were questioning the party line. They were regretting their 25 October front-page lead story, which began: 'Workers in Budapest factories yesterday formed armed groups to protect the factories and the country against counter-revolutionary formations that had attacked buildings, murdered civilians and tried to start a civil war.' The paper was taking its lead from Budapest Radio, which called the anti-government demonstrators 'fascist, reactionary elements'.

The man who had written that story, Phil Bolsover, felt confused and betrayed. 'The Hungarians do not want the Soviet Army in the country, and to say that is not being anti-Soviet; it is recognising facts. The explanation I wrote was completely wrong,' he told a staff meeting on 29 October – though the line changed a little. The paper discovered belatedly that 'the just demands of the people' were also a factor.[139]

'Why', Bolsover now wanted to know, 'are the majority of the Hungarian people fighting against the "people's government"?'

Producing a daily newspaper is an unforgiving business, and soon the soul-searching had to give way to deadline-meeting; but it resumed two days later, on 31 October, by which time the Soviet Union had announced that its troops would leave Hungary.

The front page that morning told readers: 'The Soviet government said there had been mistakes and misunderstandings in relations between the Soviet Union and the people's democracies.' One journalist, Leo Griffith, said the unsayable: 'The trouble is that there never was a revolution in Hungary. Socialism was imposed on these countries from the outside.' Glasgow correspondent Phil Stein said there was no provision in the Warsaw Pact for calling in Soviet troops in the first place: 'Some of our loyalties have been strained to breaking point.' And another journalist pointed out that the Young Communist League had condemned the use of Soviet troops, but the *Daily Worker* had not reported the fact.

Defenders of the Soviet Union were few on the ground at this long, tortured meeting. One of them was the industrial correspondent George Sinfield, who argued that, if only the staff were not divided, the paper could mount an effective opposition to Eden's Suez adventure: 'If the comrades want a slanging match with *Pravda*, I don't think I could work on a paper that did that.'[140]

---

139 Francis Beckett, *Enemy Within* (London: John Murray, 1995; Merlin Press, 1998), p. 133.

140 Alison Macleod, *The Death of Uncle Joe* (London: Merlin, 1997), p. 133–8.

The paper was bitterly divided in a way that Sinfield had never thought possible – but, on one point at least, they all agreed with him. The *Daily Worker* would have liked to be laying into the government for the Suez invasion, but it was diverted by Hungary – and the journalists felt that even *Daily Worker* readers might wonder why the British invasion of Suez was imperialist while the Soviet invasion of Hungary was not.

There was a wrenching irony in this. The CPGB was unable to make much of its furious opposition to the Suez invasion because of Hungary, and, in much the same way, the government was frustrated at not being able to do much about Hungary because of Suez.

The British government's frustration was nothing beside the frustration on the streets of Budapest. Ferenc Furedi – now the distinguished British sociologist Professor Frank Furedi – was nine, and remembers how much his parents and their friends hoped that the British and Americans would come to the aid of the revolution: 'There was a lot of discussion about Suez. People knew that Suez would detract from Hungary. People felt that Suez could not have happened at a worse time. They felt it was a nail in our coffin and it meant that no one would be interested in us.'

Furedi remembers his father, who was a prominent member of the workers' council (the main trade union organisation in Budapest), sending him out to post clandestine newspapers in the evenings, and giving him official documents of the workers' council to carry, because a child would not be suspected and searched.

His older sister finished high school with excellent results, but was not allowed to go to university because of her father's politics. 'We talked almost two different languages – one at home with people we trusted, another at school and everywhere else,' he says.

Demonstrators on the streets of Budapest demanded, among other things, personal freedom, more food and the removal of the secret police and Russian control. The protest grew to an estimated 200,000, and they marched from Budapest's splendid Parliament building to Radio Budapest to broadcast their demands. There they were met by the Hungarian security forces, who opened fire on the demonstrators.

Furedi remembers that day clearly. His sister took him to the national museum, which was close to the radio station, and, when the shooting started, she hurried him home again. 'At that point, we all thought the revolution would succeed and there was a feeling of exhilaration,' he says.

The next day, Furedi went to play in a local park, and listened to the troubles of a boy he knew quite well. The boy was distressed because his father was in the secret police, and did not know whether to go into hiding.

The government seemed ready to make radical changes: hardline communists were replaced, and Prime Minister Imre Nagy announced that he was ready to negotiate the withdrawal of Soviet troops.

Tony Benn wrote in his diary on 28 October:

> The Hungarian crisis reaching its climax. The spontaneous rebellion against the Communist Government has virtually succeeded. The Iron Curtain has risen and people are moving freely in and out of Hungary with supplies and relief... the red white and green have reappeared to replace the hated scarlet banner of the Communist Government. Everyone in the world is breathless with hope that this may lead to a rebirth of freedom throughout the whole of Eastern Europe.[141]

What Benn may not have understood is that the hopes in Budapest rested largely on an expectation that the British and the Americans

141 Ruth Winstone (ed.), *Events, Dear Boy, Events* (London: Profile Books, 2012), p. 257.

would, when necessary, give armed support to the rebels. Hungarian opponents of the government listened to Radio Free Europe, the CIA-funded propaganda station aimed at Iron Curtain countries, and were certain the West would ensure that their freedom was not snuffed out.

'RFE had an irresponsible role,' says Frank Furedi. 'Everyone listened to it, not to the BBC World Service, and there was more than a hint that we could rely on the West to help and support us.'

The mood in Britain was, however, far from heroic. The idea of war in Suez had been sold to some of the people by a relentlessly jingoistic press, but the chance of selling a war on the European continent was just about nil. The very thought of it was enough to make some otherwise rational people behave very strangely, as twelve-year-old Richard Callaghan discovered. He was called to his headmaster's office and told to go home straightaway:

> I rushed straight home and found Kenny, our housekeeper, packing bags for us to go away. Dad had rung up and told her to take me down to Hove in Sussex for a few days.
>
> An unexpected holiday was not something I was going to worry about, just enjoy. We took the train down from Ashtead, and, in those days, the second part of the journey, from Horsham to Hove, was by steam train – a great thrill for me, being careful not to get smuts from the smoke in my eyes when I looked out of the window, and running up the platform to the front at Steyning to watch the engine taking on water.
>
> We stayed at Kenny's friend's B&B just back from the seafront. It was above a restaurant, which the friend also ran. I remember having my favourite cake of all time: ice-cream cake.
>
> It was not until many years later that the housekeeper explained that Dad had been very worried that the West would declare war

> on Russia when it invaded Hungary to crush the Revolution, and he wanted us well away from London just in case.

Mr Callaghan Senior must have felt vindicated when, on 1 November, Imre Nagy announced that Hungary was withdrawing from the Warsaw Pact, and appealed through the UN to the USA and UK to support it as a neutral state. The hardline Stalinist János Kádár left the government in disgust and established a rival government in eastern Hungary, supported by Soviet tanks. On 4 November, an estimated 1,000 tanks attacked Budapest before dawn. After heavy fighting, Soviet troops entered the city.

Nagy's last appeal for help was broadcast at 5.15 a.m. At 8 a.m., his government was ordered to surrender by noon – or Budapest would be bombed. Less than three hours later, Radio Hungary was silenced, and, just after 1 p.m., Moscow Radio announced: 'The Hungarian counter-revolution has been crushed.'

The UN called for Soviet withdrawal. Nagy was deposed and replaced by Kádár.

Britain was in Suez, and was therefore quite unable to even say anything useful about Hungary. As Violet Bonham Carter wrote in her diary at the time:

> Tanks are moving in everywhere and a massacre is going on. All youth is rising and being mowed down. Children are hurling grenades at tanks. It is an extraordinary example of sublime courage against hopeless odds. Heart-rending. One feels guilty at one's impotence – and our *folly* has distracted the attention of the world from this tragedy. I cannot forgive it.[142]

142 Winstone (ed.), op. cit., p. 259.

Communists whose faith had survived Khrushchev's secret speech were now faced with another hideous dilemma. Geoff Woolfe was fifteen, and his parents were loyal members of the CPGB:

> I remember watching the news with my parents ... they sided with the Russians. My father followed the party line as detailed in the *Daily Worker*.
>
> My father took me to a CP meeting in Watford at the time of the Hungary crisis. I don't remember any of the discussion, but it was quite heated – most of the members there wanted to hear the Russian side of the story and, as far as I know, most local members stayed loyal.
>
> At the time, I was unaware of Peter Fryer's reports that gave a very different story – they were censored by the paper.

It was hardest of all for Peter Fryer. He was the *Daily Worker*'s man in Budapest, and he had a story – a cracker of a story. He eventually managed to find a phone and file it.

He had watched the Russians roll into the city. 'I'd never seen a dead body before,' Fryer said later. 'I saw a crowd of demonstrators and the police just mowed them down with machine guns, including women carrying their children.'

He reported that Soviet troops acted with great brutality, killing wounded people and dragging bodies through the streets as a warning to protestors. An estimated 30,000 people were killed, and another 200,000 fled to the West to escape the Soviet reprisals they expected, leaving behind all they possessed.

Fryer had also met one of his predecessors as the *Daily Worker* correspondent in Budapest, Edith Bone. In 1949, as she was leaving Hungary, Bone had been accused of spying, arrested and detained in solitary confinement without trial for seven years, in appalling conditions. She had developed a series of mental exercises, including reviews of geometry, language and vocabulary, to retain her sanity.

Bone was released during the last days of the Nagy government when a student group briefly seized control of the prison where she was held. Fryer's report was gutted before it appeared in the paper. According to Llew Gardner, then a *Daily Worker* journalist: 'The dispatches became banned reading. Instead of being distributed in the normal way, every copy of his story was rushed to the editor's room. Those who had access were forbidden to speak of what Fryer had written.' Instead of printing what their man on the spot had written, the paper reported that 'gangs of reactionaries began beating communists to death in the streets'.

And no one believed a word of it. Communist historians John Saville and E. P. Thompson – against all communist discipline – had founded a magazine called *The Reasoner*, whose third issue, out just before the tanks arrived in Budapest, said: 'One thing might have restrained the Soviet forces from their final criminal action – an outspoken call from the Communist Parties of the world. In this crisis, when the Hungarian people needed our solidarity, the British Communist Party has failed them.'

The CPGB expelled Thompson and Saville, but the party itself was finished. Some 7,000 people – more than a quarter of the membership – left the CPGB because of the events of 1956. To leave the CPGB was more than just to change your political allegiance; it was to abandon your faith and your friends. Old friends would cross the street to avoid you.[143]

And what about Peter Fryer? He resigned from the paper and wrote his most influential work, a book called *A Hungarian Tragedy*, in ten days. The CPGB expelled him for it, and then this talented and

---

143 Beckett, op. cit.

passionate socialist journalist lost himself in the muddled wasteland of Trotskyist politics – teaming up with Gerry Healy, quarrelling with Gerry Healy, writing some good but largely ignored books, and becoming an authority on black life in Britain (1956 wasted the bravest and the best of its young idealists). He died in 2006, and was posthumously awarded the Knight's Cross of the Order of Merit of the Republic of Hungary.

But did it matter outside the narrow confines of the faithful? Yes, it did. Communism was a home for idealists – pretty well the only one left to them, unless you could believe in the ungainly coalition that was the Labour Party, or you wanted to get involved with one of the permanently warring and confusingly named Trotskyist sects.

Idealism was eventually to find a home outside the political organisations, but, in 1956, Osborne's Jimmy Porter was right. Harry Pollitt would have dismissed his despair as middle-class angst, but there really were no more good brave causes.

In mid-November, the first Hungarian refugees began to arrive in Britain. Judit (she asked us not to give her full name) recalls the atmosphere:

> In November 1956, Radio Free Europe and Voice of America, those two purveyors of information and misinformation, broadcast every evening the number of refugees who managed to cross the border to Austria. Six thousand crossed the border yesterday, ten thousand today. How did they do it? Should we try? Communist propaganda filling our ears for a decade had one sure result: the certainty in our minds that beyond the Iron Curtain was El Dorado.
>
> We might get caught trying to escape, we might be put in prison for a long while, we might even get shot at the border or step on a mine. If the young went and the older generation stayed behind would we ever see each other again?

The same debate was going on in the Furedi household, as Frank Furedi reports: 'We realised everyone was fleeing. We heard about it from Radio Free Europe. My sister said we must go too; my father was at first indecisive.' But, when the decision was made, Furedi's father acted swiftly. He managed to sell everything their house contained, in order to raise the money for rail fares and bribes, and they walked for several days to a house 35 kilometres from the border, sleeping where they could – the first night, in a barn with twenty or so folk on the same mission.

Judit travelled in greater comfort:

> We got in touch with a cousin who had a son of conscription age and was eager to leave with him. Special permission was needed to travel to the border area; this of course we did not have. But my cousin had contacts at the sugar refinery near the border, and my husband carried a letter from his boss at the Institute of Applied Mathematics that he was urgently required at the refinery to solve a mathematical problem.
>
> I put a change of underwear and plenty of warm socks into an old rucksack. My husband stuffed his publications and his unfinished work into a briefcase. Later, in Vienna, we met people who had more foresight and made their escape wearing several shirts.
>
> Next morning we ate a copious breakfast. We left the dishes on the table, there did not seem to be any point in doing the washing up. (The sight of the settings puzzled my mother when a couple of weeks later she entered the flat. She thought that intruders breakfasted there after our departure.)
>
> We caught a tram, arrived in good time at the station and met up with my cousin and her son. As we entered the carriage, we found a couple of young men already seated there. I recognised a friend and his brother. My friend was clutching a large X-ray tube, and,

when asked where he was going, he explained that he was sent to an institute near the border that had to have its X-ray machine repaired. We told them of our mission to the sugar refinery. They left the train a couple of stations after we did and arrived safely in London a few days later. Since then, we celebrate our deliverance together every year with a good dinner.

We were met at Petöháza station by someone from the refinery and were taken to his house. Being late autumn, a pig had just been slaughtered and we had a *pig-wake* dinner: several kinds of fresh sausages, cracklings. We were introduced to our guide and made the necessary financial arrangements with him. Then we retired for the night, sharing the host's best bed, a high affair with a huge eiderdown duvet. They woke us up at four in the morning. We got dressed in the freezing cold and started our walk in complete silence. The ground was frozen solid and crunchy under our feet. On our way we met other defecting parties and walked with them. Coming closer to the canal, the border between Hungary and Austria, whispers went round that a boat was available. The guide volunteered to pay the boatman and asked us for the rest of our money. We gave him whatever we had, and were safely rowed across the canal.

We clambered up on the bank on the Austrian side and made our way to the nearest village, Pamhagen, or Pomogy in Hungarian. The school building was already crowded with refugees sitting or lying on hastily spread straw. It was obvious that some had already spent a few days there waiting for transport. It was Sunday morning and the local council had arranged for the refugees to be invited for Sunday lunch by the more prosperous farmers.

In the evening we managed to get in touch with my cousin in Vienna and he promised to send someone to fetch us in the morning. We bedded down on the straw. Next morning a well-dressed woman picked us up in her car (this was exciting in itself, since in

> Hungary nobody we knew had a car), took us to her home, gave us money for the bus fare and put us on the bus to Vienna. My cousin had booked a hotel room for us.
>
> The next five days passed in a frenzy of activity. First we had to go to the police and register as refugees. There was a long line outside the police station; we spent most of the freezing day there; luckily someone had the kindness to provide seats, so we did not stand in line but sat in line. With our registration certificate we could now make the rounds of the charities. We went to the Joint, where we had to prove our Jewishness by reciting a prayer in Hebrew. I could say the first sentence of the *Shema* and that was enough. We got some money from them. Then we went to the Catholic charity, the Caritas, where we were not asked to say a few Hail Marys, although my knowledge of that and of the Lord's Prayer was much better than that of any Hebrew prayer. Caritas gave us some clothes, a blanket and a small suitcase.
>
> We took ourselves to the Red Cross and asked to be taken to Switzerland where I had further family.

The Furedis spent three or four months in Vienna, deciding where to go. Frank Furedi makes the point that Hungarians in 1956 had far less hardship and suffering than is the lot of most refugees. Most people in the West were sure they had escaped an inhuman tyranny, and perhaps felt guilty at having done nothing to help them: 'We could go anywhere. Any country would let us in. Hungarian refugees in 1956 were treated unbelievably nicely by everyone. We were the poster refugees everyone wanted to help. There was a genuine affection for us.'

Judit's family went first to Switzerland:

> We left Vienna on a cold and overcast morning. We sat on the train all through the night. We were tired but not hungry because every

now and then *Zwischenverpflegung* [snacks] appeared. We stopped in Liesthal and were immediately taken to the barracks and disinfected. We were shown to a large hall where beds in a row stood waiting for us. This was our dormitory for the next three weeks. We were allowed to walk around the compound but not to leave the barrack area. We were given no information as to what was going to happen to us. Strangely, no one objected to this treatment. The only thing people objected to was the macaroni cheese we got for lunch. In Hungary pasta was eaten sweet with walnuts or poppy seeds or jam, never with cheese.

After a few days a school was set up to entertain the children. We made playing cards for ourselves. We had to clean the place but the implements we were given were strange and we misused them to the annoyance of the soldiers guarding us. We did the laundry by hand standing at large tubs.

After three weeks we were free to go and we travelled to Lugano where my uncle and aunt were living. We spent a few weeks in Lugano at the expense of my uncle, then moved to Zürich for a couple of months and finally made our way via Paris to London. We borrowed money from my uncle to tide us over the first few months and meticulously repaid him within six months.

Britain was a culture shock to Hungarians – the more so since they were expecting an earthly paradise. Judit felt let down at Folkestone:

The train we boarded was grimy, the upholstered seats seemed dirty and I refused to sit down on them. The view from the window was disheartening. No hills, no woods, houses everywhere. Little houses in rows with chimneys. How will I be able to live here?

Victoria station was alive with City gents in their uniform of pin-stripe suits, bowler hats, newspapers under their arms and

> umbrellas in their hands. My cousin Milan met us and took us to his house in a suburb of London. His wife opened the front door with a loud 'hello'. Not being used to this greeting I thought it was rude. In Hungary you said 'hello' when you picked the phone up, but you would greet relations who just escaped from communism with more enthusiasm.
>
> DIY was a new experience for us. So was the toilet that we could not flush, the heating that did not exist, and many other British peculiarities. In time, we got used to them.

The Furedis were repelled by the state of Britain as soon as they saw Liverpool, which they passed through en route to Southampton and a boat to Canada (Furedi settled in Britain in 1969, after graduating from McGill University): 'We were shocked at how grim and threadbare Liverpool was compared with Budapest. We felt very pleased that we were not staying in Britain.'

Wartime austerity was still very much in evidence in Britain in 1956. Hungarians – who had heard communist propaganda about how louche and debauched the West was, and Radio Free Europe propaganda about how wonderful free-market capitalism was – were dreadfully disappointed to find a poorer and dingier nation than the one they had left.

And that's before they had tasted the food. Hungarians like rich food and have sophisticated culinary tastes. Food and cooking play a big part in their lives and their conversation, and the dull, sparse, unimaginatively prepared food in Britain came as a shock to them. 'For Hungarians in 1956, the limited food options in Britain were traumatic,' says Frank Furedi.

It worked both ways. Alverie Weighill's father worked for the Ministry of Labour and was seconded to work with male Hungarian refugees who were billeted in prefabricated huts in a wartime camp at Plawsworth, north of Durham city. He got to know them well, and one day the Hungarians invited all the families of the people who worked with them for a meal:

> I was ten and my brother fourteen at the time and like most of my friends I don't think we'd ever met foreigners before and had certainly never eaten foreign food – we were used to meat and two veg, and rice was eaten sweet as a dessert. So to be given rice with meat was completely alien. I did not enjoy the meal but would have eaten it all as we were never allowed to complain about or leave food offered by others.
>
> And, even though communication was very limited, they were so friendly. I certainly remember the event as something rather special, a bit of a privilege. I guess now that they must have been missing their homeland and family life and would of course have been very concerned about the people they'd left behind and their future.

There was a lot of goodwill towards the Hungarian refugees. British propaganda had been more effective than communist propaganda in Hungary: most people were sure the refugees had fled an inhuman dictatorship.

Sandra Reekie's father was the village policeman in Loughton, Essex, and one day he came home and told her that some Hungarian refugees were being put up at Grange Farm, a centre for foreign visitors:

> Clearly my father was moved by their plight so, with my friend Marcia, we searched through our few toys and collected together what we could and held what must have been one of the first garage sales. We raised about £9 as I recall, which we sent off to the Lady Mayoress's Fund.

Meanwhile, Patricia Clipson, a mature student at Birkbeck College, University of London, saw that there was little provision for teenage Hungarian refugees: 'We managed to acquire an empty house on Kingston Hill in Surrey and renovated it, appealing for materials, furniture etc. from manufacturers and suppliers.'

The day after the tanks went into Budapest, on 7 November, the *Manchester Guardian* reported the fate of a much earlier refugee from Soviet power: 55-year-old Prince Alexandre Yourievsky, a grandson of Tsar Nicholas II. For six years he had been working as an £8-a-week storeman in Thornaby-on-Tees, and, in 1932, he had been made bankrupt for £621 9s 1d. He wanted British citizenship, but couldn't have it while bankrupt. Judge Clifford Cohen released him on the condition that he paid £20 in weekly instalments of 10s to the official receiver to cover the costs of his case. He told the paper's reporter that the men where he worked did not know his title and called him Alex: 'I'm sure they would look down on me a little if they knew about the title. I never use it now.'

On the very day that Imre Nagy announced Hungary's withdrawal from the Warsaw Pact and appealed for international support (1 November), a curious transaction took place outside the Royal Exchange in the City of London. The Lord Mayor Alderman Sir Cuthbert Ackroyd gave the Postmaster General Dr Charles Hill a pound note.

They were not settling a debt or a bet. Sir Cuthbert was engaged in probably the most memorable thing he ever did: he was buying a Premium Bond. The first Premium Bond.

The idea – essentially a strategy to control inflation and encourage personal saving – had been presented to the British people in the April Budget. (It was not a new concept: it had been proposed during the First World War, but never implemented.) It was, in effect, a national lottery: the public was invited to purchase from the Post Office numbered £1 Bonds that would be entered in a monthly draw for tax-free prizes. The winning Bonds would be selected by a computer known as ERNIE (Electronic Random Number Indicator Equipment), built by the Bletchley Park team that had created the Second World War codebreaking machine Colossus.

The scheme was launched by the Chancellor of the Exchequer Harold Macmillan, accompanied by the slogan: 'Saving with a thrill.' Before the Lord Mayor and the Postmaster General conducted their small negotiation in the City, the Chancellor stood in Trafalgar Square and told the crowd that Premium Bonds would be 'an encouragement to the practice of saving and thrift by those members of the community who are not attracted by the reward of interest, but do respond to the incentive of fortune. My object is to invite people to save for the chance of a prize.'

Some £5 million worth of Bonds were bought on the first day, and, by the time the first draw was held on 1 June 1957, the public held £82 million in Bonds. Since then, more than £9 billion has been paid out in prizes. The initial top prize of £1,000 rose steadily over the succeeding decades, and now stands at £1 million.

The second Bond was bought by the Mayor of Lytham St Anne's, which was where the office that administered Premium Bonds was located. Until far into the '80s, women who worked there had the privilege of entering an annual 'Miss Premium Bond' competition, held at the civil service sports & social club. These first Bond girls were required to promenade on a catwalk, smile at the judges and answer questions, just like in the 'Miss World' contest.

The enthusiasm of the public for Premium Bonds was not shared by some of the great and good. Shadow Chancellor Harold Wilson dismissed the scheme as 'a squalid raffle' and 'a national demoralisation', though these were not opinions he voiced when he became Prime Minister eight years later. The Archbishop of Canterbury Dr Geoffrey Fisher thought the buying of Bonds 'a cold, solitary, mechanical, uncompanionable, inhuman activity ... all things considered the best course of action is to leave the whole thing alone'.

For all that, Premium Bonds have been an enduring success, outlasting most of the legacies of the Macmillan era. At the time, they competed only with the football pools; today they contend with the National Lottery. But it is estimated that 23,700,000 people in the UK – more than a third of the population – invest £47 billion in Premium Bonds. The odds of winning the top prize are 'slightly worse', in the opinion of the financial expert Martin Lewis, 'than a bookie would give you for an alien landing in Trafalgar Square then tossing a coin that lands on its edge'.[144] And yet, sixty years on, Premium Bonds remain the UK's most popular savings product.

Neither Suez nor Hungary could stop Premium Bonds. But those events did cast a pall on that venerable showbiz institution the Royal Variety Performance (est. 1912). With British troops engaged in Suez, on the afternoon of 5 November, the dress rehearsal just finished, the impresario Val Parnell received a message from the Palace: 'Her Majesty regrets that, in view of the mounting international crisis, she is unable to attend at the Palladium tonight and therefore wishes to send the cast the sincerest apologies.'

Why on earth should her ministers have told her to stay away? It was not as though her advice might be needed on some strategic decision or other; they were all taken by a very small circle, of which Her Majesty was not a part.

Did the government fear that the populace might be appalled at the sight of Her Majesty enjoying the theatre when her troops were about to invade? That, too, sounds implausible.

It seems likely the government had in mind not so much the effect in Britain but the effect in Washington. The very next day was the US

---

144 Martin Lewis, 'The Truth Behind NS&I Premium Bonds', *Daily Telegraph*, 4 February 2015.

presidential election, at which President Eisenhower was expected to be re-elected, and perhaps it had belatedly occurred to Eden and Macmillan that Eisenhower might not be entirely pleased at what they had done; and that it might be as well not to give him the impression of a partying nation. Since the Eden government went to such lengths to cover its tracks, we will never know for certain.

Headlining the Royal Variety Performance was Liberace, still smarting from the trashing he had received from the *Daily Mirror*. This new blow was too much, and he collapsed weeping into the arms of Gracie Fields, 'watched', as Gracie's biographer David Bret notes, 'by a bemused Vivien Leigh and Laurence Olivier'. Bret continues:

> More hilarity was provided by the comic Jimmy Wheeler, who barged into the master dressing room brandishing his violin and announced at the top of his voice: 'I've been rehearsing this fucking piece for a fortnight, so somebody's going to hear it!' This brought a smile to Liberace's face, and he, Gracie and the Crazy Gang ... commandeered the Palladium kitchen and made tea.

Later they decamped to Winifred Atwell's place and partied until the early hours.[145]

Olivier was no stranger to transatlantic temperament, having spent a good deal of 1956 trying to work with the wayward Marilyn Monroe on the set of *The Prince and the Showgirl*, a period romcom (as they didn't then call it) adapted by Terence Rattigan from his stage play *The Sleeping Prince*. Olivier thought Monroe desperately needed direction but was not willing to take it from him. Monroe found Olivier overbearing and intimidating, and preferred to take advice from a

145 David Bret, *The Real Gracie Fields: The Authorised Biography* (London: Robson Books, 1995), pp. 155–6 in 2010 paperback edition.

woman friend she had brought with her – advice Olivier considered pretentious and worthless, based on the American acting technique called the Method, which Olivier despised.

Olivier, who had been flattered at first because the mega-star wanted him to direct her, concluded contemptuously that Monroe was not an actress but a model.

Monday 5 November also saw the first episode of one of TV's great perennials, *What the Papers Say*. It would run for fifty-two years, first on Granada and ITV, and subsequently on Channel 4 and BBC Two. The idea was to offer an insider's view of how the week's news had been treated in the British press. Quotes from newspaper articles, or their headlines, would appear on screen, an actor would read them out, and the presenter – almost always a journalist – would comment on them, sometimes disapprovingly, sometimes disbelievingly, wherever possible wittily. As a format, it was as immovable as *Desert Island Discs*.

What the Papers Say 'was one of the main reasons I became a journalist', recalls Jim White of the *Daily Telegraph*, who presented it on and off for twelve years. 'It seemed the most glamorous programme on TV.' In the early days, it was frequently presented by Brian Inglis of *The Spectator*. Among other press people who took that role were Paul Foot, Janet Street-Porter, Simon Hoggart and Ian Hislop. The show finally left TV in 2008, but was revived on Radio 4 two years later, and has remained there ever since.

Meanwhile, a scholarship boy from Gloucestershire, in his first term at New College, was beginning to make his mark in the

Oxford Union, speaking from the floor for the motion: 'Modern man does not require religious belief in order to be moral.' Actually 'boy' is not quite right: he was twenty-one and had just come from a couple of years' National Service, learning Russian (as Alan Bennett had, a year before him) in order to work in the intelligence corps. The young man's debut in the debating chamber was described by the Oxford magazine *Isis* as 'an excellent maiden speech'. Within a couple of years, Dennis Potter would be one of the leading figures in the Union and editor of *Isis*.[146]

Almost forty years on, he would look back on this period with a mixture of affection and infuriation in his six-part TV drama *Lipstick on Your Collar*, shown on Channel 4 in 1993.

The play is set in 1956. There are glimpses of Pathé newsreels about the Rainier–Kelly wedding, the arrival in London of Liberace and the Motor Show. Characters visit the 2i's Coffee Bar. The principal setting, inspired by Potter's own experience and rendered with gleeful malice, is a department of the War Office dedicated to the translation and analysis of Russian material, where young clerks relieve their boredom by dreaming of girls and pop music. Since it's Potter, the girls are unfailingly nubile and frequently naked, and the music is flawlessly evocative of the '50s.

The song 'Lipstick on Your Collar' actually dates from three years after the events of the drama. This seems to Potter's biographer W. Stephen Gilbert to be 'embarrassing' and 'illustrat[ing] the lack of proper rigour in its making'.[147] At a remove of several decades, such a small anachronism seems trivial. Potter's manipulations of musical meaning and gesture, in this as in *Pennies from Heaven* and *The Singing Detective*, are inventive and dramatically apt; to require them

146 W. Stephen Gilbert, *Fight & Kick & Bite: The Life and Work of Dennis Potter* (London: Hodder & Stoughton, 1995), pp. 51ff.

147 Gilbert, op. cit., p. 285.

also to be discographically precise is a failure of imagination. If it comes to that, some other featured songs aren't from 1956 either, but from a few years either side.

Hovering over this characteristically Potteresque tale of love and lust, chapel-goers and cinemagoers, is, as in *The Entertainer*, the slowly gathering storm cloud of Suez – the end of the world and all that that entails, as Peter Cook would say in *Beyond the Fringe*. To some, the kicking away of one of the props of empire really did seem that momentous and that shocking. Potter's office chief Col. Bernwood, lifting his head from his hands, says: 'Something has happened to us. As a people, I mean. I never thought I'd live to see the day. Or rather the night. The long, long night. The darkness and the shame.'

But Potter is more concerned with the young lovers, the new world they yearn for, and the music that will lead them towards it. In the closing speech he gives to the young clerk Hopper (Ewan McGregor in his first screen role), he tells us what that music is:

> The sort where moon don't rhyme with June, and you're not up to your backside in bloody buttercups. Songs that aren't about your mum and dad. A bit rough, a beat that busts up the old way, the old stodge, the empire and knowing your place and excuse me and the dressing up and doing what you're told.

A better definition of the meaning of 1956 it would be hard to find.

CHAPTER 12

EDEN AND MACMILLAN'S GREATEST FOLLY

By the end of October, Colonel Ariel Sharon was reporting to chief of staff General Moshe Dayan that the attack on Egypt was succeeding beyond all expectations. Egypt's poorly led army was in full retreat.

The politics seemed to be going swimmingly as well. Britain and France had issued a joint ultimatum to Egypt and Israel to cease fire and withdraw to a distance 10 miles from the Suez Canal, and Egypt, on cue, had told them to get lost. Grumblings were coming from the White House, but Eden and Macmillan were supremely confident that, in the end, they could square their old wartime chum Ike.

The only problem appeared to be whether Britain and France could scramble over there fast enough to engage the Egyptian Army, and force them to make peace, before peace broke out anyway.

On the last day of October, British bombers attacked military airfields in Egypt, and, within days, had grounded – and more or less destroyed – the Egyptian Air Force. Within forty-five minutes, all Egyptian resistance on the airfield had been overcome, and Royal Naval helicopters were bringing in supplies.

Resistance at home was not so easily overcome. On the popular British TV talk show *Free Speech*, there was an especially bitter debate in which the historian A. J. P. Taylor and the Labour journalist (and future party leader) Michael Foot accused the other panellist, Tory MP Robert Boothby, of being a 'criminal' for supporting the war. On 1 November, the day that Soviet tanks rumbled into Budapest, an opposition motion of censure on the government's Middle East policy was tabled in the House of Commons. It was defeated, of course, but this was a war that did not have cross-party support.

As the *Manchester Guardian* reported:

> A passionate debate in the House of Commons was to have been foreseen, but it released more violent anger on the part of the Opposition than anyone could have expected; more, indeed, than has been experienced for years ... the gravest in its content that the House of Commons has heard for a long time. When before has the Leader of the Opposition (or anyone else) been able to report of an act of government policy that it does not command the support of the Commonwealth countries – that India condemns it; that the Canadian government regrets it, and its foreign secretary says it was not consulted in advance about it; that Australia has been unable to support the British government in the Security Council; that the Prime Minister of New Zealand also regrets what has been done?

The Labour Party opposition, said its leader Hugh Gaitskell, would use every constitutional means to oppose this 'reckless war'.

Eden was booed as he came into the chamber. 'Let it be said, however,' reported the *Manchester Guardian*, 'that the Prime Minister was not in the least daunted.' He was 'self-possessed, firm and unapologetic', and asked: 'Does anyone think we could await [the UN Security Council]?'

A Labour member shouted, 'Yes: Eisenhower.'

Eden said:

> I have been accused of living in the past and being obsessed with the events of the 1930s. However that may be, is there not a lesson to be learned from that period which cannot be ignored – that you best avoid great wars by taking even physical action to stop small ones. Everyone knows that the United Nations is not yet in a position to do that. We and the French had forces available.

The Labour motion is interesting even today – it could have been moved in exactly the same terms at the time of the Iraq War nearly half a century later, except, of course, for the bit about straining the Atlantic Alliance:

> That this House deplores the action of Her Majesty's Government in resorting to armed force against Egypt in clear violation of the United Nations Charter, thereby affronting the convictions of a large section of the British people, dividing the Commonwealth, straining the Atlantic Alliance, and gravely damaging the foundations of international order.

The Prime Minister, as prime ministers do on these occasions, accused Labour of betraying 'British troops going into action'. The *Daily Mail* led the cheers for the war with a 2 November headline 'Nasser's army routed', a report of the House of Commons debate headed 'Eden triumphs with record 69 majority' and a front-page editorial that described the invasion as 'a police action': 'Britain has not sent a force to the Middle East to punish Egypt or Israel, but to hold the ring between them. She is trying to prevent a big war by stopping a small one.' By contrast, a headline inside the paper talked of 'the murder of Hungary'.

The nation, like the House of Commons, was bitterly divided. And so were the men at the front. Donald MacLean was one of them and, among his comrades, he made no secret of his view that it was a ghastly mistake.

Having left the army nine years previously and gone to work at the BBC, MacLean had been recalled to lead a small 'press communications' unit of Royal Signals, which aimed to help journalists to cover the conflict. He was flown to Malta

> [in an] old Hastings aircraft, full of sleepy, khaki-clad figures and kitbags. My envelope was marked: 'Secret – not to be opened until arrival.' I opened it immediately. It contained a cryptic message about reporting urgently to 'CSO at UKHQ'. I answered Pete's enquiry with: 'Can't tell you ... our destination's so secret they've omitted it.'

In Malta he boarded a ship:

> Vehicle ferries on the Irish Sea at the time were ex-wartime tank landing ships. One of them, like me, had been press-ganged back into service and had spent the summer (with our untested vehicles baking in its hold) in the Grand Harbour of Malta. I joined it that afternoon. The next morning we were at sea and sailing eastward at a snail's pace in an armada stretching to the horizon.

> The temperature rarely dipped to 90 degrees even at night. Flying fish were spectacular. BBC World Service was reporting widespread public opposition to military action – and ministerial condemnation of the BBC for reporting that.

The BBC always gets it in the neck when there's a military adventure on – exactly the same thing happened almost half a century later when Tony Blair led Britain to war in Iraq.

> Sweating with me in the tiny ward-room were two professional infantry officers. We argued constantly. Their theme was: 'Why all this discussion – we need to teach the wogs a lesson, let's get on with it.' I suggested this was precisely why the UN had been created and that our intervening might be counter-productive and cause the canal to be blocked (it was) – but their mind-set was still in the imperial era.[148]

Nineteen-year-old Hugh Armstrong of the Royal Navy was in another ship in that great armada, HMS *Forth*. He too had not been told where they were going. Starved of news from home, he did not know of the anti-war protests in London, but he knew what he thought:

> The action was relatively popular among the crew, not a view I shared. The Soviet invasion of Hungary had stopped me in any communist leanings but shades of empire were too much. I was threatened with court martial for expressing my views. We were called to action stations up to seven times a day, usually because birds showed up on the radar as suspicious blips.

148 Donald MacLean's blog autobiography, www.the-life-of-me.

On 3 November, Egypt seized the property of the Anglo-Egyptian Oilfields Company. That day, Hugh Dalton wrote in his diary: 'House of Commons ... adjourns in uproar. Loud booing, and gestures at Eden, cries of "Resign", "Go" and "Get out".'[149]

On 4 November, at an anti-war rally in Trafalgar Square attended by 30,000 people – making it easily the biggest rally in London since 1945 – the Labour shadow Foreign Secretary Aneurin Bevan accused the government of 'a policy of bankruptcy and despair':

> We are stronger than Egypt, but there are other countries stronger than us. Are we prepared to accept for ourselves the logic we are applying to Egypt? If nations more powerful than ourselves accept the absence of principle, the anarchistic attitude of Eden and launch bombs on London, what answer have we got, what complaint have we got? If we are going to appeal to force, if force is to be the arbiter to which we appeal, it would at least make common sense to try to make sure beforehand that we have got it, even if you accept that abysmal logic, that decadent point of view.
>
> We are, in fact, in the position today of having appealed to force in the case of a small nation, where if it is appealed to against us it will result in the destruction of Great Britain, not only as a nation, but as an island containing living men and women. Therefore I say to Anthony, I say to the British government, there is no count at all upon which they can be defended.
>
> They have besmirched the name of Britain. They have made us ashamed of the things of which formerly we were proud. They have offended against every principle of decency, and there is only one way in which they can even begin to restore their tarnished reputation and that is to get out! Get out! Get out!

149 Ruth Winstone (ed.), *Events, Dear Boy, Events* (London: Profile Books, 2012), p. 257.

The crowd in Trafalgar Square chanted: 'One, two, three, four, we won't fight in Eden's war' and 'Eden must go!' They marched to 10 Downing Street and tried to storm it. The clashes between police and demonstrators, captured by TV cameras, had a demoralising effect on the Cabinet, which was meeting there.

Michael Rosen, the children's writer, remembers that day:

> I am in Trafalgar Square for an anti-Suez War demonstration. I'm ten years old, and I'm with my parents and my older brother and another family, the Flowers – two boys about the same age as me and my brother.
>
> Aneurin Bevan is speaking and my parents seem glad he's speaking. We're standing by the fountain that is on the left of the square looking out from the National Gallery. Waves of sound come out of the speakers and my father and mother are nodding appreciatively.
>
> Suez? The *Daily Worker* had shown a picture of Egypt from a few days earlier and it showed, as I remember, Port Said, bombed by 'our' side. 'Their' side wouldn't show this, the paper had said.
>
> Bevan spoke on. I played with the water. I didn't understand what he was saying.
>
> Suddenly the brother of the dad in the other family appeared – John. He looked grave. He tightened his lips.
>
> 'They've gone in,' he said.
>
> The family group stopped listening to Bevan.
>
> 'The tanks are in Budapest,' John said.
>
> My dad seemed shocked. He brushed his hand up over his forehead into his hair.
>
> Budapest? Budapest? Is that in Egypt? I wondered. No, my brother and I often used to play capital cities quizzes. Hungary. So why would they send in tanks to Budapest if they were at war with Egypt over the Suez Canal?

> I knew, from often being in situations like this, where my parents spoke in some kind of shorthand about world affairs, that there was no point in asking questions yet.
>
> Later, I got it. The Russians. The Russian tanks had gone into Budapest. It was nothing to do with Suez.
>
> Well, except that it was.
>
> And of course, looking back, that moment, when John Flower said, at a demonstration about the Suez War, 'They've gone in,' represented a moment in the history of the left that broke up many of the certainties and allegiances that had kept it stuck together for fifty years.

That same day, Eden broadcast to the nation – and opposition leader Hugh Gaitskell demanded a right of reply. His emissary Tony Benn did a good deal of arm-twisting with the BBC, and Gaitskell put out a statement that he would be replying, so that everyone would know that, if he were to be refused airtime, it was because he had been gagged by the government.

Gaitskell got his broadcast. It was an extraordinary situation. Normally opposition leaders row in behind the government at times of war – and the *Daily Mail* questioned whether he should have been allowed to broadcast – but to suppress Gaitskell's fiercely anti-war view would be to suppress the view of a great many people.

'We have violated the Charter of the United Nations,' Gaitskell told the nation:

> In doing so, we have betrayed all that Great Britain has stood for in world affairs ... Only one thing can save the reputation and honour of our country. Parliament must repudiate the government policy. The Prime Minister must resign. The Labour Party cannot alone achieve this. We are a minority in the House of Commons. So the

> responsibility rests with those Conservatives who like us are shocked and troubled by what is happening and who want a change.

It seemed as though 1956 was going to signal one of those shifts of the tectonic political plates that Jim Callaghan identified in 1979 – the sort that had marked the general elections of 1905 and 1945 – and if it, or even 1967, had been an election year, it probably would have done. Labour had put its internal war behind it. At the party's annual conference the previous month, Hugh Gaitskell had finally brought Nye Bevan into the tent, and had made him shadow Foreign Secretary, and Bevan and Gaitskell were both genuinely shocked by what Eden had done – even though they still did not know the full story, for they knew nothing of the Israeli conspiracy.[150]

There were student demonstrations all over the country. Anyone who thinks the '60s invented student demonstrations should look at the pictures of Manchester University students, among others, marching through their city with banners and placards on 1 November 1956.

The literary critic D. J. Taylor wrote:

> Surely no writer with even the vaguest interest in politics could fail to be moved by the fight for Nasser's canal, or be in any doubt that it symbolised the loss of Britain's ability to exercise influence over its more powerful allies, and the collapse of the Butskellite consensus? In reality, novelists do not seem to have been greatly concerned by Suez. Kingsley Amis attended a Labour Party meeting on the crisis, but played down its importance, for which he was roundly rebuked by a hot young radical named Paul Johnson [later editor of the *New Statesman*, later still a convert to Thatcherism]. A *Times Literary Supplement* editorial of the time lamented the

150 Brian Brivati, *Hugh Gaitskell* (London: Richard Cohen Books, 1996), pp. 277–8.

> fact that young writers seemed too committed to a sceptical and empirical attitude to be roused by political causes.[151]

Even the Conservative Party was not united behind the action. The Conservative-supporting *Spectator*'s editorial that week said:

> A time may come when a nation can only do what it has to do; when treaties and technicalities are swept away on the surge of events. That time, the government decided on Monday, has arrived. [But] was the action taken appropriate? And if so, was it timely? The answer to both questions, it is now clear, is – no.

At the very moment Bevan was speaking, President Eisenhower was mobilising a force far more frightening to the British government than British public opinion. For the first time ever, the USA combined with the Soviet Union at the United Nations to condemn Britain and France. Britain had to use its veto in exactly the same way as the Soviet Union had done in the past – and been roundly condemned for it by Britain.

Eisenhower hated the fact that the British had forced him to rely on the Soviet Union just as it was crushing Hungarian freedom. He blamed the bumbling British for the Hungarian disaster too – and with some justice, for it was part of the Soviet leaders' calculation that the West was too distracted with Suez to oppose them effectively. Eisenhower had been placed in the position of sending out very similar messages to Eden and Bulganin, asking them to withdraw their forces.

The next day, 5 November (Guy Fawkes Day), soldiers of the

---

151 D. J. Taylor, *After the War: The Novel and English Society Since 1945* (London: Chatto & Windus, 1993), pp. 81–2.

Parachute Regiment dropped onto El Gamil airfield, while French paratroopers landed south of the Raswa bridges and at Port Fuad.

That day, Donald MacLean's ship reached Port Said, just in time to watch RAF jets blasting the town with rockets and the Commandos swarming out onto the beach:

> A hail of bullets clattered around us every few minutes, answered by tracers arcing up to the many rooftops whence the sniper fire was coming. I guessed that UKHQ [where he had been told to report] might be the Canal Company office and on the way there the jeep was fired on – getting my head down rapidly I smashed my front teeth on something.
>
> When I got there, no one was expecting us. The building was empty. Watching the battle through a broken window it became apparent that we were ahead of the game – it was almost an hour before three armoured cars bumbled into the courtyard and a squad of infantrymen 'secured' UKHQ.
>
> By the end of World War II, several war correspondents had achieved legendary stature by their bravery as well as their reporting – and they all seemed to be there. I was besieged by these daunting characters, each demanding a table and a typewriter, which we could give them – and communication with London and Washington, which we could not. I contrived a temporary solution involving a 'borrowed' aeroplane and a cable office in Cyprus ... and the less said about that very unofficial operation the better.
>
> With radio communication established, I visited one of the majestic battleships anchored offshore, where a naval dentist conjured up my first set of dentures and I had my first shower in weeks. I was urged to stay for dinner but one look at the room with its white-coated stewards and gleaming silver sent me, in my filthy battledress, back ashore to my hard-working colleagues and baked-beans in a billycan.

While we Brits had apparently elected to invade this downtown part of Port Said our gallant French comrades were installed in the upmarket area across the canal entrance – Port Fuad – with its broad avenues and night clubs and, well, the sort of recreational support required by the city's new upper class of well-paid canal-pilots.

There was a rumour that the Royal Navy were shipping fresh water daily to our allies' warships, whose starboard cisterns were filled with a well-known product of Burgundy and the port ones with a demi-sec white from the Loire valley.

Shortly, the spasmodic sniping paused – discouraged by enthusiastic responses from our infantry colleagues. During the lull, I dared to explore a little of the city. I ventured inside a small temple that dominated the square behind our base on the beach-head, and was appalled by the luxurious interior. Every bit of intricate plasterwork seemed decorated with gold leaf. I find it very hard to accept that families who cannot afford to feed their children nevertheless fund the obscene extravagances of their religion.

Only days after that we were subjected to sniper fire which emanated from the roof of the temple. I requested advice from the infantry. Three stocky Glaswegian members of a venerable Scots regiment cocked their Sten guns and disappeared in the direction of the temple.

Half an hour later they returned and said, 'Ye'll no be having ony mair trouble from that direction, sir.' I thanked them, adding, 'I hope you didn't need to shoot anyone?' Their corporal said, 'Och no, that wisnae necessary.' As they departed, I thought they were smiling. Moments later there was an almighty explosion and the whole temple crumbled into dust and rubble. When my time comes, I hope Saint Peter will know that that wasn't my idea.[152]

---

152 Donald MacLean's blog autobiography, www.the-life-of-me.

Sharing the Canal Company office with him was Bob Ball and the rest of the editorial staff of 2 *Corps News*, which aimed to keep the soldiery supplied with such information as it was good for them to have. Bob had been called up as a reservist in August 1956, and allocated to a small group of six, whose role in the event of hostilities was to produce a small daily newspaper for distribution to army units in Port Said.

'We were based in Canal Company House right by the side of the canal within sight of the ships,' he says:

> The captain organised and supervised the operation and was responsible for resources. One of the three sergeants had the task of news gathering and writing reports, one translated the main articles into French and the third was tasked with the daily distribution of the published newspaper to units based around Port Said. My role was to find fill-in pieces and to oversee the physical production using typewriters, Gestetner skins and a duplicator. The paper was normally put to bed by 2 a.m.

The newspaper – usually four sides of A4 paper – was first published in Port Said on Remembrance Day.

Arriving on HMS *Forth*, Hugh Armstrong counted seventy ships in Port Said, mainly British and French ones, and saw plumes of oily smoke from the land. He heard afterwards that the US Navy ships were within 100 miles, because that entitled the crews to danger payments.

HMS *Forth* tied up to the quay by the old Navy House. The canal was blocked by vessels the Egyptians had sunk:

> It appeared that war planning hadn't foreseen that, as lifting craft had to be despatched from the UK. We got ashore twice in the two months at Port Said, but were allowed only in pairs. The town was

regarded as dangerous and it was known that an army lieutenant had been kidnapped and died.

The Egyptians had withdrawn their planes to the south of the country, but small depth charges were set off routinely to discourage any frogmen. Life on the ship was pretty normal and the war didn't stop the Egyptian sellers of trinkets doing business. I was fooled in[to] buying a photo album that I eventually threw overboard in disgust.

John Knox, a National Serviceman who was working as a mechanic in the navy, was on board HMS *Dalrymple*, moored at Valletta, Malta, and diverted from a planned Tobruk survey to 'Operation Musketeer' – the codename for the Suez invasion – on 27 October:

I could see Royal Naval ships, of all sizes, to the horizon in all directions. My letters during this time were read by a censor and never reached my parents who were anxious and waiting for news.

The crew was informed that our mission was to support other armed services which would retake the canal. *Dalrymple*'s role would be to help to clear wrecks sunk in the harbour and entrance to the canal itself.

As the ship approached Port Said the hatches were battened down and all internal doors secured to make each compartment watertight. No unnecessary crew were allowed on deck. In fact there was no danger as the Egyptians had no warships and no aircraft. Before we reached Port Said on 6 November 1956, crew members were allowed on deck in turn to see our jets overhead and huge columns of smoke rising from the Egyptian oil tanks they had attacked.

There then was a brief period of army occupation of Port Said and the ship got down to work on clearance of wrecks.

There was not much in the way of entertainment but there was

> a forces' concert on a shore beach featuring Lita Roza, who had the sort of reception performers must dream about. There were attempts to play football on the beach but they failed because of the soft sand and nearby helicopters.
>
> The Egyptians were not entirely passive. An army lieutenant went missing in Port Said. His dead body was found in a bricked-up alcove in the town.
>
> The feeling of the crew was that 'we should have finished the job'. I don't recall any serious discussion among crew members about the issue or that we had any indication of the political dissent in London, the nature of the American pressure, the Israeli involvement or the Russian suppression of the Hungarian revolt. We had the outdated mindset of British imperial power.

The war was being won, yet nothing but harm was being done, said the *Manchester Guardian* leader on 5 November:

> Not until the government has been changed can British military operations be stopped. The United Nations twice in three days has called upon Britain and France to halt their attack on Egypt, but Sir Anthony Eden has refused ... Plainly the present government will not turn back from its disastrous course. If and when a new government is formed, it can consider how to meet the United Nations wishes.

Gaitskell called on dissident Tories to help him get rid of Eden, and pledged to work with a new Conservative Prime Minister who wanted to bring the troops home.

Even the *Daily Mail* thought it was 'a tragedy that Britain intervened in Egypt when world attention should be fully focussed on Hungary'. However, no blame was attributable to the government, and the *Mail*'s US correspondent Don Iddon speculated that Americans might refuse to re-elect President Eisenhower because of his failure to support the British: 'The Egyptian crisis and the holocaust in Hungary give Adlai [Stevenson, the Democratic candidate for President] an outside chance.' This was pretty desperate stuff, since Adlai Stevenson, if elected, would certainly have proved at least as hostile to Eden's Suez adventure as Eisenhower, if not more so, and Mr Iddon was forced to admit two days later that 'a last-minute landslide of votes attributed to the international crisis have given the old war leader [Eisenhower] victory in today's presidential election'. The headline over his think piece on the election was: 'Cease fire rocketed votes for Ike the Peacemaker.'

On 6 November, the sea- and helicopter-borne assault went in. Royal Marine Commandos, together with British and French airborne forces, supported by British tanks, soon defeated the Egyptian forces, capturing men, vehicles and many of the newly purchased Czech-manufactured weapons.

They were just in time. That very day, a ceasefire was announced, demanded by UN secretary general Dag Hammarskjöld with the backing of President Eisenhower on the last day of his re-election campaign. The Anglo-French forces had reached El Cap, just south of Port Said, but were not yet quite in control of the entire canal. Militarily, the operation was a great success.

But Chancellor of the Exchequer Harold Macmillan reported to the Cabinet a serious run on the pound, orchestrated deliberately in Washington, where sterling was being sold vindictively. Britain's gold reserves had fallen by an eighth, and only a ceasefire by midnight would bring American support for an IMF loan to prop up the pound. The IMF would not even allow Britain to withdraw her own money until it had begun its withdrawal from Suez.

The Americans also refused to sell oil to Britain, which, when the canal was not usable and several Middle East pipelines were out of action, would bring Britain to its knees, even without the attacks on the pound.

The day after the ceasefire, 7 November, President Eisenhower was re-elected, and the roof fell in on the British government. Eisenhower now knew that – just six days before polling day in the presidential election, without telling him – his old Conservative friends in Britain had thrown sand in his face. He knew that they had been lying to him for months. He was concerned about the image of the US in the Arab world. And he had stood as the President for peace.

His wrath was terrible. He had had to contain it while campaigning for re-election, confining himself to statesmanlike sentences such as: 'We do not accept the use of force as a wise or proper instrument for the settlement of international disputes.' But those close to the President reported that, whenever he could get away from the campaign trail and be private, he filled the air with 'barrack-room language' about the British government.

It is very hard to see just how Eden and Macmillan failed to predict this. Their position was now dreadful. Eden's troops may have been in Nasser's backyard, but Eisenhower's tanks were on Eden's lawn. The Chancellor, who had spent months plotting to get Britain into Suez, told the Cabinet the day after they had landed that they must come out at once because of the collapse of sterling. Then he heard that the UN was threatening oil sanctions: 'Macmillan held up his hands and theatrically exclaimed, "Oil sanctions! That finishes it!"'[153] Harold Wilson's jibe that Macmillan had been 'first in, first out' of Suez was wounding because it was absolutely true.

Two days later, a new British ambassador presented himself at the White House. Eisenhower read him a letter he had received from Imre

153 Clarissa Eden, *A Memoir* (London: Orion, 2007), p. 254.

Nagy saying that, had it not been for the invasion of Egypt, the Hungarian uprising would have succeeded.

Donald MacLean went home in luxury:

> I escaped the rubble and fleas of Port Said to be transported home in an almost empty luxury liner, SS *Asturias*. The premier stateroom was a suite of generous proportions and as I sat on its private terrace with a cold Daiquiri to hand and a lovely Swedish girl manicuring my broken fingernails, the danger and discomfort of the previous weeks began to recede. Had I not wanted to be home for Christmas I might have wished for the snail's-pace of the outward journey.[154]

But while Donald MacLean was sipping his daiquiri, his country's victory was disappearing like water down a plughole.

On 7 November, the UN demanded withdrawal of British, French and Israeli troops. Eden, trying desperately to salvage something from the wreckage, said he wanted to stay and clear the canal, and use his control of part of the canal as a bargaining counter. Nasser refused to allow the canal to be cleared, and refused to negotiate 'as long as there is a single foreign soldier left on Egyptian soil'.

Israel asked to be allowed to hang on to Sinai and the Gaza Strip, and France was in favour of allowing it, but Britain was forced to promise to ensure that Israeli forces were withdrawn. Israeli Prime Minister David Ben-Gurion felt Britain had betrayed him, but had little choice: he did what Eden asked of him.

Also on 7 November, Noël Coward's play *Nude with Violin* opened at London's Globe Theatre, and, on 8 November, judicious last-minute changes were made to the script. Its leading actor and director John Gielgud later wrote to Coward: 'We removed [references to] "Cairo"

---

154 MacLean, op. cit.

and "Port Said" last week. I felt the audience chill as we uttered them. (We have already had to change "Cyprus" in *The Chalk Garden*, first to "Suez" and then – hastily – to "Potsdam".)'[155] This tact was uncharacteristic of Gielgud. More typical was his remark in front of the company when Coward came into rehearsal: 'We've been working like blacks,' he said. Then, remembering the West Indian actor Thomas Baptiste, added, 'Not your kind of black of course, Tommy.'[156]

But the changes to the script were probably just as well. Noël Coward's audiences were not like John Osborne's; they did not like controversy. 'The kind of audience that goes to a Noël Coward play in mild and middlebrow expectation was not let down,' wrote Philip Hope-Wallace, reviewing *Nude with Violin* in the *Manchester Guardian*.

On 10 November, the *Daily Mail* did its best for Eden with a story headed: 'Reds had master plan to seize canal.' An 'intelligence expert' had apparently discovered a Russian plot to seize the canal and make Egypt a Soviet satellite, which was fortunately pre-empted by the British invasion of Suez. But no evidence of this plan has emerged in the last half century or so.

Nasser did agree to accept a UN force, and some British servicemen were told to stay and exchange their British Army uniform for a UN one. Hugh Armstrong was among them:

> We were issued with marines' boiler suits minus badges as civilian gear and transferred to HMS *Striker*, a tank landing craft, as the British and French ships departed. It was an uncomfortable day as the Egyptians blew up the de Lesseps statue and we tried to be invisible although directly across the harbour from the action. We were unarmed and vulnerable.

---

155 Barry Day (ed.), *The Letters of Noël Coward* (London: Methuen, 2007), p. 625.

156 Jonathan Croall, *John Gielgud* (London: Methuen, 2011), p. 422.

> The Canadian carrier, the *Montcalm*, came in and I was amazed to find that it had a burger bar and a Coca-Cola bar for the crew.

The Suez affair, he says, 'left me ashamed of the actions of my government and reluctant to go back to Egypt. It was nearly forty years before I did.'

Bob Ball stayed on too, probably because *2 Corps News* was needed more than ever, if Britain's soldiers were not to become too demoralised, and every day it tried to make the best of the situation. A full three weeks after Britain's humiliation, on 29 November, it reported on another New York trip by Foreign Secretary Selwyn Lloyd to beg the Americans and the UN to give the British government a figleaf to wrap around its shame:

> Mr Selwyn Lloyd has arrived back from New York. At London Airport yesterday he said in answer to questions that Britain and the USA must get their policies regarding the Middle East more closely aligned. At present, Mr Lloyd said, the only people benefitting by the present situation are the Communists. There is no reason why the Anglo-American Alliance should be irreparably damaged but there are still points on which there is not yet agreement.

Meanwhile: '100 Conservative MPs have tabled a motion deploring the attitude of the United States to the British policy in the Middle East and the United Nations order to withdraw immediately.'

2 Corps News also reported that Egyptian police had been expelling British subjects from the country, and it is a fact that several British citizens lost their homes, businesses and livelihoods in November 1956, and were not well looked after when they came back to Britain to look for work. The paper added some rather random snippets from home:

> Because of losses due to bad weather, day trips from Brighton and other south coast towns are to be discontinued by the owners of the familiar paddle steamers providing them ... The Alderman Jack Cohen Health Centre at Sunderland, officially opened by Mr Aneurin Bevan, is the first health centre in north-east Britain.

And just in case anyone thought that Americans were now our enemy, *2 Corps News* also noted: 'US airmen stationed at Wethersfield, Essex, and Woodbridge, Suffolk, will act as Santa Claus to well over 800 children in charitable homes ... A spokesman said: "Each child will receive a toy, clothing and a stocking full of candy."' Perhaps readers were reassured that Uncle Sam still had his protective arm around us.

HMS *Dalrymple* was one of the ships placed under the UN blue flag in place of the white ensign, says John Knox:

> Crew members wore overalls and berets in place of Royal Naval uniform and working dress. A number of UN personnel from armies of other countries were stationed on board. They carried machine guns and used them in a bizarre incident over Christmas when a few crew members lowered one of the ship's boats and set off saying they were going to Cyprus. It only took a single burst of machine-gun fire for them to turn back to face the consequences of their action.
>
> Christmas was my first away from home. The navy did its best to recognise the season and I have a copy of the traditional British menu for the day. Bacon and eggs for breakfast, roast turkey, pork and Xmas pudding for (midday) dinner, Xmas cake and mince pies for tea, and a cold meat supper. There must have been carol singing and, equally certain, special rum rations. A week or so later I received a parcel from my mother which I rushed to open. It contained a small and very very green roast chicken.

> I received a Naval General Service [medal] for my part in the Suez adventure which was stolen in a burglary of my house about thirty years later. I have not missed it.

Nasser's victory was complete. Egypt kept full ownership of the Suez Canal, and got Soviet support for the construction of the Aswan Dam, which was completed fourteen years later. Nasser was an instant hero in the Arab world. The Suez affair was as gross a miscalculation as any British government has made. Macmillan said later:

> We altogether failed to appreciate the force of the resentment that would be directed against us. For this, I carry a heavy responsibility. I knew Eisenhower well ... and thought I understood his character ... I believed the Americans would issue a protest ... in public; but that they would in their hearts be glad to see the matter brought to a conclusion.[157]

Macmillan was not only an old friend of Eisenhower; he was also Chancellor of the Exchequer, and knew the vulnerability of Britain's economy. Eden was supposed to be Britain's greatest foreign affairs expert. It is extraordinary that two men with the experience, sophistication and long-standing international contacts of Eden and Macmillan could have got it all so utterly wrong.

Between them, they ensured that for many decades to come – it is still the case today – no British government would act in any international matter of the slightest importance without first obtaining American permission, and that, if the American government required action from a British government, it got that action. It was, of course, high time Britain's now absurdly inflated idea of itself as a great

157 Nigel Fisher, *Harold Macmillan, A Biography* (London: Weidenfeld & Nicolson, 1982).

imperial power was punctured, but Eden and Macmillan's incompetence ensured that it was done in as sudden, painful and humiliating a way as possible.

Of course, it took time for Britain's radically changed status in the world to sink in. *The Spectator* struggled against the inevitable conclusion. In mid-November, it would still say, defiantly:

> The prospects of a settlement in the Middle East have deteriorated to the point at which negotiations could break down at any moment. Encouraged by the overwhelming support his cause has received at the UN and in world opinion, Col. Nasser has been trying to insist on terms which the French and British governments could not, without total humiliation, accept.

Britain did accept them, though, no matter how total the humiliation. Negotiations could not break down, because Britain had no leverage.

The magazine added wistfully: 'The British and French governments, once they had committed themselves to the assault on Egypt, ought to have gone through with it to the point where the canal was wrested from Nasser's hands.'

By the end of the month, the magazine was observing the newly invigorated anti-Americanism to be seen around the land. It did not note – but it might as well have done – that the government had placed British foreign policy permanently in American hands, where it would remain. The one notable act of defiance throughout the next half-century was when Harold Wilson kept Britain out of Vietnam – a stand that was neither understood nor forgiven in Washington, where President Lyndon Johnson frequently reminded Wilson that his was not a wealthy country, and could be bankrupted at will by Washington.

In 1956, Britain had not been a great power for at least a decade; but neither the people nor the government quite understood or accepted this. After 1956, no amount of self-deception could hide it. A curt instruction from Eisenhower to Eden to give up the invasion or be ruined forced Britain to face the finality of the wartime settlement, in which it was financially and militarily a vassal to the USA.

Every Prime Minister since Eden has remembered that lesson. When American presidents say 'Jump!', British prime ministers ask, 'How high?' Of all the prime ministers since Eden, only Harold Wilson has dared conduct a serious rebellion, and only Edward Heath has rejected the idea that British foreign policy should revolve around our 'special relationship' with the USA.

Heath, who in 1956 was Eden's Chief Whip, saw British foreign policy as centring on Europe, and his thinking was influenced by having watched that terrible moment in November 1956 when Britain withdrew from Suez. He – unlike the Prime Minister he served in 1956 – understood that, while British politicians were thinking of nothing but Suez and Washington, the European Economic Community (EEC) was taking shape, and was going to matter more in the long term.

Before Eden told Parliament about his capitulation on the morning of 6 November, he had to tell French Premier Guy Mollet, whom, up until then, he had dragged along with him. It placed Mollet in an appalling position. But Mollet, unlike Eden, had something more important at the top of his mind. Roy Hattersley describes what happened:

> Mollet was in a meeting which he left with the greatest reluctance and only after he was told that the British Prime Minister must speak to him at once. In the Palace of Westminster, Parliament was about to take part in one of the great manifestations of faded glory. The Queen, crowned and robed and preceded by the Sword of State and Cap of Maintenance, was about to address the ermine-robed peers of the realm. In the Elysée, the leaders of France and

> Germany were discussing equal pay for equal work and support for French industry. Agreement on these prosaic subjects was all that was needed to enable the two countries to join together in a common market. Konrad Adenauer had travelled to Paris to overrule the German officials whose detailed reservations were standing in the way of European unity. When he heard of the collapse of sterling he observed that America could not be trusted to defend Europe. As the old order was crumbling on one side of the channel, a new one was being created on the other.[158]

Britain's anti-Americanism has, since the Second World War, been a little like a child's dislike of a parent. The rest of Europe had America in better proportion, and, in November 1956, was taking steps to establish its independence of Uncle Sam.

For it was not the United Nations that persuaded the British government to end its Suez adventure; it was not international condemnation, nor domestic unpopularity; it was not the Labour Party, nor the Church of England. The Cabinet minute on 28 November – three weeks after the enforced ceasefire, when Macmillan was urging instant withdrawal without even a figleaf by way of conditions – could not be clearer on this point. Britain must get money from the IMF and 'in other ways. For this purpose, the goodwill of the United States government was necessary; and it was evident that this goodwill could not be obtained without an immediate and unconditional undertaking for withdrawing Anglo-French forces from Port Said.'

That is the clue to much of what followed, for decade after decade: Macmillan's and Heath's eagerness to join the EEC; Harold Wilson's determination to stay in it; the subservience to Washington of successive British governments. Even today, though it is often unspoken,

158 Roy Hattersley, *Fifty Years On* (London: Little, Brown, 1997), pp. 114–15.

it is part of the newly revived Europe debate – if we make ourselves free of Brussels, are we simply tying ourselves yet more tightly to the whims of Washington?

Which is almost all you can say about the Suez affair. Except, of course, that men died. And we should say that, because it's often forgotten. We remember the national humiliation, but forget the men who never lived to see it.

The numbers were small – about 100 British and French soldiers died – but that was 100 young lives thrown away needlessly, and their families must have wanted to know what it was they died for, or to be helped to convince themselves that it was for something worthwhile.

Macmillan and Eden never gave them an answer, for there was no answer except: we screwed up, and your son paid for that with his life. They were protected from the loathing levelled years later at Tony Blair because those were more deferential times, but Suez was one of the moments that changed all that. Not the least of its many legacies is that governments are now held to account for the lives they sacrifice in war.

John Osborne's 1957 play *The Entertainer*, set in 1956 during the Suez crisis, has one of those young men in it. *The Entertainer* is, in its way, an even more political play than *Look Back in Anger*. It is not just about the death of music hall, but also about the death of the England in which music hall had flourished; an England in which Archie Rice's father Billy Rice could carry audiences with him while he sang songs pleading with the government to keep up a strong navy; an England where a young man off to fight in the Suez adventure (and, as it turns out, die in it) can say: 'Life isn't as bad as all that, and even if it is, there's nothing we can do about it.' That England was dying with indecent speed in the first week of November 1956, and John Osborne was ready to dance a jig at its funeral.

CHAPTER 13

ANOTHER FINE MESS YOU'VE GOT ME INTO

So, by the end of the first week in November 1956, there really were no great brave causes left. The British government's arrogant foolishness and cruel pride destroyed the old, brave, patriotic causes, and the Soviet government's cynical brutality destroyed the brave, egalitarian cause of communism.

And, right on cue, in Paris on 12 November, the last remaining symbol of the last great brave cause departed – quietly, because he had said his goodbyes years earlier. Juan Negrin, the last Prime Minister of Republican Spain – the symbol of the great brave cause for which many young men in the '30s had sacrificed their lives, and Jimmy Porter's father had sacrificed his health – died in exile, aged sixty-four.

This end-of-an-era moment passed almost unnoticed in London. 'No one thinks, no one cares. No faith, no belief and no enthusiasm,' Jimmy Porter had said, and, in November 1956, you would not have thought you were in a country that had just failed to prevent the destruction of one nation because its leaders were intent on the destruction of another. Getting enough petrol to fill our cars seemed a far more vital concern, and many of us who were children in 1956 have memories of our fathers coasting down hills to save a drop of petrol.

If we blamed anyone, it tended not to be Eden and Macmillan, but those who had stopped Eden and Macmillan. There was almost as much resentment against the Americans in 1956 for stopping us going into war in the Middle East as there was, forty-eight years later, for dragging us into war in the Middle East. And, as for the domestic opposition, those in Britain who had warned of the impending disaster were punished severely.

The Observer and the *Manchester Guardian*, which had opposed the Suez adventure from the start, suffered massive losses of circulation and of advertising. The Labour Party, as Roy Hattersley puts it:

> Paid the price for both predicting disaster and for proposing the solution which was eventually imposed on Britain by world opinion. When, on 14 November Gallup published the first post-Suez opinion poll, the opposition's six point lead over the government had disappeared. The news that a UN peace-keeping force was supervising a withdrawal and ceasefire led to neither services of thanksgiving nor dancing in the streets.[159]

Somehow, Labour's opposition to the war from the start made Britain's eventual humiliation their fault.

159 Roy Hattersley, *Fifty Years On* (London: Little, Brown, 1997).

The humiliation was felt most severely in the army – the prop of Britain's imperial pretensions. The soldiers, sailors and airmen felt demoralised, even betrayed. They had done the work that was asked of them faultlessly; now they were effectively being told that it was all a mistake.

People die in war, and men had died in this one. But generally, in the past, their grieving families were able to cling to the idea that the sacrifice was in a noble cause – the defeat of the Nazis in Europe; the defeat of communism in Korea. This time, no one could pretend that the sacrifice achieved anything, or even that it was designed to achieve anything particularly noble. Such a dreadful thing was not to happen again until Tony Blair's government invaded Iraq.

So instead of pride there was bitterness and cynicism, made worse among soldiers because the post-Suez cuts in military expenditure bit deeply.

The popular press – what we would now call tabloid newspapers, though, in 1956, no newspapers were produced in the tabloid size – did its best for the cause by talking up the red menace. Russia, they assured us, had been about to establish satellite countries right across the Middle East, and was only prevented from doing so by the British action in Egypt. 'Reds' were burrowing their way to the top of trade unions, apparently, and the gallant struggle against them by ordinary, decent, industrious British workers was compared to the struggle of the Hungarian people. Dr Hewlett Johnson, the 'Red Dean' of Canterbury, was a target of sustained abuse. He was busy 'whitewashing the Russians', according to the *Daily Mail* of 13 November, and had said that the British invasion of Egypt was worse than the Russian invasion of Hungary.

The *Daily Mail* also treated as a major news story the decision of the annual conference of the London women Conservatives to pass a motion of confidence in Sir Anthony Eden. By conventional news standards, it would only have been a story if the women Conservatives had refused to pass such a motion, but the *Mail* was determined to row in heavily behind the beleaguered Prime Minister.

Lady Clarissa Eden was there, apparently to thank her Conservative sisters. 'We have been encouraged and stimulated by such resolutions, which are arriving in thousands, from all over the country,' she told delegates. Thousands? Well, maybe.

The women Conservatives might have been less pleased with the star treatment given them by the *Mail* if they had been reading its series 'Men writing about women'. The day the paper published the hot news of their resolution in support of the Prime Minister, it was the turn of Wolf Mankowitz (author of the novel *A Kid for Two Farthings*, a semi-fantasy set in London's Jewish East End, which had been turned into a popular film in 1955, starring David Kossoff, Diana Dors and Celia Johnson). Mankowitz wrote that he had

> never met a professional woman who didn't regret. Either she regretted not having been pretty enough to find a mate. Or, being pretty enough and having found one, regretted that it interrupted her work. Or, attractive but skilled in defence, regretted that the ideal man didn't exist – someone who pays bills and ... prepares neat little dishes for her to come home to.

Mr Mankowitz's article was headed 'Never a career girl without a regret', with the strapline: 'One of Britain's top writers (yes, he is married) takes a long, sour look at women and jobs.'

On the same page as Mr Mankowitz dispensed his wisdom, the paper's agony aunt Ann Temple reported a letter from a man who had fallen in love with a woman but discovered that, before they met, she had had several affairs. What should he do? 'Don't marry this girl, you're not her type,' was Ms Temple's crisp advice.

On 14 November, it was John Osborne's turn to examine the modern woman in the *Daily Mail*. 'What's gone wrong with women?' he asked. Just two days after the death of the symbol of the last great brave cause, you might have thought Osborne would have had something more interesting to write about. Perhaps he did, but the *Mail* – then as now – was the best payer in Fleet Street.

Osborne could see dimly that there was a revolution brewing in the relationship between men and women – and it was one revolution that this revolutionary playwright did not like at all:

> Never before have women had so much freedom, so much power, or so much influence ... It seems very obvious to say that women have arrived, that at last they are coming into their own, but what is not so obvious is the price we are all paying for it.

What this price was exactly, he did not explain, but he was quite clear what the shortcomings of women were. 'What distinguishes a woman', explained Mr Osborne, 'is her lack of imaginative vitality. She will hardly ever do anything for its own sake. Her roots are so deep in sexuality that she is the natural enemy of the visionary, the idealist.' (He went further once with Colin Wilson, describing an actress they knew as 'the kind of girl who needed to be fucked by a syphilitic gorilla'.)[160]

No doubt the London women Conservatives would have been relieved to learn from Mr Osborne that:

> Women are born conservatives. Their very nature demands that they preserve and consolidate society. Men until now have always set out to change the pattern. Progressives have always been men.

160 Colin Wilson, *The Angry Years: The Rise and Fall of the Angry Young Men* (London: Robson Books, 2007), p. 65.

> Women have followed a long way behind. Most women want to retain the death penalty and bring back the cat.

But they would have been less pleased with his view of women Conservatives: 'Go to any Tory conference, let anyone even dare to discuss the abolition of capital punishment, and watch these overdressed bullies with blue hair leap to their feet and bay their lungs out like a herd of outraged seals.'

In the light of this, perhaps we should not be surprised that, two days later, the paper reported Osborne seeking a divorce from his wife Pamela. Alongside the story, apropos of nothing in particular, was a picture of actress Mary Ure. Readers were informed that she had starred in *Look Back in Anger*, but were told nothing else about her, and the uninitiated reader might have wondered what relevance she had to the story. Or perhaps we are underestimating the sophistication of *Mail* readers in 1956; perhaps they would quickly have worked out what the sniggering sub-editors already knew.

John Osborne and Mary Ure married in 1957.

Two days later, on 16 November 1956, radio and TV personality Frank Tilsley took the *Mail*'s 'women' slot to ask: 'Are wives too independent?'

The BBC was certainly too independent, in the *Mail*'s view and in that of many Conservative MPs. Just as they were to do forty-eight years later over Iraq, the *Mail* and the harrumph tendency in the Conservative Party united to mount a furious attack on the BBC for its reporting of opposition to the war.

Peter Rawlinson complained in the House of Commons about 'matters of tone, matters of emphasis, matters of selection, the use of adjectives and the use of tone'. Apparently, according to Mr Rawlinson, a programme called *Press Comment*, which went out at 6 a.m. in the European News Service, had quoted the *Manchester Guardian*, which called the Suez invasion 'an act of folly without justification' and 'a disaster of the first magnitude', with no adequate balancing quotes. It sounds a little like Andrew Gilligan on the *Today* programme, forty-eight years later and very early in the morning, saying that Downing Street probably knew there were no weapons of mass destruction in Iraq. Mr Rawlinson feared that the broadcast might have reached the troops in Cyprus, and would create doubt and division among them (though, as we have seen, the troops did not need the BBC to instil doubts about the war into them – they had formed those by themselves). And, he added, the BBC was publicly funded – with the usual sinister, unspoken implication: if it's going to do this sort of thing, how long will we go on allowing it to be publicly funded?

But there was worse:

> Mr Robert Grimston (Con, Westbury) said he had watched the television broadcast of the Lord Mayor's dinner. He heard from friends who were at the dinner that when the Prime Minister sat down at the end of his speech he received an ovation. But the BBC faded out the applause ... There was no need to cut out the applause 'except by deliberate intent'.

Now, this is quite odd, because, even in those much more acquiescent times, broadcasters knew that to focus lovingly on polite applause from dinner-jacketed diners for any length of time was terminally tedious for viewers and listeners. Mr Grimston was probably reflecting an Eden obsession. Eden – vain and insecure – did not forgive people who cut short his applause. Clarissa Eden never forgave Rab Butler for doing that the previous month at the Conservative Party conference: 'In the afternoon, Anthony had to speak for over an hour. Rab was in the chair and I noticed he stopped the applause at the beginning by holding up his hand and at the end, after a sidelong glance, by sitting down.'

Rab Butler's sin in apparently stifling the applause for Anthony

Eden must have counted against him when it came to choosing Eden's successor.

Of course, in October, it did not look likely that a successor would be needed for some time to come. But then came Suez, and next, on 20 November, the newspapers reported that Sir Anthony Eden was ill, and was being forced to hand over his duties temporarily to Butler.

The ever loyal magazine *The Queen* commented:

> The heavy burden that Sir Anthony Eden has shouldered must have made everyone marvel at his stamina ... His work in Downing Street alone was a full time job, and to be forced, as he was, to attend debate after debate in the House of Commons, defending his actions against a mob of howling jackals headed by Gaitskell, was more than could be expected of any man. Here was a gang of cheap opportunists, itching for office.

And much more in that vein.

Poor Sir Anthony, having to defend his actions in the House of Commons! But *The Queen* knew nothing. The Prime Minister was a very sick man, and this is probably part of the reason – though only part of it – why the Suez affair was handled so ineptly.

Eden had been in constant pain for years, and dependent on painkillers. In April 1953, he had had an operation to remove gallstones from his bile duct. It should have been routine, but it was botched. The senior surgeon was reduced almost to a nervous wreck by Prime Minister Winston Churchill's constant messages reiterating the eminence of the patient and the national importance of a successful outcome – the last arriving when Eden was already anaesthetised and unconscious. The surgeon made an error, a vital organ was cut, the patient lost a huge amount of blood, the surgeon's nerve deserted him completely, and it was left to the junior surgeon to clear up the mess.

Before the end of the month, the junior surgeon had to carry out a second operation, during which Eden nearly died. Eden was then taken to America for a third operation, using the latest medical procedures and lasting eight hours. Before this operation, the American surgeon told the British ambassador that there was a 50/50 chance Eden would die under the knife, a 20 per cent chance of regaining a measure of his earlier fitness, and only a 10 per cent chance of a full recovery.

As Eden told the Cabinet when he resigned on 9 January 1957:

> It is now nearly four years since I had a series of bad abdominal operations which left me with a largely artificial inside. It was not thought I would lead an active life again. However, with the aid of drugs and stimulants, I have been able to do so. During these last five months, since Nasser seized the canal, I have been obliged to increase the stimulants necessary to counteract the drugs. This has finally had an adverse effect on my rather precarious inside.

In 1956, he had been looking forward to a summer holiday, which he desperately needed but felt he could not take after Nasser announced the nationalisation of the Suez Canal. In October, he was taken ill and spent a few days in hospital.[161]

Eden's constant irritability, his micro-management – all were partly due to the fact that the Prime Minister, throughout the Suez crisis, was ailing. And when the Suez affair collapsed, so did the Prime Minister. On 20 November, the day the newspapers announced that he would have to take a break from his duties, Eden wrote to French Premier Guy Mollet:

161 Peter Hennessy, *Having It So Good: Britain in the Fifties* (London: Penguin Books, 2006), pp. 407–11.

> My dear friend, I am so sorry to be laid up like this. It will not be for long. I hope that in three weeks' time at most I shall be completely active again. Meanwhile, if I go away for a short spell, Butler will look after everything here and uphold our friendship.

He and Clarissa had been offered the use of Ian Fleming's home Goldeneye in Jamaica – though, from correspondence now in TNA, it looks as though Fleming was initially not quite clear who was borrowing his house. The intermediary was Colonial Secretary Alan Lennox-Boyd, who, because of security considerations, seems to have given Fleming the impression that he wanted to borrow the house himself. Fleming assumed that Lennox-Boyd was planning an extramarital fling. In a handwritten letter to the Cabinet Office on 1 November, Lennox-Boyd noted: 'The sooner I can tell Ian Fleming the truth naturally I shall be glad – as I do not want to deceive him even in so good a cause for a day longer than is absolutely necessary.'

Fleming must have been told the truth within the next two days, judging by Eden's reply to a message from Lord Beaverbrook.

A note to Eden says:

> Max Aitken rang up this morning to say that he has had a telegram from Lord Beaverbrook offering you his house at Montego Bay, which is isolated and has everything you need. He thought this worth passing on, though he knew you were fixed up.

Eden sent a telegram to Beaverbrook in Nassau:

> Deeply touched by your generous offer, which I should have been delighted to accept. Have however fixed up with Flemings a day or two ago. I wish I had not got to travel at all at this moment but

doctor is firm and I shall not be much use until I have had a break. If you are in Jamaica hope we may meet.[162]

That day, Tony Benn wrote in his diary:

> [Eden] is leaving for Jamaica without even a Private Secretary. William Clark, his PR adviser, said this was because all his staff were united by an intense loathing of the man but that is not the whole story. He has deliberately not made Rab Butler acting Prime Minister but only charged him ... with 'presiding over the Cabinet'. As one Conservative Member put it to me, 'You all underrate Rab. When the smoke has cleared you'll find him there on top of a mound of corpses with his knife dripping with blood and an inscrutable smile on his face.'[163]

Ian Fleming wrote to Lennox-Boyd (the handwritten letter in TNA is undated, so it is unclear whether he yet knew the truth about his guest's identity):

> One or two afterthoughts.
>
> 1. Don't forget to spit on the inside of the masks before use or they will fog up.
>
> 2. There is a coal black, but good, doctor called Dr Harry at Port Maria. He was trained in Edinburgh and is perfectly all right for all the normal things.

162 The National Archives, PREM 11.

163 Ruth Winstone (ed.), *Events, Dear Boy, Events* (London: Profile Books, 2012), p. 259.

> P.S. Naturally we both refuse absolutely to accept any rent whatsoever and will be much offended if there is any talk of payment, except perhaps for tips for servants when you leave.

On 23 November, Eden left for Jamaica, and on 28 November he telegrammed Butler: 'Thank you so very much for your message STOP everyone here from governor downwards is most kind STOP this is a real rest but I still feel badly not being with you STOP love from us both.'

Butler, whom Eden did not trust and whom Clarissa by now loathed, wrote to Eden the same day:

> The Party did not flare up again til last night ... An anti-American resolution [was] backed by 130 members; the resolution also welcomes the work of the Foreign Secretary ... Anyway don't worry. Things are well in hand. All your people at No. 10 and Bobby are in on everything and are lending a hand ... Much depends on our talk with Selwyn today ... There is no major issue [on] Anglo-American policy at the moment. Harold is doing his best with his problem.

But Eden was finished, and Butler and the rest all knew it. Even if his health permitted him to return to the premiership – which was unlikely – the Americans would not. His old friend Eisenhower would not talk to him about anything that mattered. Eisenhower's note to Eden was the least he could politely do: 'My dear friend, I understand you are recuperating in Jamaica. This short note brings you my very best wishes for an enjoyable and restful vacation and a complete return to health. As ever, Ike E.' It made no mention of their ever working together again.

Eden replied: 'My dear friend. Thank you so much for your very kind message. It is very pleasant and peaceful here and I am sure I shall be quite fit in a week or two.' He added, hopelessly: 'Meanwhile I am of course available if you should want to call on me at any time. Every good wish, yours ever, Anthony.'[164]

This book is not really the story of Anthony Eden's personal tragedy but of the transformation of the Britain he led, in a few short months, and this is a key moment in that transformation. The British government had learned the harsh lesson that it cannot have a Prime Minister with whom the Americans would not do business, and they would no longer do business with Eden.

That, more than Eden's health, was the reason why, when they returned in mid-December, Clarissa noted: 'Everyone looking at us with thoughtful eyes.'

His doctors were sure he could not continue anyway, which allowed both Eden and his country a veneer of dignity. They could always say that the Prime Minister would have continued had his health allowed, but it was not true. Eisenhower wanted him gone. And that was that.

Fifty years later, the veteran right-wing American senator Pat Buchanan described it like this:

> Eden's government fell, and, so legend goes, his successor Macmillan telegraphed Ike: 'Over to you!' Macmillan meant that Britain's responsibility and role in securing the Middle East would now have to be assumed by the United States. For, without Suez, the Brits could no longer secure it.
>
> At the time, many felt Ike should have let the Brits take down Nasser. But Eisenhower was not only enraged at not being informed of the operation, he had come to believe British imperialism was finished, that Arab nationalism was here to stay, that the Suez Canal was now irretrievable, and that we had to deal

164 The National Archives, PREM 11.

> with the new Arab world rather than attempt futilely to reconstruct the old.[165]

Among his many other quarrels with the British action in Suez, Eisenhower was sure that, without British bungling in the Middle East, there could have been a better outcome in eastern Europe; and, though we cannot know for certain how much Suez affected Khrushchev's and Bulganin's thinking, it is certainly the case that the British action in Suez muffled international attempts to restrain Khrushchev, and robbed the West of the moral high ground.

As soon as Imre Nagy was deposed, thousands of Hungarians were arrested and eventually 26,000 were brought before the Hungarian courts, 22,000 were sentenced and 13,000 imprisoned. Most of these were free again by 1963. But several hundred were executed or deported to the Soviet Union. Sporadic armed resistance and strikes continued until mid-1957.

Janos Kádár led a Revolutionary Workers'-Peasants' Government, and the old leadership was purged. Kádár spent November establishing control of the whole country, and the next year the Soviet Union increased its troop levels in Hungary, while Kádár agreed to a treaty whereby Hungary accepted the Soviet presence on a permanent basis.

The Hungarian Catholic Cardinal Mindszenty was granted political asylum at the United States embassy, where he lived for the next fifteen years, refusing to leave Hungary unless the government reversed his 1949 conviction for treason.

Imre Nagy and some of his colleagues, along with Julia Rajk, the widow of László Rajk, who had been executed as a Titoist spy in 1949, took refuge in the Yugoslav embassy. They were promised safe passage out of Hungary if they came out, but they were arrested when they

165 http://www.antiwar.com/pat/?articleid=9941

tried to leave the embassy on 22 November and taken to Romania. There was no secret about it: the Yugoslav officials who were protecting them, and were forced away at gunpoint, made a public protest and told the world's press. But Nagy and his party were kept in prison and tortured, and in 1958 they were tried in secret and executed.

Julia Rajk, who in October under the Nagy regime had seen her husband reburied with full honours, was in prison for two years, but later became a leading campaigner for dissident intellectuals, and offered the compensation she received for the loss of her husband to a fund supporting talented university students. She died in 1981.

The *Daily Worker*'s Peter Fryer sent a despatch from Budapest to the paper's editor on 11 November. It was not printed, and even the paper's staff were not allowed to see it:

> I have just come out of Budapest, where for six days I have watched Hungary's new-born freedom tragically destroyed by Soviet troops.
>
> Vast areas of the city – the working class areas above all – are virtually in ruins. For four days and nights Budapest was under continuous bombardment. I saw a once lovely city battered, bludgeoned, smashed and bled into submission. To anyone who loves equally the Socialist Soviet Union and the Hungarian people it was heart-breaking.
>
> The people of Budapest are hungry today. Many are almost starving ... Corpses still lie in the streets – streets that are ploughed up by tanks and strewn with the detritus of a bloody war: rubble, glass and bricks, spent cartridges and shell cases ... Budapest's workers, soldiers, students and even schoolboys swore to resist to the very end. And every foreign journalist in Budapest was amazed that the resistance lasted so long.[166]

166 Alison Macleod, *The Death of Uncle Joe* (London: Merlin Press, 1997), pp. 178–95.

Fryer had seen evidence of crimes committed throughout the time the communists had controlled Hungary. As Hungary's prisons opened, hundreds of gaunt men and women crawled out, seeing the sun for the first time for years, with dreadful tales of torture and ill treatment to tell.

He found out that László Rajk had been forced to confess in return for a quiet life in which he and his wife and child would be looked after in the Soviet Union. Then his wife was forced to watch his execution. Fryer cursed himself for writing to the *Daily Worker* saying the confession was genuine.[167]

Suez should have been the moment that Britain's communists had waited for, ever since the foundation of the CPGB in 1920. Suddenly, in 1956, at the moment of its greatest opportunity, the party imploded. It left a vacuum so vast that in the half-century that has elapsed no one has yet found a way of filling it.

Before 1956, young idealists impatient with the caution and reformism of the British Labour Party could find a home in the Communist Party. It had worked ruthlessly and successfully for two decades to make itself the only party on the left. The Independent Labour Party, a force in the land in 1931, was reduced to virtually nothing by 1945, because communists were told to join the ILP, get themselves elected to important positions in their branch, and then expel all the other members for deviating from the line.[168] The party had managed to keep its enemies on the Trotskyist left confined to tiny, warring, discontented factions.

But the left could no longer fool itself about the Soviet Union. The world in which radical idealists had lived for three decades was suddenly uninhabitable.

167 Macleod, op. cit., pp. 99–100.

168 Douglas Hyde, *I Believed* (London: Heinemann, 1950).

Yet there were signs in November that the CPGB still hoped to regain its position as the great brave cause of radical youth. 'Britain's top fourteen communists – the members of the political bureau – are meeting at the King Street headquarters today to consider what they should do to ride the storm that threatens to destroy their party,' reported the *Daily Mail* on 15 November. The CPGB's King Street headquarters in those days was a rather fine corner office building just off Covent Garden, bought in 1920 with money provided by Lenin. The party had done pretty well since 1940, so well that it had not actually required any Soviet money. The popularity of Stalin and the Red Army during the war had helped bring in members, and the party's reputation as an uncompromising opponent of fascism had bought it the loyalty of several Jewish businessmen who made up what was called the 'commercial branch' and provided funds.

The year 1956 saw the end of the commercial branch, for it saw confirmation that Stalin had persecuted Jews. The next year, the new general secretary John Gollan was forced to go cap in hand to Moscow and ask for a renewal of subsidies, and the long, slow decline eventually ended up with the King Street building becoming the Covent Garden branch of Lloyds Bank.

In 1956, newspapers still thought the CPGB mattered enough to report the arrival in, or departure from, the Communist Party of even the most obscure trade unionist. On 15 November, some papers announced the defection of Mr T. Parry of Stoke-on-Trent fire brigade. This would be Terry Parry, who in 1964 became general secretary of the Fire Brigades Union.

More importantly, John Horner, the FBU's communist general secretary since 1940, decided he could not live with what the Communist Party was doing any longer and defected to Labour, later becoming a Labour MP.

Horner was a serious loss – he had built his union's considerable industrial muscle and political influence, and was widely respected. The defection of the two historians and founders of *The Reasoner*, E. P. Thompson and John Saville, was more newsworthy but less serious, for the Communist Party could more easily shrug off the loss of intellectuals. The loss of top trade unionists mattered terribly.

Daily Worker journalist Alison Macleod told a staff meeting that only one thing now kept her in the party: 'I can't bear to think of seeing my name in the capitalist press.' She complained that editor Jonny Campbell had told the staff they were 'infected with Trotskyist lies' and she commented: 'That's the language used when one side in the controversy is going to hand the other side over to the secret police to be tortured in a dungeon, and if you haven't got any dungeons or secret police, you'd better not use it.'

But there were still young idealists ready to try to save the party. Prominent among them was nineteen-year-old Mick Costello, who went to Manchester University in September 1956 and joined the Communist Party after the Russian invasion of Hungary:

> I thought, this is a testing time, this is a time to say where you stand. I went down to Manchester's speakers' corner and people were giving Communist Party speakers a hard time.
>
> I went to a meeting addressed by Harry Pollitt and someone asked him what he was doing while Khrushchev was denouncing the crimes of Stalin. He said: 'I was doing what I am still doing, fighting for the interests of the working class.'

Costello's campaign worked. By 1957, the Communist Party at Manchester University eclipsed all the mushrooming Trotskyist sects that were building their membership on the apparent eclipse of communism, and Costello was elected student union president on a communist ticket, beating the future newscaster Anna Ford to the job.

Costello is one of the most interesting and sophisticated people who ever attached himself to the CPGB. He is probably the sort of man who, despite his attachment to communist discipline, would feel instinctively uncomfortable if, by some mischance, he found himself swimming with the tide. He rose to be the *Daily Worker*'s powerful industrial editor and then the party's industrial organiser and the best known communist in Britain, and at the height of his powers he was a key figure in the Trades Union Congress. Because he was a fluent Russian speaker, a false rumour went round Fleet Street that he was a Soviet spy, and *The Sun* once called him 'the most dangerous man in Britain'.

After the CPGB collapsed in 1991, he became a consultant on trade with the former Soviet Union, and in 2015, aged seventy-nine, he was awarded a PhD from Kent University in social anthropology. He still insists that there was a 'strong pro-Soviet feeling in the working class in 1956. Remember, this was only eleven years after the end of the war.' He says that the party survived 1956 and could have recovered in the long term. What finished the CPGB, says Costello, was not 1956: '1968 was the hellhole.'

Maybe it was. But 1956, despite Costello's efforts in Manchester, was when the rot seriously set in. 'If defending the Soviet Union gives you a headache, take an aspirin,' said Harry Pollitt to his comrades in 1956, but after Khrushchev's speech, after Hungary, there was not enough aspirin in the world to make international communism look like a great brave cause.

CHAPTER 14

ONWARDS AND UPWARDS, COMRADES, THE FUTURE LIES AHEAD

Britain's colonial problems did not cease just because the US President had declared the British Empire redundant. On 19 December, proposals were announced for a new constitution for Cyprus. They had been drawn up by Lord Radcliffe, a lawyer and former director-general of the Ministry of Information, who in 1947 had drawn the border between India and Pakistan.

Charles Foley, editor of the *Times of Cyprus*, considered that Radcliffe did the best he could for the stability of the turbulent island, giving the Greeks an elected majority in the assembly and six out of seven ministries, and protecting the rights of the Turks by a new system of checks and balances. But in one detail the proposals fell short of what governor Sir John Harding had promised Makarios a year before: 'Internal security – the control of the police – would remain permanently in British hands.' Radcliffe nevertheless saw some room for negotiation, but Harding did not: 'The constitution, he told me, had all the symmetry of a Chippendale chair; you could not touch the design without destroying the whole effect. The British could take no risks with internal security – the Cyprus Emergency had already cost £30 million.'[169]

Alan Lennox-Boyd, Eden's Secretary of State for the Colonies, laid Radcliffe's proposals before Parliament, adding that, if they proved to be effective, the government might, in due course, consider the case for Cypriot self-determination. In such circumstances, if the Greek majority sought union with Greece, there would be a second vote for the Turkish minority. If they in turn sought union with Turkey, the island would be divided between the two nations.

'The idea of partition in Cyprus thus sprung upon the world', as Foley observed, 'dismayed those with memories of Ireland, India and Palestine.' It would certainly have troubled Radcliffe, who had seen the appalling human cost of partition along the line he had drawn in the Indian subcontinent – an estimated half a million people died in the violence that followed independence – and consequently refused to accept the salary for his work:

> Still less would partition suit Cyprus, an ethnographical fruit-cake in which the Greek and Turkish currants were mixed up in every town and village and almost in every street. Half the population

169 Charles Foley, *Island in Revolt* (London: Longmans, 1962), p. 132.

> would have to be uprooted and moved and any frontier between the two races would be entirely artificial.[170]

The Turkish government, however, was all for partition. 'Until Lennox-Boyd dropped the word,' wrote Foley, the Turkish Prime Minister Adnan Menderes had supported British rule in Cyprus. 'Now he said that if Turkey were not given half the island, she would take the whole.' The idea of partition was 'hammered into Turkish Cypriot heads through speeches, newspapers and broadcasts from Ankara ... A new slogan was coined: "Turks and Greeks cannot live together" and to prove it came a series of Turkish riots.'

Foley tried, through his paper, to calm things down. It had become routine for the Cyprus government to attribute violence between troops and Cypriots to 'provocation'. 'Now when Turks burned and looted Greek homes "provocation" excused that too. In an 8-inch editorial, [we] used the word eight times, once in capitals ... We proposed that provocation from all sides, including the Government's, should cease.'

The official response was a letter by special messenger saying that the governor intended to close the paper down 'unless it stopped creating ill-will between the communities.'

The *Times of Cyprus* responded in its turn by publishing the letter and its reply. In London, *The Observer* devoted a large part of its next day's front page to these documents. *The Spectator* remarked that *The Times* 'had printed daily articles over the past fortnight "warning the government of the danger of allowing Graeco-Turkish relations to flare into a forest fire" and had also made "the first constructive suggestions to stop mob violence"'. MPs attacked what they called 'totalitarian threats' to shut down a newspaper that 'had done its best to reconcile Greeks and Turks ... Mr James Callaghan said that

170 Foley, op. cit., p. 133.

he had read the articles in question and had found not the slightest justification for complaint.'[171]

Ministers did not defend the governor's letter and the *Times of Cyprus* continued to be published.

Radcliffe thought the proposals should be put to Archbishop Makarios, still in exile on the island of Mahe in the Seychelles, but even this apparently straightforward process was grotesquely mishandled:

> Five prominent Greek Cypriots heard for the first time on CBS that they had been invited to the Seychelles by the Cyprus Government to advise Makarios on the Constitution. Those named on the radio indignantly replied that it was for the Archbishop, not the British, to say who his advisers would be. The whole operation was performed without personal contact between the Government and the Greeks.

Envoys from the Cyprus government arrived in Mahe to

> explain the proposals to the Archbishop but on no account to enter into negotiations on them. Their task was lightened by the fact that Makarios had already received a copy direct from London, together with a new official pamphlet denouncing him as the instigator of terrorism and a major obstacle to the return of peace on the island.[172]

Unsurprisingly, the archbishop told his visitors that the proposals did not need to be explained to him – 'he had read and rejected them already'.

Makarios's exile lasted only a year. Forbidden to return to Cyprus, he based himself in Athens and continued to work for *enosis*. Greece,

171 Foley, op.cit., pp. 134–6.

172 Ibid.

however, came to see more future in an independent Cyprus, and Makarios was eventually converted to that view. Talks between Britain, Greece, Turkey and Cyprus led to the Zürich Agreement of February 1959 and the end of EOKA, and then, in August 1960, to Cyprus achieving full independence.

Though that, of course, was not the end of the matter. Charles Foley lived to witness the Turkish invasion in 1974 and the partition of Cyprus that Harding had thought 'the worst of all solutions' and Foley and his paper had always opposed. In December 1956, however, Cyprus was in a state of, certainly not equilibrium, but at least uneasy coexistence. 'For a year to come,' said Foley, 'the communal peace was almost undisturbed.'

At this point, Britain suddenly found that it had to deal with another place of turmoil, much closer to home.

Irish Republican opposition to British rule in Northern Ireland had been subdued for a decade or more. In 1948, the Irish Republican Army (IRA) had ruled out armed action against the Republic; henceforth its attention would be focused on Northern Ireland. In a series of raids on British military bases in the early '50s, the IRA considerably increased its armoury, but its perceived failure to take decisive action in the North led to splinter groups doing so themselves. In order to preserve unity, the IRA devised a campaign of border attacks, codenamed Operation Harvest, in which they would target military bases in Northern Ireland and set up IRA cells there, or – as it was phrased in an IRA 'general directive' – 'guerrilla warfare within the occupied area and propaganda directed at its inhabitants ... [in order] to liberate large areas and tie these in with other liberated areas[,] that is areas where the enemy's writ no longer runs'.[173]

173 Patrick Bishop and Eamonn Mallie, *The Provisional IRA* (London: Corgi, 1988), p. 41.

The campaign was initiated on 12 December with a statement from the IRA:

> Spearheaded by Ireland's freedom fighters, our people have carried the fight to the enemy ... Out of this national liberation struggle a new Ireland will emerge, upright and free ... our aim [is] an independent, united, democratic Irish Republic. For this we shall fight until the invader is driven from our soil and victory is ours.[174]

There were simultaneous attacks on border targets by about 150 IRA fighters, followed on 14 December by actions against three Royal Ulster Constabulary (RUC) posts.

A week later the Northern Ireland Prime Minister Basil Brooke invoked the Special Powers Act to imprison several hundred suspected Republicans without trial. On 30 December, an IRA column made a second foray against Derrylin RUC barracks and killed a constable, John Scally, the first man to die in the campaign.

Operation Harvest grew in intensity through 1957, executing more than three hundred attacks, but it declined thereafter and was finally terminated in February 1962. The IRA stated that: 'Foremost among the factors motivating this course of action has been the attitude of the general public whose minds have been deliberately distracted from the supreme issue facing the Irish people – the unity and freedom of Ireland.'

In other words, the IRA's campaign had failed – catastrophically, some members thought – to accrue the support it had hoped for from its sympathisers in Northern Ireland. Divisions in opinion over how to proceed would lead, at the end of the '60s, to yet another partition, between the official and the provisional IRA, and to the provisionals'

---

174 Ibid.

almost thirty-year paramilitary campaign, effectively ended by the Good Friday Agreement in 1998, but leaving all Ireland with scars of social and psychological damage that are still visible.

The post-Hungary new left was starting to take shape by spring 1957, when the first issue of *Universities and Left Review* declared:

> Those who feel that the values of a capitalist society are bankrupt, that the social inequalities on which the system battens are an affront to the potentialities of the individual, have before them a problem, more intricate and more difficult than any which has previously been posed. That is the problem of how to change contemporary society so as to make it more democratic and more egalitarian, and yet how to prevent it from degenerating into totalitarianism.[175]

At first, Trotskyist groups mushroomed to fill the void left by the decline of the Communist Party. But, in the '60s, single-issue campaigns increasingly absorbed radical energy: banning nuclear weapons (the first Aldermaston March was in Easter 1958), getting the Americans out of Vietnam.

Not, of course, that the Communist Party of Great Britain thought of itself as finished. The young Mick Costello was not the only person to take the view that now was the time the cause needed his loyalty most. The Scottish poet Hugh MacDiarmid decided that early 1957 was the moment to rejoin.

Even if all the accusations made by 'the enemies of communism' were correct, he wrote:

> The killings, starvings, frame-ups, unjust judgements and all the rest of it are a mere bagatelle to the utterly mercenary and unjustified

175 David Kynaston, *Modernity Britain* (London: Bloomsbury, 2013), p. 38.

> wars, the ruthless exploitation, the preventable deaths due to slums, and other damnable consequences of the profit motive, which must be paid to the account of the so-called 'free nations of the West'.

But at least the left was thinking, says Frank Furedi, whom we last met escaping from Budapest. He became involved with the Trotskyist groups and went on in the '70s to found the Revolutionary Communist Party. 'Nineteen-fifty-six was a catalyst year because the ruling elites on both sides had lost confidence in their way of life,' he says. 'Khrushchev's speech acknowledged that, but there was no appetite among the leaders to change anything.'

The year's last issue of NME, on 28 December, found the year's first chart-topper, Bill Haley, still with a foothold in the Top 10, this time with 'Rip It Up'. In the paper's annual poll, the results of which had been announced on 16 November, Haley had been voted 'The World's Outstanding Musical Personality'. The following week, the NME analysed these results:

> This time last year, Elvis Presley, the Platters, Pat Boone, Fats Domino, Tommy Steele, The Teen-Agers, Gene Vincent, Freddie Bell's Bellboys, Gale Storm and Alan Freed were completely unknown; at the same time, Bill Haley was not placed in any section of the poll – while Lonnie Donegan ... was known to a handful of club habitués only. But examine the situation today!

There had been several efforts to exploit Haley's success in the UK by getting him over here on a tour, but he was doing too good business at home to have time for a Transatlantic jaunt. He would finally arrive in the UK in February 1957, to be mobbed by fans at Southampton and Waterloo. 'Well, just dig those happy cats!' says the newsreel commentator indulgently. 'The thing is an abomination, a perversion,' trumpeted *The Times*, which was the sort of thing *The Times* was expected to say.

What happened next depends on who you ask. For Pete Townshend: 'The birth of rock 'n' roll for me [was] seeing Bill Haley and The Comets ... God, that band swung!' Paul McCartney shelled out £1 4s 0d for a ticket and was glad to do it – 'I knew there was something going on here.'

'I've still got the ticket stub in my wallet from when I went to see Bill Haley and The Comets play in Manchester in February 1957,' says Graham Nash. 'My first-ever concert. Over the years I've lost houses, I've lost wives, but I've not lost that ticket stub. It's that important to me.'[176]

Some teenagers were not so captivated. It's been suggested that they were bored by the supporting acts, as well they might have been, since the entire first half of the bill was devoted to the swing orchestra of Vic Lewis and a comedy-and-song duo.

George Melly, perhaps because he was no longer a teenager like Townshend, McCartney or Nash, felt that Haley had 'killed his own image dead ... Whereas it had been possible to ignore the fact on film, in the flesh it became painfully obvious that this perspiring fat person was quite old. One of "them" pretending to be one of "us".'[177]

'Quite old' is not entirely fair. When he came to the UK, Haley was thirty-two – only eighteen months older than, say, Johnnie Ray. It was more a matter of style: the plumpness, the tartan jacket, the aw-shucks amiability of the man. Had anyone shouted from the back of, say, the Hayes Essoldo, in the words of the girl in the movie *The Wild*

---

176 'This Day in History: Feb 05' at www.history.com

177 George Melly, *Revolt into Style* (Harmondsworth: Allen Lane The Penguin Press, 1970), p. 45 in 1972 Penguin edition.

One, 'Hey, what are you rebelling against?', we may be sure kiss-curled Bill would not have drawled, like Brando, 'Whaddya got?' Although FBI chief J. Edgar Hoover believed rock 'n' roll was a communist conspiracy to attack American values, and Haley was duly investigated (and became so concerned that he took to carrying a gun on tour), it is hard to believe that any serious threat to the Western way of life was to be expected from the man once famed throughout Pennsylvania and Connecticut as 'The Silver Yodeller'.

With hindsight, we can see Haley more clearly. 'This was never proper rock 'n' roll,' the Staffords observe in their biography of Lionel Bart.[178] 'It was Western Swing ineptly gene-spliced with Big Joe Turner and dressed in rayon.' But Big Joe Turner was a name only to jazz fans, Western Swing not even that, and for a while, as the writers ruefully admit, the Haley synthesis 'pressed several of the right buttons'. Harry Goodman, the publisher of 'Rock Around the Clock', quoted in the *Melody Maker* in April, had been less analytical: 'Until something better comes along, we're going to have rock 'n' roll. I'd say it'll always be here. It always has, but the public don't know it.'

While it passed, Haley's comet threw its light in some unexpected places. In that year's-end issue the NME also reported, under the headline 'Rock 'n' roll for lunch!', that:

> Lunchtime rock 'n' roll sessions are the newest innovation at the Locarno Ballroom in Leeds.
>
> Believing that young local workers needed an interest during their spare lunchtime break, manager Alan Farris, in company with bandleader Lew Stone, has thrown open the Locarno with an admission charge of only 3d.

---

178 David and Caroline Stafford, *Fings Ain't What They Used t' Be: The Lionel Bart Story* (London: Omnibus, 2011), p. 41.

> Teenagers at the rate of 2,000 a day are packing the ballroom in this new and successful venture.
>
> Local industrial firms have welcomed the idea, believing that it allows bright relief to some of the tedious factory jobs that local teenagers might be employed in.
>
> Strong feeling has been shown by local high school headmistresses who have put the ballroom 'out of bounds'.
>
> The patrons are allowed to eat their lunchtime sandwiches in the hall, and rock 'n' roll to the music of Lew Stone and his Band, and to the Quartet led by Larry Cassidy.

Lew Stone had been a popular bandleader of the '30s, with residencies at London's Monseigneur Restaurant and Dorchester Hotel. He was also an arranger of considerable skill, capable of producing big-band jazz that would not have shamed an American orchestra. In 1938 his was the first 'name' dance band to play a season at a Butlin's holiday camp. But this was not at all the background from which rock 'n' roll had emerged, and it's hard to imagine what kind of music Lew Stone played for the dancers at the Leeds Locarno to rock 'n' roll to.

But such peculiar juxtapositions were far from uncommon in the pop music of 1956. Consider, for example, Radio Luxembourg, one of the small number of continental commercial stations whose signal could be picked up, if somewhat erratically, in the UK. As the '50s turned into the '60s, Luxembourg would become a haven for musically curious listeners, playing at least occasionally records that were seldom or never heard on the BBC. It also provided, every Sunday, the only Top 20 countdown programme on air, sponsored – who can forget? – by Sta-Blond and Brunitex shampoos and by Horace Batchelor of Keynsham (which he always spelled out, 'K, E, Y, ...') and his 'Famous Infra-Draw Method' for the football pools.

Admittedly, to reach the good stuff one had to pass through strange programmes by American evangelists such as *The World Tomorrow*, presented by Herbert W. Armstrong, founder of the Radio Church of God, and subsequently by his son Garner Ted Armstrong.

Luxembourg's December 1956 schedule found Mr Armstrong Sr sharing his radio pulpit with Billy Graham's *The Hour of Decision* and the Dawn Bible Students Association. Quizmaster Hughie Green offered to *Double Your Money* and his fellow inquisitor Michael Miles asked you to *Take Your Pick*. The latter had transferred to ITV in 1955, the first game show on commercial television and the first ever on a British network to offer cash prizes. Dance-band leader 'Uncle' Eric Winstone presided over *Butlin's Beaver Club*, the Italian State Tourist Office demonstrated that *Italy Sings*, and minor celebrities presented label-sponsored shows promoting new releases on Capitol, Philips, Columbia and Parlophone.

David Jacobs, not yet occupying the magistrate's bench on the BBC's *Juke Box Jury*, had a show, while another DJ who would become nationally known in the '60s, Keith Fordyce, had two: *Lucky Number* on Tuesdays and *Rockin' to Dreamland* on Wednesdays. A couple of months before, Fordyce had taken over the NME pop reviewer's post from Geoffrey Everitt – who happened to be the general manager of Radio Luxembourg's London operation. Pop pundits, like cricket commentators, were a close-knit bunch.

The most progressive segment of the Luxembourg schedule in December 1956 was *Jamboree*, between 8 p.m. and 10 p.m. on Saturday night, 'exciting, non-stop, action-packed radio' with a slot for the American disc jockey Alan Freed to present rock 'n' roll in.

As Christmas approached, the new, raucous and disrespectful sounds were everywhere; so much so that on 20 December the *Kent Messenger* reported: 'A prankster switched on the record "Rock with the Caveman" in place of "Good King Wenceslas" in the procession through Ashford, Kent, last night. Carollers walked to rock 'n' roll.'[179]

But not quite everywhere. The last day of the year witnessed the first night of a musical revue that would enchant a generation.

Michael Flanders and Donald Swann had been writing and performing songs since they were schoolboys at Westminster, and had placed some of their compositions with celebrities of the time such as Joyce Grenfell and the popular bass-baritone singer Ian Wallace. After giving a well-received lecture on songwriting at the 1956 Dartington summer school, they decided to create what they called 'an after-dinner farrago' of songs for the London stage, and perform them themselves.

On 31 December, the curtain of the small New Lindsey Theatre in Notting Hill rose on a stage bare except for a piano and a wheelchair, Swann seated at the former, Flanders (who had contracted polio while in the navy) in the latter. In agreeable and well-modulated voices, the two youngish men in dinner jackets sang about a reluctant cannibal, a romance between a honeysuckle and a bindweed, and the delights of 'a London Transport diesel-engined 97-horse-power omnibus'. They sang of gnus, warthogs and hippopotami. Unpromising material, one might think – but it was transformed by the pair's exuberant wit and clever songwriting. The reviews were excellent, and in January 1957 *At the Drop of a Hat* transferred to the larger Fortune Theatre, where it ran for more than two years.

The show's best numbers were recorded on an LP and repeatedly heard on radio request programmes: the tale of an Edwardian seduction – 'Have some madeira, m'dear. You really have nothing to fear'; the elaborate wordplay of 'A Gnu' – 'I'm a g-nu, the g-nicest work of g-nature in the zoo'; and the stirring chorus of 'Hippopotamus

---

179 David and Caroline Stafford, op. cit., p. 50.

Song' – 'Mud, mud, glorious mud, nothing quite like it for cooling the blood.'

It's difficult to overestimate the impact of these skilfully silly songs on '50s teenagers who fancied themselves as wits. They learned them by heart and, along with the people who could imitate all the characters in *The Goon Show* (some overlap here, one suspects), became a bit of a bore, singing them – as Flanders and Swann once put it, though they were not talking of their own songs – 'much too often, much too loudly, and flat'. For all that, like rock 'n' roll, though by completely different and utterly English means, the songs of Flanders and Swann opened receptive ears to a new way of interpreting the world around them. Some of those ears were surely attached to the humorists and satirists of the '60s who created *Beyond the Fringe*, *Private Eye* and *That Was The Week That Was*.

At the start of *At the Drop of a Hat*, Michael Flanders would tell the audience that the job of modern theatre was to strip away the hypocrisy, the veneer of modern civilisation, 'and our job, as we see it –' slight, almost imperceptible pause '– is to put it back again'.

It was a good line, delivered with Flanders's perfect timing, and it never failed to get a laugh. But it also went close to the heart of a nation reeling out of 1956 – a nation that would love to have back the hypocrisy, veneer and self-delusion that 1956 had stripped away, and thought it would be nice if 1956 were to turn out to have been a bad dream.

If the real England were the one in William Douglas-Home's *The Chiltern Hundreds*, not the one in John Osborne's *Look Back in Anger*.

If Britain's place in the world were summed up by that picture of Churchill, Stalin and Roosevelt at Yalta in 1945, the big three deciding the fate of the world; and not by the shaming image of Eden flinching as Eisenhower cracked the whip while Khrushchev made free with his tanks in eastern Europe.

If our soldiers were commanded by Kenneth More, not Bill Fraser, and young people listened to Perry Como, not Lonnie Donegan. If the British Empire was still the British Empire. If we could still say 'patriotism' with a straight face, which people who reached adulthood before 1956 could do, and people who were children in 1956 often cannot do.

If the left could wake up and find that communism was still a great brave cause, that the secret speech and the invasion of Hungary were just nightmares; and if the right could wake up and find British communism still powerful enough to be a credible enemy within, and a British Empire upon which the sun never set.

None of that was possible, of course. The year 1956 was the beginning of the end for the '50s and all they represented, and Britain spent the rest of the decade and most of the decade after that trying to pretend it had not happened, while gracelessly coming to terms with the fact that it had.

On 9 January 1957, Eden resigned. There was no election for his successor. In an exercise that reeked of the past, Tory grandee Lord Salisbury called the members of the Cabinet, one by one, into his room at the House of Lords and asked each of them: 'Well, which is it to be, Wab or Hawold?' Pretty soon it was clear that the answer was going to be Hawold.

Rab Butler had made the mistake of being right about Suez – he never pushed it, but everyone knew he had doubts. Macmillan had been safely and enthusiastically wrong about Suez, and he was an officer and a gentleman. Butler seemed, in those frenetic days, to be none of these things.

Completely by accident they had managed to make the right choice, in fact the only choice that could stave off disaster for their party and perhaps for their country; for Macmillan turned out to be a great realist who learned from his mistakes. The first thing he did was take himself off to Washington in the guise of a genteel mendicant, with all the dignity he could muster (which wasn't much). Britain had stayed aloof from the discussions that were soon to lead to the creation of a European common market, so without US patronage there was nowhere in the world for Britain to hide.

He appealed for help in getting a face-saving agreement with Nasser which 'we can claim as reasonable, if not quite what we would like ... I hope you will denounce Nasser and all his works'. His idea for a figleaf behind which Britain could hide its shame was that fees for using the canal would be paid to an international body, not to the Egyptian government. But he found the president unsympathetic, and was left to do the best he could with Nasser.

He eventually settled, as he had to, on Nasser's terms. The French were furious, and felt betrayed for a second time. They wanted to boycott the canal. French politicians were becoming surer by the moment that Britain had decided to put US friendship above European unity. They were right, of course. The myth of the special relationship, which is still with us today, was the one great survivor of 1956.

Macmillan knew that Britain's wounded pride would heal faster if people thought they were better off. 'I am always hearing about the middle classes,' he wrote to the head of the Conservative research department. 'What is it they really want? Can you put it down on a sheet of notepaper and I will see if we can give it to them?'[180]

That is pure Macmillan: the self-mocking lordliness; the apparently effortless superiority; the ruthless appreciation of political reality. It enabled him swiftly to beat off the early monetarists – it was almost another two decades before they were able to recover and place one of their own in the party leadership and eventually in Downing Street.

Part of what the middle classes wanted was an end to National Service for their children, and they got it: fewer international responsibilities

---

180 John Charmley, *A History of Conservative Politics* (London: Macmillan, 1996), p. 160.

enabled Macmillan to announce the end of conscription in time for the 1959 election. With the Americans once again allowing Britain's economy space to breathe, the government could reduce income tax and purchase tax and go into the election with the slogan: 'Life's better with the Conservatives – don't let Labour ruin it.' It was in that campaign that Macmillan said: 'Most people in this country have never had it so good.'

Eisenhower, now once again willing to help the Conservatives to victory as he had in 1955, came to Britain for five days and appeared on television with the Prime Minister, giving the appearance of two elderly, trusted statesmen making the world a safer place. The cartoonist Vicky christened the Prime Minister 'Supermac', and, on 8 October 1959, he won a stunning victory with 365 seats to Labour's 258 – just three years after he and Eden had led the country to its greatest humiliation.

The year 1956 had shown that the British Empire was a thing of the past, and that Britain's imperial pretensions were irritating the American President. So it all had to go, and, as soon as the election was over, Macmillan set about jettisoning it, over the dead bodies of many of the men who had made him premier.

He went to Africa, toured newly independent countries and British colonies, and ended up in South Africa, where he was to address both Houses of Parliament. He paid elaborate compliments to South Africa's progress and courage in war, and then he said:

> The wind of change is blowing through this continent ... As a fellow member of the Commonwealth, it is our earnest desire to give South Africa our support and encouragement, but I hope you won't mind my saying frankly that there are some aspects of your policies which make it impossible for us to do this without being false to our own deep convictions about the political destinies of free men.

As a Prime Minister, Macmillan is in the top rank. He was not a great change maker, not an Attlee or a Thatcher, but he was a great change manager, rather like Baldwin, and a great change manager was exactly what Britain needed after 1956.

He managed to make great change at headlong pace feel like a gentle amble over a grouse moor. And the way we lived was changing as fast as our place in the world. For, while Macmillan was smoothing Britain's release from its pre-1956 delusions of grandeur, a procession of writers and directors helped free the country from what film director Lindsay Anderson called 'its straitjacket of middle-class respectability'.

'Nineteen fifty-six was an extraordinary year,' said Anderson thirty years later.

> The end of World War II had been followed, in Britain at any rate, by a sort of freeze, a paralysis of exhaustion. The freeze lasted for ten years. In 1956, the tragedies of Suez and Hungary shattered the fantasies of imperialists and communists and created the hope of a true social-democratic New Left. And sympathetically, at home, the cultural scene showed extraordinary changes. From the north of England, a whole new generation of writers began to make their mark. Alan Sillitoe from Nottingham. Shelagh Delaney from Salford. Willis Hall from Leeds. John Arden from Barnsley. David Storey was from Wakefield; so were John Braine, Stan Barstow, David Mercer. And in London Tony Richardson from Bradford was George Devine's assistant at the Royal Court Theatre and making history with a play turned down by every management in London, John Osborne's *Look Back in Anger*.
>
> In the conformist climate of postwar Britain, dissenting voices began to make themselves heard.[181]

181 *Free Cinema 1956 – ?: An Essay on Film by Lindsay Anderson* (Thames TV, 1986).

These writers helped at the birth pangs of sexual intercourse, which, as Philip Larkin has told us, began in 1963; but its conception, if we can put it that way, was really in 1956, in teen culture and Teddy Boys and rock 'n' roll. (Rock always had a sexual connotation, and 'Rock Around the Clock' was a boast of sexual prowess.) Yet its birth was slow and difficult, and it had certainly not quite emerged from the womb in 1962, the year in which Ian McEwan's 2007 novel *On Chesil Beach* is set.

The wedding-night meal for McEwan's newlyweds begins with 'a slice of melon decorated by a single glazed cherry' while 'in the corridor, in silver dishes on candle-heated plate warmers, waited slices of long-ago roasted beef in a thickened gravy, soft boiled vegetables, and potatoes of a bluish hue'.

With a flourish, Edward gives Florence his sticky cherry, and she eats it flirtatiously, thinking, 'If only eating a sticky cherry was all that was required.' For the real dread is not the meal, bad as it is, but the nameless horror that she knows is supposed to follow it.

Edward and Florence are 'young, educated, and both virgins on this, their wedding night, and they lived in a time when a conversation about sexual difficulties was plainly impossible'. The subsequent coupling is so complete a disaster that it spoils their love for ever.

If Edward and Florence had been a very few years younger – if they had been part of the baby-boom generation born between 1945 and 1955 – everything would have been different, though not necessarily better. The '60s really began in 1956 with John Osborne's *Look Back in Anger*; but most people did not notice until the Beatles released 'Love Me Do' in October 1962. By then, the oldest of the baby boomers were seventeen years old, and soon they were to know everything there was to know, from the secrets of the universe to the correct way to roll a joint.

In the short '60s – from the release of 'Love Me Do' to the student sit-ins and the Paris *événements* of summer 1968 – young middle-class folk thought they had been liberated, and that New Jerusalem was round the corner, its arrival hindered only by the conservatism of Harold Wilson's Labour government. They did not realise that they were living in New Jerusalem; that it would all be downhill from then on; and that their generation, which benefited from this dazzling array of freedoms, would, within twenty years, destroy them.

For the first time since the Second World War, there was money, there was safe sex, there was freedom. Within a decade the world before 1956 – poor, penny-pinching, conservative and conventional – had, for a great swathe of British society, disappeared without trace. Even the memory of that world was very soon forgotten, for the '60s generation rather despised the past, a small faraway country of which they knew little.

And yet how much of a revolution was it, really? As with many good things, the richest and the upper classes had had sex for years. The '50s were remarkably tolerant about the peccadilloes of celebrities and the political and upper classes, so long as they were conducted discreetly. The same politicians who upheld laws against homosexuality quietly covered up for their colleague Tom Driberg, whose exploits with young men were common gossip in the Strangers' Bar. It was well known in political circles that Harold Macmillan's wife had for years had an extramarital affair with Robert Boothby, and that the fourth and youngest of the Macmillan children, Sarah, born in 1930, was biologically Boothby's child. In a middle-class family this would have been an intolerable embarrassment. But, in the circles in which they moved, it does not seem to have affected the way in which Macmillan, Boothby or Lady Dorothy were regarded, and it was no obstacle to Macmillan becoming Prime Minister.

Larkin was wrong. Sexual intercourse was not invented in 1963. It was starting to be democratised by 1963. The real long-term legacy of 1956 is that people started to say: 'If it's good enough for them, it's good enough for us.'

Once, before the Second World War, the House of Commons was a little like a barrack room; MPs were regularly drunk there at late-night sittings, and some, like Arthur Greenwood, deputy leader of the Labour Party in the '30s, were known to be pretty well permanently drunk, but no one outside the Palace of Westminster ever got to hear about it. In the '60s, George Brown's drunkenness was in all the newspapers; today it would have him drummed out of the House. The House of Commons is now probably a soberer place than at any time in its entire history.

The freedom of Tom Driberg to have homosexual affairs, and Lady Dorothy Macmillan to have heterosexual ones, spread down for the first time to the middle classes. Politicians today know that they cannot get away with behaviour that those who elected them cannot get away with. In fact, as we write, they are probably judged by harsher standards than other people are.

We have not managed, so far, to extend that principle to billionaires and national newspaper editors and other powerful folk, but it's a start.

This is the real legacy of 1956: it began the erosion of automatic respect for politicians, for ministers of religion or teachers, for those who are richer or older than we are. When 1956 opened, we were walled up in an intensely subservient society. John Osborne, Anthony Eden, Ike Eisenhower, Gamal Abdel Nasser, Nikita Khrushchev, Elvis Presley, Arnold Wesker, Lindsay Anderson – they ganged up, some of them unintentionally, to start to pull down those walls.

There have been setbacks. High levels of unemployment and insecure employment breed submissiveness, for nothing makes a person so obsequious as the knowledge that the boss could consign his family to poverty. Politicians understand that lack of respect damages their power, and every so often one of them makes an effort to bring it back. In 2011, David Blunkett called for a National Volunteer Programme to be 'an integral part of growing up in Britain, a rite of passage into adulthood, just as National Service used to be for the 1950s generation' and despite the word 'volunteer' he wants to deny unemployment benefit to young people who do not join. David Cameron once described a good school as a school where children wear uniforms and the class stands up when an adult enters the room. And politicians frequently call on us to be respectful to those they call 'wealth creators' (they mean rich people).

There is still a long way to go, and we frequently stumble on the road, but the lasting legacy of 1956 is the decline of deference.

ACKNOWLEDGEMENTS

Several friends and colleagues have contributed ideas, memories and suggestions, and we have to thank, particularly, the late Hetty Bower, Alan Clayson, Linda Cohen, Mick Costello, John H. Cowley, Andrew Dearing, Alan Fountain, Frank Furedi, Richard Rawles, Keith Richards, Michael Rosen, Iris Russell, Sarah Ryle, Paul Vernon and Katrina Whone. Thanks also to our excellent editors Olivia Beattie and Melissa Bond.

An appeal in *Third Age Matters*, the national magazine of the University of the Third Age, brought, as it always does, a host of interesting ideas and memories. We are grateful to the U3A for allowing the TAM editor Francis Beckett to abuse his position by placing the appeal, and to those who responded to it – including Hugh Armstrong, Bob Ball, Anne Black, Richard Callaghan, David Clark, Patricia Clipson, Peter Cooley, Marian Cox, Jenny Field, Richard Hackford, Donald

Hatton, Terry Hitchen, Tom Jones, John Knox, Sandra Reekie, John Rimington, Stuart Smith, John Tween, Alverie Weighill and Geoff Woolfe.

INDEX